GIVING AND TAKING HELP

GIVING AND TAKING HELP

by Alan Keith-Lucas

The University of North Carolina Press
Chapel Hill

Copyright © 1972 by
The University of North Carolina Press
All rights reserved
Manufactured in the United States of America
ISBN 0-8078-1183-1
Library of Congress Catalog Card Number 70-174784
First printing, March 1972
Second printing, June 1973
Third printing, March 1974
Fourth printing, January 1976

CONTENTS

Preface / *vii*

I. *The Nature of Help* / *3*

II. *Taking Help* / *20*

III. *Choosing to Do Something About It* / *33*

IV. *The Helping Relationship* / *47*

V. *The Helping Factor* / *66*

VI. *The Helping Person* / *89*

VII. *Suggestions for Practice* / *109*

VIII. *Helping and Current Value-Systems* / *136*

IX. *Exceptions and Alternatives* / *151*

X. *Helping in Various Settings* / *169*

XI. *A Short History of Helping* / *185*

XII. *Helping and Religious Belief* / *200*

Index / *215*

PREFACE

This is a book about helping. It attempts to describe what happens, or should happen, when two people come together, one to get help, the other to help. It pays some attention to what happens when one or the other, or both, are a group, but its main thrust is in personal helping. And out of this discussion it moves towards the formulation of a unitary, general theory of helping which can be used in many different situations.

To say this involves no claim that the process could not be formulated with equal validity in other terms. Most theories dealing with a process are of necessity nothing more than models, or metaphors, devised to illustrate the sort of thing that happens, rather than factual statements about objective, measurable things. One would have to be very naïve, for instance, to believe that Freud, Adler, and Jung are actually describing wholly different observable phenomena, rather than creating different models to explain the relationship between many facts observed in common. There is actually no such "thing" as an "id" or a "superego," but in analytic psychology, Freud's model did illustrate a process and give the psychoanalyst ways of describing what he saw. The same is true of the concepts developed in this book. They do offer such a model which would appear to illustrate help as it appears to take place in most helping situations. But if someone can produce a more useful model the world will be his debtor.

Although, as will be apparent from many examples, the writer is a social worker, or rather a teacher of social work, this is not primarily a book for professional social workers. It is directed much more towards those new professions that have grown up in the last few decades that have to do with helping—professions such as vocational guidance, probation counseling, welfare work, special education—and those older professions, such as medicine, law, nursing, and the ministry, that have found personal helping to be a large part of what they do.

But it does not stop with these. It is addressed also to the volunteer, to the civic or church group that wants to help people, and, even more specifically, to the private citizen who finds himself called on to help his neighbor. Particularly is it intended for those who have found, somewhat to their chagrin, the effort to help somewhat frustrating or unexpectedly difficult.

The origins of the book are to be found in a paper I was asked to give in 1958 to the Mental Health Society of Florence-Darlington, South Carolina, called "The Nature of the Helping Process." This paper apparently encountered a thirst for knowledge of the basic principles of help among many kinds of helping people, lay and professional. It, or a slightly expanded version of it, which I called "The Art and Science of Helping," has been reprinted many times, and mimeographed much more often, by such different organizations as Alcoholics Anonymous, the Federal Extension (Agricultural) Service, church conferences, and welfare departments. It has been presented in lectures, at their request, to college deans of students, VISTA volunteers, dental health educators, teachers in special education, and rural missionaries. It has become core material in courses for vocational guidance counselors for the mentally retarded, welfare workers, probation officers, home economists, houseparents, and administrators in Children's Homes. It is used in some schools of social work, and enlarged somewhat in the form of a fifty-page manual by church groups engaged in helping (*This Difficult Business of Helping,* John Knox Press, 1965).

In each of these settings the basic theory has been the same, with additions or modifications as my own understanding grew. In adapting it to a new group all I found that I had to do was to change the examples used, or have the class or the audience supply these from their own setting. It therefore seemed right and proper to expand this theory into a book.

The book is empirical and pragmatic. It is not a sociological or a psychological treatise. It has not been researched in any formal way. I doubt that it could be. Help is not a measurable thing except in terms of specific helping goals, which depend ultimately on values, and on what one means by help. It is rather the result of observations made during thirty years of helping practice, both directly and in association with many other helping professions. The conceptualization of these practices into a unified theory or model is largely my own work, although it draws heavily at times on the so-called "functional" school of social work practice which I have come over the years to respect as offering the most consistent account of this process.

It will be objected by some that the kind of help described in this book is of a personal nature and perhaps enshrines a middle-class philosophy of individualism, at a time when most social theory and practice is centering on the community and the group. While I would agree wholly that individual help will not solve society's most pressing problems of poverty, crime, delinquency, and the like—indeed I believe that the effort to do so on an individualized basis is the single most potent cause both of society's failure to solve them and the deterioration of individual helping in the past thirty years—people still need help on an individual basis. The interests of the individual are not always met by an improvement in society. Both community action and individual help are necessary, and this book deals with the individual part. This is one of my strongest reasons for saying that this is not a social work book. It is applicable to the social worker only where he is engaged in the giving of personal help and not, except in a limited way, where he is acting to change society or to exercise social control.

Others will see in the book's insistence on the use of reality as a helping factor the attempt to adapt people to society rather than to make needed changes in society itself. Social work has in fact been accused of doing exactly that. But in discussing "reality" there is no implication that this reality is good. A welfare grant, or an unjust law, is reality. We may wish passionately to enlarge the one or repeal the other, but for the moment we have to live and work with them. It would do a sufferer from cancer little good if we failed to provide him with medical care but urged him to contribute to medical research. To do both—to face the present reality and to try to change it for the future—would indeed make good sense. But at the moment the present reality represents the greater need.

One's debts, in writing such a book, are always multifarious. I owe a great deal to my colleagues at three universities—the universities of North Carolina, London (through the London School of Economics), and Pennsylvania, for their encouragement of the project, while I was working with or for them, and even more, perhaps, to my students in these places and in many social agencies. Although comparison is invidious I would single out in particular the welfare workers of the State of Maine, my students in administration at The University of North Carolina at Chapel Hill, and the executives of many children's institutions for trying out my formulations in practice and showing them to work, or not. I owe to the administration of the universities, and of their schools of social work, of North Carolina and Pennsylvania, time to write and facilities to do so. I owe to a number of secretaries, and in particular Mrs. Pauline Seawell, Mrs. Janice Ingles, and Miss Emilie Boyle, much assistance in disentangling much over-written manuscript. I owe to hundreds of clients and students includ-ing many children insights into what help means to them and what they have done with it. I owe much to my teachers at Cambridge, Western Reserve, and Duke, to employers and supervisors, particularly in the Louisiana Department of Public Welfare, and to my pastors, including Robert McMullen, Vance Barron, and Harry E. Smith. And I owe in particular to my wife the criticism of my earlier attempt to present this material that I hope put me on the right track.

Truly, no man is an island, even when he writes about individual-ized help, and the best way to learn about helping is to have received help oneself.

GIVING AND TAKING HELP

I. THE NATURE OF HELP

There is no question but that this is the century of the helper. Not only have many new helping professions—social work, vocational guidance, clinical psychology, marriage counseling, and the like—developed and become part of the social structure, but older professions such as medicine, law, and the ministry have redefined their practice much more in terms of their helping function. Governments have become involved in helping on an entirely new scale. Welfare departments, poverty programs, and mental health clinics are part of the daily scene. Help, too, has gone international, through foreign aid, the Peace Corps, technical aid, and alliances for progress. More and more young people, notably perhaps young men who previously would have gone into business, are becoming probation officers, vocational guidance workers, or child care workers. Higher education, from university to community college, is preparing workers for helping fields. People think, too, much more in terms of helping than they used to think. Law and the public think of rehabilitation of the offender as much as they do of his control or punishment.

There is also no doubt that much of this help and the good intentions behind it are going to waste. To this, perhaps, our state department could, if it would, be a powerful witness. But such wastage exists on every level, from government programs to individual attempts to help. In some parts of our society this wastage has become so obvious that there is something of a revulsion against helping in any form.

What is wrong in this situation? It does not lie in the basic quality of those who are trying to help. One of the most encouraging things about the present situation is the quality of those who are entering the new helping professions.

It lies more in a general ignorance of what it means to give and take help, and perhaps, first and foremost, in a misunderstanding of what help means, or is. "Help" is in fact a difficult word. Many people, and not only the unthinking, see help as something that is given by one person to another, put down in front of him, as it were, for him to use or not to use. The thing given may be material, such as money, clothing, a new house. Or it may be intangible, such as advice, instruction, or even psychotherapy.

When the person, or group, or nation, does not use this help, or uses it unwisely, two things begin to be said. First there must be something wrong with the recipient. He is weak, sorry, ungrateful, either unworthy of help or not in need of help at all. What he needs is a good swift kick in the pants, to be left to his own efforts, to suffer the consequences of his untoward behavior. This was, indeed, the theory on which the Poor Law operated for the best part of three hundred years, with its deliberately bleak and unpleasant workhouse for those guilty of not accepting the opportunity to cease to be poor.

Or, the observer might conclude that the wrong kind of help has been given. Maybe money was an inappropriate kind of help. What the helped person needed was a job, new clothes, or a measure of good advice. Maybe this was not the kind of help that this person could use. This has led, on the popular level, to a sort of stratification of help. Tangible help is down-rated and intangible elevated. Money is bad, advice is good. On a more sophisticated level it has led to much research and much individual diagnosis to try to determine what it is that people in general, or this individual, need.

There are truths in both these positions. There are some people who appear, at least in the present state of our knowledge, to be unable to take help. The cure for this is not however to try to shame them or starve them or punish them into doing something about it. This, too, rarely works, although the idea lingers on, especially in popular opinions about public relief. And it is undoubtedly true that people often give quite inappropriate kinds of help from lack of knowledge of the feelings, the needs, or the condition of the person they are trying to help.

The trouble comes when we accept either explanation, or even both of them together, as the cause of all failures to help. It is probable that these are in fact rather small factors in the total situation. This is particularly true of the first, where modern methods are finding ways of reaching more and more people who were formerly thought of as hopeless. Inappropriate help is certainly still a problem, but even there the problem is often not inappropriate measures but quite appropriate things given in an inappropriate way.

Help has in fact a second meaning, which has to do not with *what* is given, but with *how* it is given and used. We can, and do, say of a situation, that so-and-so got help from somewhere, but it does not seem to have helped him much. This is what we try to express in the very curious statement that we ought to help people to help themselves— curious, since if help is something one person conveys to another, it is hard to see how one can help oneself. This meaning of help which has to do with growth, or change, or betterment, in some way, immediately makes one thing clear. What may be wrong with much of our helping may not lie in the recipient, or in the thing which is given, but in ourselves, as helping people. And this is for some an unpleasant thought.

We can all see it in obvious cases. It matters how help is given. If it is given in such a way as to degrade the recipient, he will not be helped by it. Nor will he, which may not be quite so obvious, if it is given grudgingly, patronizingly, punitively, or, let us say, indulgently. Lord Beveridge once said, even of public money, that the purpose for which money was given would determine the way in which recipients would use it. Although one could cavil that he made no allowances for reaction against this purpose, there is much truth in what he said.

But is there more to it than this? Is the *how* simply a matter of avoiding certain unproductive attitudes; not that that is an easy task? Is the how simply a matter of establishing rapport, a good relationship with people? Can it be taught in a few simple principles, such as, say, "Start where the helped person is?" or "Listen to him?"—not again that these are easy things to do. Or is there a body of helping knowledge and theory, a more or less unitary process, adaptable in general to all sorts of helping situations and to the great majority of people? Can one, in fact, learn to help?

There are at least two groups of responsible people who would answer in the negative. The well-known British sociologist, Barbara Wooton, for instance, says that the "common elements," by which she means the helping theory, in social casework "does not amount to much. Good manners, ability and willingness to listen and efficient methods of record-keeping are the principal elements required."[1] This point of view is largely taken, in my experience, by those who have given their lives to learning about people, not to working with them. It is hard to refute except by the simple statement that when two people work together much more happens than Lady Wooton describes, and that help often occurs out of this encounter and not from the review of a record. Unfortunately, perhaps, the best analytical brains, dealing with measurable facts, conceiving help as a thing, not a

1. Barbara Wooton, *Social Science and Social Pathology* (London, 1959), p. 291.

process, are not always the most sensitive to people in action, and, although I would not suggest it in Lady Wooton's case, sometimes discount knowledge of a less measurable kind because they are ill at ease with it. They need the security of incontrovertible facts. Their contribution may be great, but it limits as well as adds to our knowledge.

Perhaps a more formidable objection comes from those who in the name of human difference find it important to deny any but the most obvious generalizations about people as a whole. They see each individual as unique, which in a sense, of course, he is. All too often, even in trying to help, we have lumped people, or classes of people, together and treated them with no recognition of their individuality.

These people would hold, therefore, that there can be few or even no rules. The problems in helping, say a prostitute in Chicago who would like to find some other way of life, and a freshman at Harvard having problems with his grades, are so completely different that few common elements could apply. Moreover, because of their past experience, their heredity, their goals, helping two prostitutes in Chicago may be as different as night and day. This applies not only to the what but just as strongly to the how. There can be no unitary method, but only a number of different methods, each helpful under certain conditions. One helped person may need encouragement, another challenge, a third support, a fourth being looked after by a kindly "parenting" person, a fifth tranquilizing. It all depends on the situation, which must be carefully diagnosed in all of its psychic and social implications. In fact, without such diagnosis, or where the diagnosis is wrong, helping had better not be attempted. It is likely to do more harm than good.

Again there is truth in this position. One can do a sick person harm by ill-advised attempts to help—by sympathizing, for instance, with a depressive or trying to force a neurotic to face a bit of reality that is too hard for him to take. It may not do much good to say that to do either to anyone, depressive, neurotic or not, to sympathize rather than empathize, to face someone with reality without the empathy and support that alone makes reality bearable, is very poor helping practice. Both are quite common helping mistakes, innocuous, although basically sterile, in the majority of cases, but in these two actually harmful. It is good to know when to be especially careful. And there can be no doubt that where there is real pathology diagnosis is a must. Where there is not, it is usually helpful to know as much as one can about the person one plans to help. It prevents a good deal of floundering and sometimes mistakes that have to be painfully retrieved.

Nevertheless there are good reasons for not accepting this position too completely or exclusively.

The first is purely pragmatic. Psychosocial diagnosis, if it is to be reasonably accurate, is an extremely difficult thing. To attain any proficiency in it one not only has to have considerable skill in identifying clues but fairly rigorous training. Amateur diagnosis is notoriously fallacious. It is too easily skewed by personal rationalizations. Paul Halmos, in a book largely ignored in America, but which made quite an impact in England in 1966, even holds that anything less than full psychoanalytic training as preparation for counseling is a "short cut" inconsistent with theory.[2] Even the diagnosis of graduate social workers has been shown on several occasions to be extremely suspect.[3] And, increasingly, it is becoming obvious that to arrive at any sort of comprehensive evaluation of so complex a situation as a human being reacting to his social environment, one needs knowledge of psychology, sociology, epidemiology, economics, and anthropology at least.

This is not to say that such knowledge may not be extremely helpful, but as a sine qua non for beginning to help people it is clearly most impracticable. A great deal of the helping that goes on today is being done, and must be done, by those who have neither the training or the knowledge to make this kind of diagnosis. What is more, much of this helping is being given in situations in which there is no time, or possible opportunity, to gather the facts on which diagnosis can be based.

Indeed, as many people who naturally think in diagnostic terms—and we all do to some extent—have discovered, any strict sequential process of history-taking, diagnosis, and treatment denies two of the things that we know about help. The first is that the process of helping begins from the very first moment of encounter between the helper and helped persons, and the other that some of the most productive helping situations are those of acute crisis in the helped person's life, where something has to be done at once.

Then, again, there is some question as to whether those who insist on the necessity for intricate diagnosis and many "helping methods"

2. Paul Halmos, *The Faith of the Counsellors: A Study in the Theory and Practice of Social Casework and Psychotherapy* (London, 1965), p. 123.
3. See, for instance, Alfred Kadushin's "Diagnosis and Evaluation for (Almost) All Occasions," *Social Work* 8, no. 1 (January 1963): 12-19.

are talking about help to all. They are talking, actually, much more about control, and the two things are not the same.

This arises because any theory that dwells exclusively on the differences between people has, by its very nature, to subsume some sort of norm. People become distinguished by their difference from this norm. What we become concerned about is their failure, their dysfunction. It becomes the job of the helper to restore them to some condition that is considered desirable or acceptable. This is why, so runs the argument, one has to develop a variety of helping methods. Each is a tool to be used in a particular situation. Yet, however appropriate these are, however much the helper person may have agreed to their use, however much even participated—a somewhat slippery word—in their selection, the choice of tool and the treatment goal is more in the mind of the helper than it is in that of the helped. Like it or not, the helped person is being manipulated, having things done to him, more or less subtly being controlled. He is being encouraged, challenged, loved, limited, supported with the purpose of restoring him to some socially acceptable or less dysfunctional condition, or even a more comfortable one.

Now there are dysfunctional people, or people in situations in which they have lost the power to function in a reasonably comfortable, productive, or acceptable way. It is possible that some of these people do need to be controlled for a period of time, or in certain respects, before they can begin to live on their own. But to limit our concept of help, or even to define help as principally related to restoring people to comfort, to productiveness, whatever that may really mean, is again to deny much of what we know about it. I suspect that an overemphasis on restoring functional ability is largely due to the social work profession, which has always been caught in a tension between its desire to help people with what they want for themselves and a responsibility to society not to permit too great a dysfunction; a group of people moreover, that is used to dealing with more or less serious dysfunction. To social work as a profession what is inclined to matter is deviation, delinquency, or deprivation, not the conditions of normal living, although there are individual social workers who feel quite otherwise.

Deviation, delinquency, deprivation are of course very real things, but they are not the whole of life. Nor does dealing with them comprise all that we mean by help. Help is not simply something given by the well part of society to those who are sick. Its goal is not simply, as we were taught when social work first tried to measure its results, such things as "adaptive efficiency" or "absence of disabling conditions" or even such qualities as being satisfied, getting along, being independent, managing, or not getting into trouble.

Indeed, there is some danger in thinking of help primarily in these terms. The concept of the "sick" and the "well" person, or the "sick" and "well" segment of society, leads only too easily into confusing the helping process with the process or processes of control. Help is something a person finds. He is the one who acts on it. The decisions in it are his. He may not ask for it directly. It may be offered to him, even presented to him as a virtual "must." But he cannot be given it. Control, on the other hand, is society acting on him. He is no longer the "subject," as it were, of the sentence, the one who acts. He has become the "object," the one who is acted upon. Fundamentally these are two different processes.

Yet the line is a very fine one, and this is where confusion begins. Undoubtedly some people do, in the present state of our knowledge, need acting on for a while before they can act for themselves. How many such people there are is anyone's guess. One thing we do know, however. The tendency, in any helper, when he feels that the other person is not making use of help, is to begin to control. Usually he rationalizes it in terms of the helped person's good. "He will be happier if I can get him to . . ." do what the helping person thinks would be good for him. Often, too, the helping person conceals from himself how much control he is in fact exercising. He is not "telling so and so what to do." He is not ordering or commanding. But he is manipulating, persuading, shaming, praising, approving, creating an emotional dependence in which the helped person would be most uncomfortable if he did not do what the helper wants.

The situation is further complicated by the very fact that, as we shall see, a measure of temporary dependence, trust, or acknowledgment of the helper's ability to help is part of a true helping process. The problem is, then, for the helper not to prolong this passing phase, and if the helper is one who finds controlling easier than giving help, he may not only not know where to stop but may go under the impression that what he is giving is really help.

Apart from obvious control situations, such as the enforcement of law, control of another's life and actions may be necessary in some situations, where a social problem is concerned or where the person to be helped is, it appears, quite unable to make use of help in the sense that we have been discussing. These situations must not, however, be confused with those where the helping person is frustrated, has offered inappropriate help, or has a tendency to control. For this reason the decision to manipulate another, even for his own good, should be a professional one, backed by adequate diagnosis. It should always be made reluctantly and with the knowledge that the failure to help may be as much due to our own lack of knowledge, or ability to put it into practice, as it is to the person being helped.

If control is necessary, moreover, it should always be intended to lead to the helped person's ability to make use of help on his own. A general theory validating control, manipulation, or "authority" in the sense of claiming the right or the responsibility to represent eithei society's interests or the interest of the helped person himself, is a very serious thing. It might possibly be assumed by a socially-based profession, such as social work, although even there it is often assumed too glibly. It is much more questionable in other professions, such as the ministry, vocational guidance, or various forms of counseling. It is quite inexcusable between nonprofessional adults, except in as far as the helped person is willing to grant it, and even here, as we shall see, it is often most undesirable.

Indeed the political implications of a theory that permits, or encourages, control or manipulation for the helped person's good or which thinks in terms of "sick" and "well" are at their best a little frightening. If they are allowed to develop too far they can become the rationale of paternalism, colonialism, and even totalitarianism. The right to decide that another person needs to be manipulated, and that one has the right to do this, is one that needs very careful guarding. This is true even of the scientifically trained. Even the best of the social sciences, putting aside for the moment all questions of accuracy, new discovery, or changes in fashion, is to some extent the slave of the existent culture. Its value system, however acceptable it may seem, is not susceptible to proof and is all too often simply assumed without too much thought. The same, let me say, might be said of some of the values on which this book is predicated, but that is one of the reasons why I teach a helping method as free as possible from controls.

Control, manipulation, and the like should not however be confused with helping people in a framework of authority such as exists in probation, protective services for children, or work with those committed to an institution.

Some of the clearest examples of the helping process can be found in such services. It would be entirely false to think of the helping process as "permissive" or careless of the demands of society on the individual. The difference between the two processes does not lie in the existence or nonexistence of external controls, nor in the kind of conditions which the helped person may put on his ability or willingness to help—indeed, as we shall see, some such controls and conditions are necessary to constructive helping. It lies, rather, in one's concept of what "to help" someone else means—whether it is to offer someone one's skills, one's knowledge, one's self in relationship and one's resources for him to use as he finds it possible to do so within the limits of society's demand and the possibility that failure to use help may involve him in unpleasant or even disastrous consequences, or whether one has in the back or even the front of one's mind some goal for the other person which is ultimately one's own decision and not his, however good this may seem for him. And, curiously, it may be discovered that to give up this goal for another is in many cases to make it more likely to be achieved.

Despite some present moving in the opposite direction in social work, which has quite lately become impressed once again with its social responsibility, experience has on the whole tended to enlarge the number of people who can make use of a true helping process. The mentally ill, in the "well" part of themselves, the mentally retarded, some of whom can use help very well, and children, even very young children, are good examples. This is a constantly encouraging fact. Hopefully, it will mean in the end that control processes will need to be used less and less, unless more and more people become sick in a way that they cannot use help. And this is good, not only politically and philosophically, but because help, in the form of a process in which the individual makes use of help in his own way and acts as subject, not as object, does lead to firmer decisions and more lasting results. Some decisions can be reached by manipulation, especially perhaps decisions that although at first induced become possible a second time, as when a child, cajoled into the water, finds that he really can swim, and afterwards is not afraid. But often this does not happen. And those decisions one has to live with, question again and again, the sort of decision, for instance, that an unmarried mother makes when she gives up a child for adoption, have to be one's own. Manipulation may help one to make the decision but when questions arise later cannot carry one through.

The two processes are in fact quite different. Indeed there is some question whether there really are valid "processes" of control. What people appear to use as control measures are a mixture of all the old and well-tried expedients for getting someone to do what one wants. Some of these are not so bad—cajoling, challenging, persuading, influencing, reassuring, rewarding, praising, even some forms of conditioning. But they can become a process only if we can see people moving through them in some sort of logical order or sequence. Yet the very nature of control is that its methods are selective. At one time one preaches. At another one praises, blames, or encourages. The only consistency evident appears to be in the helper's perception of what might be effective at the moment. Even though consistency be maintained in terms of a diagnosis of the helped person's psychosocial situation, this differs from one situation to another, and to teach such methods of control would involve that very emphasis on diagnosis we have suggested as impractical or indeed unwise for the ordinary helper. It had better be left for the professional social worker or psychologist who is concerned with specific treatment situations.

Indeed to attempt to teach control methods within the scope of this book would be confusing. Sometimes for instance, a method which is harmful if used in trying to help the majority of people is appropriate in a control or treatment situation. False reassurance is a distinct pitfall in helping but might conceivably be used as a manipulative method. For this reason I have not dealt with control methods, except negatively in this book, with the exception of the discussion of "parenting" in chapter 9. I shall concentrate on the helping process.

What then do we really mean by help? What are its goals? How does it transcend "adaptive efficiency" or the "absence of disabling conditions"? We can perhaps get some clues to its nature when we say, as some people do, that one of the goals of help is something called "self-fulfillment."

This rather undefined concept does point to two characteristics of help. It emphasizes that help is something that occurs in the self. It has to do with growth and change. And it carries the implication that help also has to do with living life more fully, which might mean quite a number of things. Social work in one of its semiofficial statements, speaks of man's innate drive towards self-fulfillment, which is, I think, open to question, although there is no question but that self-fulfillment is what man perhaps blunderingly looks for and knows for good when he finds it to any degree. This is recognized even by those who practice many kinds of control.

Those who believe strongly in manipulative methods often justify what they are doing by saying that when normal functioning is restored the helped person will now be free and possess the resources to pursue self-fulfillment.

Again, perhaps this is a partial truth. Some people seem able to experience life intensely, to be particularly alive, to make decisions confidently, to surmount apparent disaster, and in particular to be capable of man's two most satisfying, prized, and ultimate emotions, which he has called love and joy, as it were on their own. These are not necessarily people who are adaptively efficient or free from disabling conditions, although perhaps they tend to be. Certainly they have, perhaps, a better chance if they are. Others, however, who would appear to have much the same opportunity remain for some reason half-alive, indecisive, incapable of any emotion that could be called either love or joy except in a most superficial sense. Still others arrive at the first condition, or something much nearer to it, in a relationship with another through a process known as help.

Philosophically what is being asserted here is the difference between personality and individuality.[4] Individuality sees each person as unique in his difference from other people, as for instance, the number 17,194 is different from 17,195, in its possible factorization, absolute size, sum of its digits, etc. It forces one, on the one hand, to recognize this difference, but on the other to find ways to reconcile it with others, by perhaps, adding 1. This is the individualization that has permeated our public relief system and in the name of individuality created a rather horrible instance of personal control on the part of welfare workers. It is an essentially self-centered concept in which difference becomes so important that mutuality is often lost.

Personality, on the other hand, is not a category of comparison. It is what is truly unique, not just different, in any human being, his self, his style, his feelings, his capacity for love and joy, his face, his expression, which are not reducible to any but the broadest and usually rather meaningless differences. It is what one falls in love with in another person, and at the same time what makes it possible for one person to overcome and another to be overwhelmed by the same set of social and psychological circumstances. And perhaps paradoxically, what nurtures personality is not so much treating people as different but treating people the same with appreciation of how differently they will make use of a process, a grant, or a law.

This is very different from forcing conformity on them; it is in fact the individualist who actually demands conformity, for as C. S. Lewis says, "The power of man to make himself what he pleases . . . means

4. This distinction is somewhat similar to that made by Nicolai Berdyaev in his *Slavery and Freedom*, trans. R. M. French (New York, 1944), chap. 1, but has been developed somewhat differently.

the power of some men to make other men what they please."[5] The power to treat people differently always means the denial of their rights to be treated as people.

Love and joy are factors in personality, not in individuality. And personality always requires, or, rather, results in, a mutuality quite different from that of the individualist. It is my contention here that help, which is a mutual process, has to do more with personality than it has with individuality.

The actual "help" given may be very small, even what might be thought of as trivial, such as assistance in mending a tire or a small indication of concern. The same thing, given a little differently, may mean nothing at all or may increase some inward fear or sense of defeat. But this time something happens. The helped person gains some little measure of courage, some little clarification of how things really are, some little more ability to meet the next situation, which he did not have before.

Sometimes the change is quite dramatic. Sometimes it comes bit by bit. But one thing we do know about it. In nearly every situation there is some point in time at which the human organism seems to decide—a poor word, but perhaps the best we have—whether to use this help or reject it. The original decision may have to be reaffirmed again and again, but it has to be made in the first place. Something new has to start. This leads to us talking sometimes of a "turning point in help," and we might note that this phenomenon is quite well-known in medicine. In many diseases and injuries there is a point at which the patient either gives in to the disease, and in that case often dies, or appears to decide to get well, sometimes in spite of the most logical prognosis.

At this point, too, we join hands again with the clinical helper, the man who, because he is dealing with a real pathology, must make an accurate diagnosis. He too is dependent on something within the patient, an elusive something that could variously be called coopera-tion, resolution, or decision, but which results in some change and redeployment of forces which, for lack of a better term, we will call "movement." With this movement his careful treatment has a good chance of success. Without it the best treatment, the best advice, may quite likely go to waste.

The characteristics associated with movement are probably best described as courage, purposiveness, and clarity. These should not be

5. C. S. Lewis. *The Abolition of Man* (New York, 1947), p. 37.

considered the ultimate goals of help. They are rather necessary preliminaries to achieving what one wants. One of the commonest mistakes in helping is, in fact, to try to induce a quality such as ambition or sexual morality without the realization that courage, clarity, and purposiveness are a necessary preliminary to it. This is the fault of much earnest preaching. It tries to achieve the final result without going through the steps.

Let us then summarize briefly what we have said about help. This may help us go on to the question of whether a true process exists. Help then is more than something given by one person to another. It is something given in such a way that the other can make use of it. It is more than restoring something dysfunctional to normal operation. It does not depend entirely on a process of diagnosis and treatment, and indeed its primary manifestation, movement, is necessary even where there is good diagnosis and treatment. It is more than politeness, or even listening, although both of these may be components. It is something that happens in the self of the helped person, and is characterized by new courage, clarity, and purposiveness. It begins to take place the moment two people meet for the purpose of helping. It is sometimes more effective in crisis situations. There is often a "turning point" in helping, one of the signs, incidentally, that a process does exist. Its general goal can be described in terms of "self-fulfillment" and is associated with experiencing life deeply, and in particular the emotions of love and joy. It takes place in a relationship between two people or groups of people. There are at the present some groups of people whom we do not know how to help, but these are growing fewer.

This is perhaps as near as one can come to a definition of help, but for those who like definitions I would offer the following simplification: Help is something tangible or intangible offered by one person or group to another in such a way that the helped person or group can use it to achieve some measure of self-fulfillment.

It is my contention that anything so complicated, so difficult, at points, to define, but having definite characteristics, is worthy of more detailed study. In this I am encouraged by the attempts of others to do the same.

The literature of helping is not, however, extensive, and much of it, especially in the counseling field, is little more than a collection of pragmatic rules or suggestions for practice, without any unified theory behind them. Others, especially in social work, are concerned chiefly with diagnosis and treatment but not with helping theory as such. Possibly the first major contribution to theory within the grasp of the nonprofessional was Carl Rogers's "nondirective counseling"[6] which established, perhaps for the first time, the principle that the source of movement was in the helped person himself. Herbert Aptekar, in his *Basic Concepts in Social Casework*,[7] did a great deal to clarify for us the role of will and denial when two people come together, one to be helped and the other to help. Anita Faatz in her *Nature of Choice in Casework Process*,[8] in 1953, contributed vastly to our understanding of the phenomenon of choice. These two books came from the so-called "functional" or Rankian school of social work at the University of Pennsylvania. This school made enormous contributions to the understanding of help, but, in some people's minds at least, developed something of a mystique and a specialized use of language which made it hard for what they said to be understood. I have tried in this book, as far as possible, to avoid doing the same.

Another social work book which made a definite contribution was Helen Harris Perlman's *Social Casework: A Problem-Solving Process*,[9] particularly in the way she combines diagnostic helping skills and makes use of the psychological theories of Erik Erickson. Herbert Aptekar's second book, *The Dynamics of Case Work and Counselling*[10] is also useful in distinguishing different forms of the helping method. Melvin Glasser's *Reality Therapy*[11] does indeed formulate a theory of help which emphasizes one part of the helping process—the use of reality—which is often ignored or evaded, and which certainly needed reaffirming. He deals with other elements more or less implicitly. He is also so concerned with proving the success of his method, and the mistakes of conventional psychotherapy, that his book has only limited value in constructing comprehensive theory.

Since this book was conceived, however, and indeed was in rough draft, Stanley C. Mahoney published his *Art of Helping People*

6. The term comes from Rogers, *Counselling and Psychotherapy* (Boston, 1942).

7. Herbert Aptekar, *Basic Concepts in Social Case Work* (Chapel Hill, N.C., 1941).

8. Anita Faatz, *The Nature of Choice in Casework Process* (Chapel Hill, N.C., 1953).

9. Helen Harris Perlman, *Social Casework: A Problem-Solving Process* (Chicago, 1957).

10. Herbert Aptekar, *The Dynamics of Casework and Counselling* (Boston, 1955).

11. Melvin R. Glasser, *Reality Therapy: A New Approach to Psychiatry* (New York, 1965).

Effectively.[12] This was the first book for the lay helper since Karl de Schweinitz' *Art of Helping People in Trouble,*[13] published in 1924. Dr. Mahoney's book is a genuine attempt to outline a helping theory. Readers will recognize in it a number of concepts that are stressed in mine but have otherwise rarely been expressed, notably the inclusion of rejoicing (joy) as one of the goals of helping, his recognition of humility as a helping virtue—he calls it "acceptance of our limitations" —his insistence on a "concept of separateness" and the clear distinction he makes between helping and controlling. There might almost seem to have been collusion, instead of what has actually happened, the arrival at common concepts by two people working independently and from quite a different professional background.

Dr. Mahoney's book, however, falls a little short of presenting a unified theory of helping. His major conceptualization is his division of the "art" into four factors, which he calls acceptance, presence (on which he is very good indeed), listening, and information-giving, but there is little demonstration of why these are helping factors and how they are interrelated. In my opinion he also underestimates the use of reality and the helped person's resistance to taking help.

Perhaps this is because he sees helping as an art and I see it both as art and science. It is not a science, of course, in the strict Cartesian sense of the word. Some of its formulations and quite a bit of its results are not susceptible to proof or measurement. It is hard to measure love or joy. But it does possess a body of knowledge, based on observation, and the parts of this knowledge that have been acquired do appear to have some sort of logical relationships with others. The very correspondences between Dr. Mahoney's formulations and mine would seem to argue this kind of connection.

Then, while this book was in its final stages, Robert R. Carkhuff published the first volume of his *Helping and Human Relations: A Primer for Lay and Professional Helpers,* a book hailed by a colleague in its foreword as "the first time that we have a comprehensive model for helping."[14]

Despite its subtitle the book is likely to appeal only to those familiar with social science method and vocabulary. Much of it consists of tests

12. Stanley C. Mahoney, *The Art of Helping People Effectively* (New York, 1967).

13. Karl de Schweinitz, *The Art of Helping People in Trouble* (Boston and New York, 1924).

14. Robert R. Carkhuff, *Helping and Human Relations: A Primer for Lay and Professional Helpers,* vol. 1 (New York, 1969), Foreword by Bernard G. Berenson, p. viii.

and criteria for the selection of trainee helpers or counselors. Helping theory is covered however in 121 assumptions, propositions, corollaries, and conclusions of which the following is not atypical: "A comprehensive model for helping processes must consider helpee movement towards improved capacities for understanding and action with relevant responsive and initiative helper variables."[15] Yet when Dr. Carkhuff is not engaged in constructing his model he shows himself to have real feeling for people, as when he writes of those "searching for help and yet rejecting it, seeking light yet preferring darkness, crying for life yet choosing death"[16] in terms reminiscent of Anita Faatz.

With a great majority of Dr. Carkhuff's formulations, which he claims to be scientifically validated, one cannot help but agree. Indeed this book states most of them in somewhat different terms. He sees "all effective interpersonal processes" as sharing "a common set of conditions that are conducive to facilitative human experiences";[17] in other words, he sees a common helping process. He mentions in particular empathy, respect, and concreteness as primary elements in this process, which is not far from my own formulation in chapter 5. He believes in feeling, in genuineness, in immediacy, in the helping experience as strengthening the helped person's ability to tackle other problems, and in the contribution of helping people who do not have sophisticated diagnostic skill and knowledge. Where I would part company with him is in his insistence that the helping person's ability to help is largely dependent on his own superior level of functioning,[18] his overemphasis, in my opinion, of the helped person's need to understand his problem intellectually, and in the fact that his model seems to allow little room for the helped person's will, resistance, and choice, although his more lyrical passages show his understanding of this.

How absolutely Dr. Carkhuff's model has been objectively validated depends on the measures he uses to indicate success, which are not entirely clear, the objectives he sees helping to have, which have to do with "handling difficulties," and the meaning he ascribes to such words as "genuineness." Nevertheless his is a valuable book and it is somewhat gratifying to see a theory developed within the canons of social science research arrive at so many of the same conclusions as my own more experiental, philosophical, and theoretical approach.

15. Ibid, p. 57.
16. Ibid., p. 22.
17. Ibid., pp. xii, 26, 45.
18. Ibid., pp. 45.

How much this process can be taught is a question to which we have no definite answer. Certainly its major principles can be set forth in logical form and to this extent it can be thought of as a communicable science, although obviously one in its infancy. At the same time it must be recognized that its practice requires both experience and the acquisition of a considerable self-discipline. In this respect it is perhaps an art, but not an art that operates without structure and form and that cannot be analyzed.

Some writers would appear to deny the possibility of this self-discipline being acquired in any way except, perhaps, by life experience and practice, but there is considerable evidence that a combination of theory and practice, and in particular the experience of being the recipient of help oneself can do much to help a student acquire both the self-discipline and the sensitivity that helping requires. It is also my observation that despite some vigorous statements to the contrary, it is possible for a person, once having grasped the basic theory, to advance his own skill. This is never an easy matter. It involves, as we shall see, considerable self-examination and considerable trying out of this in practice. This is certainly a less sure method than undertaking a professional education, in, say, a school of social work, which is deliberately structured to help the student acquire the necessary insights and self-discipline, but it would be naïve to suggest that all those who are or will be involved in helping could or would even want to undertake such a course. There is certainly something a helper can learn on his own.

At the same time there is need for a coherent theory of help, and perhaps even more urgently, a common language or set of concepts wherein helping people and helping professions can communicate their ideas and their experience. Is it, for instance, too much to hope that there will be some day, in universities, one or more courses in helping theory required of students preparing for any one of the helping professions, including law, medicine, the ministry, teaching, and social work and available to others, perhaps as an elective or in extension? Such a common background would add much to our ability to avoid at least the major mistakes in helping, the relationships which are from the beginning unproductive of help, that are all too common today. It might do something to prevent the waste of good intentions that is presently occurring. It might even produce a number of quite efficient helpers, adding their natural abilities to a core of understanding of basic principles. That at least is my dream. With this in mind let us turn to the problem of taking help.

II. TAKING HELP

Perhaps the most important thing to realize at the very beginning about help is that most people do not want to be helped in any significant way. The great majority even of those who ask for help are at the same time very much afraid of it. They may, in fact, actively work to render it fruitless at the same time as they ask for it.

These may seem extraordinary statements when so many people appear to be demanding help of one sort or another, when requests for welfare services are increasing on every hand and when one of the major fears of the populace as a whole is, in America at least, that we are raising a generation who have been led to expect assistance from some governmental unit rather than to rely on their own initiative. Yet it is a fact that most people who are in trouble both want help and are terrified of it. Indeed in most cases the fear of any kind of help that would really induce change or movement is greater at first than the desire for it.

We can understand this fear better, perhaps, if we consider what asking for help demands. The person who asks for the kind of help that will really make a difference to him must, in fact, do four things. He must recognize that something is wrong with or lacking in his situation which he can do nothing about by himself. He must be willing to tell someone else about his problem. He must accord to this other person at least a limited right to tell him what to do or to do things for him. And finally he must be willing to change in some way himself. This means giving up whatever adjustments he has been able to make to the present situation—adjustments that may have and probably have cost him a great deal to make and have become part of himself and wholly necessary to him—in favor of a new kind of life, which he may have some reason to believe will be more satisfactory but which, at the same time, is an unknown quantity, full of possible dangers.

But the difficulty is greatly increased if up to the time of asking for help a person's experience of permitting another to take some control of his affairs has been that he is taken advantage of; if telling another has meant that his confidence is abused; or if his attempts to live a supposedly more productive life have always resulted in defeat. And these have been the experience of all too many of those who are in need of help.

Yet for the most part this tremendous demand made on the person to be helped has gone unrecognized. People who refuse help are still thought of as ungrateful when all they really are is afraid. Others are thought to be insensitive, not to know there is something wrong, or to lack simple common sense, when in fact they are acutely aware of the wrongness but even more afraid of what it would cost them to put it right. Many are stigmatized as content with unsatisfactory or degrading conditions when all that they are is scared to act on their discontent, something that has become quite obvious in the past few years in the United States, when it has become a little less risky for the Negro population to express its wish for a better life and its discontent with its old one, and the illusion of the "contented darkey" has been recognized as such. Again it might be said that one of the major medical problems of our time is the number of people who are sick and afraid to get well, not because they like being sick any more than the rest of us, but because being well would involve expectations of them which they are afraid they will be unable to fulfill.

Is it surprising, then, that many people will do almost anything to prevent themselves from being caught in the process of receiving meaningful help? Is it surprising that many people meet an offer of help with suspicion, or work hard to limit the kind of help they will receive?

Anyone whose business it is to help others will recognize quite a number of different stages in this struggle. First are those who apparently do not recognize at all that they lack anything or are in any kind of trouble. Those who truly lack this recognition are, I suggest, rather few, although in some situations people do repress unpleasant realities and lose touch with reality.

More often, perhaps, the person is aware of some sense of wrongness, but, by putting the whole matter outside himself, either adapts to it by accepting his need to suffer and gets what satisfaction he can out of this, or persuades himself somehow that the problem is temporary and will go away if he waits it out.

Sometimes he tries to solve the problem by setting up certain conditions in which it is manageable, either consciously or unconsciously, in which case we call him neurotic. He may find, for instance, that he can live with the problem if he can claim special privileges from others by reason of his illness, or his more or less imagined status as self-sacrificing wife, loved child, business executive, martyr, or even target of misfortune. He will not usually ask help unless hard realities impinge on his privilege, and sometimes, even then, he will escape by denying this reality to the point that he becomes psychotic rather than neurotic.

Sometimes, although he apparently recognizes no need for help, he does in fact do so, consciously or unconsciously, but cannot take the second step, that of admitting it to another. Still, he needs help, and his only recourse is to act in such a way that help is forced on him, often apparently against his will. We are all familiar with the child who misbehaves in order to draw attention to the trouble he is in, although we often dismiss his action as somehow meaningless because "it was only done to get attention." Yet this is the child's way of bringing his distress to our notice. We are perhaps less likely to see an adult's behavior or even his criminal act as a plea for help, although experience has shown us that this is often what it is. Hierens, the murderer of Suzanne Degnan, scrawled on the child's mirror with lipstick a plea for the police to catch him before he did such a thing again.

This phenomenon is apparent in many court hearings involving neglect of children. The parents have often been offered all kinds of help before the matter was brought to court and have apparently either rejected it or proved incapable of making any improvement in response to urging, persuasion, or opportunity to do a better job. They are brought to court "as a last resort." The court may see its action as a regrettable act of force, but actually this is the way that the parents have chosen to yield to the demand that they be helped, a way in which they do not have to admit their lack of love for their children but can feel themselves to be deprived of their children's care against their will. Indeed if there have been adequate services which really offer help to a family before it comes to court, the chances are very small indeed that the court actually makes a decision against the will of the parents. Usually it does little more—although this little more is important—than to confirm the parents' will and give substance to it.

We are obviously caught here in something of a semantic tangle. The order of the court is clearly against the parents' expressed wishes. They may be very angry at it, and genuinely so. It is not a matter of the parents' having lied when they protested their love for their children. Human emotions are much too complicated to be expressed in such terms as "wish" or "want." We run into much the same difficulty when we use the terms "conscious" or "unconscious," which is why I find myself writing, as I have in the paragraph above, "consciously or unconsciously" as if I were uncertain which it was. A better phrase might be "consciously *and* unconsciously," for while it is possible to speak of a conscious act, such as a premeditated murder, and an unconscious one, such as blushing, when we talk about a person's desires, his "wishing" or "wanting" something, we are talking about something that has both conscious and unconscious elements.

Nor can we solve the problem by talking about someone's "real" wish or desire, as we do when we say that what a person asks for at first is often not what he "really" wants, since in fact it is this that he "really" wants at that time but not what in time he will find himself to want. The truth is that to will something—and I shall use that word, among others, to express what I think people mean when they talk of "really wishing"—is not an emotion at all. It is an act of commitment to a certain course of action, and involves being prepared to carry through with it. As such it is both conscious and unconscious, for both conscious and unconscious preparedness is necessary if the commitment is to be carried out. Quite often we find, for instance, an apparent commitment that is made with no reservations on a conscious level at all, but which is utterly destroyed by an unconscious factor. A man may apparently want a job and do all that he can to obtain it, but when its pressures become too great for him he may escape by developing an allergy to the materials with which he works. He does not do so consciously and yet it could be said of him that his will to do the job was somehow incomplete. The same is true of the neglecting parent, who may genuinely "wish" or "want" to do a better job, but does not actually have the "will" to do so.

But even should a person get to the point that he recognizes his need for help, and go perhaps to considerable trouble to seek out someone who can help him, he is still very far from accepting help. He now has the problem of telling this person about his trouble. He may, of course, lack words to do so, especially if he comes from a culture which is not accustomed to discussing how one feels about anything. But even if he has the words and wants very much to communicate what he feels, and to have this other person "understand" him and his problem, he puts a special meaning into the word "understand."

He does not want the helping person to understand him completely, to know him in all his weakness. He wants the other person to understand his point of view, to see things as he sees them, to approve of him in some fashion, to accord him some respect. He may, therefore, under- or overstate his problem. He may tell only part of the story, again either consciously or unconsciously. Nearly always he will manage somehow to put the problem outside himself, to ask not that he be changed but that some other person be talked to and made to change. If he does admit some need for change on his own part, perhaps because he feels that he ought to, this is usually some part of himself he is willing to let go and therefore not too important to him.

Sometimes he will refuse to discuss the matter at all. He will uphold that he knows the solution to his problem, which he can accomplish by himself if only he receives a certain specified bit of help. One can recognize the phase, "All I want (or need) is . . ." which actually often means, "Give me this, which may or may not solve the problem for me—and don't dare tell me what I really need." Often someone who handles his fear of help in this way is very demanding and insists on his rights to a certain kind of assistance, so that he gives the impression of being greedy or overready to accept help, when he is actually trying to ward off being helped. He is one whose courage has failed him at the point of asking for help. He wants help but is willing to take it only on his own terms, although these very terms protect him from really being helped. Again, however, he is not lying, or deliberately asking for something which he does not need. For the moment, he really wants what he is asking for.

This demand for help on one's own terms and no other is often seen among parents who bring their children to a psychiatric or guidance center. They are often quite surprised and even resentful when the psychiatrist or the social worker wants to see them as well as the child. They try to limit their participation to that of giving information about their child so that the psychiatrist may know how to help him. The last thing they really want to consider is the part they have played in the child's problem and their need to change in their relationship to him.

A related way of warding off help is to throw the whole burden of decision onto the helping person—"You tell me what to do." This way of avoiding the necessity for change is particularly difficult for some helping people to understand, since they naturally want to do things for people who want help and it does look, at least for the moment, as if the client really does want one to help. He is actually asking for advice and up to a point he will take it. But since there has been no real change in the client's view of the problem or his readiness to do something about it, the helping person's prescribed remedies generally fail to do what they were intended to accomplish. Often, in fact, this very failure of the remedy to solve the problem without calling for any change in the person asking for help will be used to deny that the helping person has any knowledge of his subject, or "really understands."

This phenomenon is well known to anyone who has been a consultant. The client follows the consultant's recommendations in great detail. He is enormously cooperative. But the course of action prescribed fails to solve the problem, not because the consultant was wrong in what he suggested, but because the client accepts the consultant's suggestions as law to be meticulously followed. He does not make the suggestions his own. He does not adapt them to the particular situation in which he finds himself, and which only he knows fully—a fact which consultants sometimes forget in their eagerness to prescribe. And, as a result, the consultant is not only wasted, he is discredited as well.

A more extreme form of warding off help by thrusting decision onto the helping person is to get that person to do what one needs to do for oneself—to find one a job, or look for a house, or inquire about a resource. This sometimes pleases the helper, who feels that he is "doing something to help," but all too often, what the helping person does or finds, turns out to be something less than the helped person feels that he needs.

Up to this point we have been considering the negative impulse, the fear of being helped, and it may seem to the reader that not only are people who need help highly ingenious and dishonest in defeating those who wish to help them, but that it is something of a miracle that help ever gets given at all. But quite clearly this is not so. Thousands of people do get effective help daily, although probably not as many as should. Even with all the protections man throws up around himself, his need to be helped is there.

Nor are these protections in themselves unworthy things. They can, and are, and ought to be used to ward off all kinds of interference, patronage, or desire to contol that may be offered under the name of help. The only reasons for dwelling on them at such a length are that they also exist in a genuine helping situation and must be recognized and worked with, and the fact that they are too often seen as moral faults which somehow could be conquered with an act of the will, instead of the almost impulsive and quite natural defenses that they are.

How universal is this resistance to help? The very fact that it is not generally recognized might suggest that we have been generalizing here in much too total a fashion.

Do all people resist help? Are there not some who genuinely seek advice, whose need for help is so much greater than their fear of it that they are ready to place themselves unreservedly in the hands of another? Is it not possible, even, that what we have been describing here is in fact the exception, the neurotic reaction, and that ordinary people do not go through this struggle? Most of us can remember times when we have been helped in which we can recall only eagerness for help and gratitude when it has been given. But if we think more deeply we can also remember our doubts and fears, our difficulty, say, in approaching the bank for a loan or in sharing our problems with a counselor. One of the exercises sometimes demanded of social work students early in their learning process is to give an account of some occasion in their lives when they have needed or asked for help. To read these accounts is often a poignant experience, so real are the fears and doubts recalled. So far from these being the outpourings of the most neurotic students, the reverse is true. It is the more neurotic student, the student who can only live with a tightly controlled artificial projection of himself, what is sometimes called a persona, and the student who is unlikely to be able to learn to help others, who does not recognize that help is hard to take or confirms this fact, without perhaps realizing that this is what he is doing, by denying stoutly that he has ever needed or asked for help in his life. The process of taking help is so painful that many of us repress it or rationalize it in some way.

Many of the occasions about which these students write may seem comparatively trivial. Some have to do with seeking help from a teacher in high school or college when they have found themselves "lost" in a course, some with such apparently unimportant happenings as being stranded with a car which stops running in an unfamiliar place. The majority have to do with borrowing money. Yet it would probably be too much to assert that there are not certain situations where the help to be given is so unlikely to touch one deeply or to demand any change in oneself that it is quite easy to ask. Some people have no hesitation in asking the way if they are lost. I myself would far prefer in most situations to be lost than to ask the way. In some situations, too—and asking the way should be one of them—the help which one asks is so obviously something one cannot be blamed for not having oneself that it is not too hard to turn to the expert. It is not too difficult, perhaps, to consult a lawyer about the law or a scholar in some other field about his specialty, as long as the answer is unlikely to affect one too deeply. But most people are somewhat less than wholly frank with their doctor.

But what about matters which do affect one deeply? Is it not possible that a person's need is so great that his resistance to seeking help has in fact been effectually answered before he comes to the helping situation?

There are such situations. They occur principally when a person is in a state of crisis, that will make a major change in his life inevitable. There is, in this kind of situation, very little of the old and familiar to cling to. If help can be offered before new resistance can be formed, it may be accepted with some eagerness. But even here the process is not one of putting oneself in the hands of another to make one's decisions for one. It is a process of discovering in oneself new methods of coping with what is essentially a new situation, calling for new roles to be played. For a while, after a crisis, people are forced into activity, even in the form of protest. This short, vulnerable period, which may result in new ways of handling things, is all too often followed, if help is not given, by despair and finally by detachment from the problem or denial of it. The helping person is not always available at a time of crisis. Most people wait until long after a crisis before they seek help. They try to solve their problem alone until they become convinced of their own inability to do so. This is true even of such obvious help as public assistance. A study of the 1950s showed that 59 percent of families eventually applying for aid to dependent children did not do so until six months after the family crisis—death, desertion, or incapacity of the father—which made assistance necessary.[1]

In the vast majority of situations the wholehearted putting of oneself in the hands of another is more likely to be apparent than real. To allow another to make one's decisions for one is more likely to be a disguised way of resisting help than an acceptance of it. It is one way of avoiding making hard decisions oneself, and although there may be occasions where this is a sign of growth it is more likely to be a sign of the opposite. The one situation in which it is a sign of growth is perhaps that in which the person has been trying to make decisions for which he does not have the equipment—perhaps trying to conduct his own case at law, or prescribing for himself medically, or needing to prove for himself facts that other researchers have established.

It might be argued, and is sometimes, that to submit oneself to the

1. Gordon W. Blackwell and Raymond Gould, *Future Citizens All* (Chicago, 1952) , pp. 26-27.

expertise of the social scientist is not, in fact, very different from doing the same with a lawyer or a physician, and that the person who more or less blithely does what a social worker or a counselor tells him to do is not so much resisting help as accepting the fact that he cannot manage his own life and finding help in doing so. Why should making the decision to trust a doctor to tell me in detail what I should do to strengthen a broken leg be so very different from, say, trusting a marriage counselor or a minister to tell me in detail what to do to strengthen a broken marriage?

The claim of the social scientist or any other expert in living to the same status as the doctor is based on the assumption that in fact I can strengthen my marriage by putting myself unreservedly in his hands. But question must be raised about the possibility of this. It is not simply a matter of marriage being a much more complicated an organism than a broken leg, which may not be in some senses true. Nor is it only a matter of the physical sciences being much older and knowing much more about their material than the social sciences do as yet, however true this be at the moment. This would suggest that the social sciences might eventually attain this knowledge, whereas the difference is more fundamental. Nor does the apparently promising answer that a leg is a concrete thing with its own regenerative process, apart from my feeling about it, while a marriage needs for its betterment the involvement of my feeling, my unconscious as well as my conscious will, which cannot be prescribed for me, entirely answer the problem. My unconscious feelings do and may enter in very largely to what happens to my leg. I may have, for instance, an unconscious desire for my leg not to get well, to claim the indulgence accorded to the man with a limp, and this may greatly affect how faithfully I follow the doctor's advice.

The difference lies in the fact that I am asking the doctor's advice only on how to deal with my leg, and I know, and can agree with him on what values are subsumed. This is a fairly simply matter—to have an operative leg or not to have one, or perhaps to have one that is partly operative. That what eventuates will have a great effect on the whole of my life is not denied, nor is the fact that I will have a number of decisions to make as a result of it. But these decisions I reserve for myself. I do not submit them to the doctor. As a matter of fact I do not believe, and he probably does not believe himself, that he is an expert in them. If he does, his relationship to me is radically altered. He is acting as expert in the whole matter of living and I will have much more resistance to placing myself in his hands.

But when I ask someone to tell me how my marriage can be strengthened and determine to follow his advice, this distinction no longer exists. Any change I make involves immediately all my relationships with people. And it is these relationships that comprise the expertise of the counselor. Having once assumed responsibility for my feelings, for my conscious and unconscious will, he cannot in fact limit the control he will exercise, or his work will be incomplete. He may require me to make decisions for myself. Any but the most cocksure or naïve counselor would do so. But if he did so he would in fact be denying the rightness of my total submission to his advice. He would be recognizing that this submission was a defense against really being helped, and would try to overcome my resistance to accepting a kind of help in which I was more active.

Moreover, in accepting his prescription without myself really making decisions about it—in deciding, that is, to let him make my decisions for me—I am accepting his values, his belief about what a marriage should be like. I must in fact do so, since his knowledge of how to achieve a goal must be predicated on some concept of this goal and will prove inadequate if the goal is altered. Whether this is, in fact, possible is very doubtful. Values, which in this case mean the whole range of human preference, both conscious and unconscious, are not only almost incredibly complex but highly individual.

It can only be assumed that the values of the helped person and of the helper (whose values are in themselves partly unconscious) can be fully acceptable to both in very general terms, in which case we are attempting to adjust a very complex machine with a very blunt instrument, or that it is really possible to know a man in such detail that it is possible to predict the whole of his response to a given situation and tailor a prescription to this. This, in turn, requires a belief that man is a wholly mechanical being, that his feelings, aspirations, even his consciousness itself is ultimately attributable to the laws of chemistry and physics, and although there are many who profess to believe this, this is usually an unprovable assertion and one that cannot be acted on with any certainty at all.

If, however, we make the assumption that there is something in man which cannot be measured or predicted, it is largely in the realms of values, or at least consciousness of values, that the difference must be assumed to lie. It would be precisely in the giving up of fine discrimination in this sphere that man would give up the very thing that makes him a man. To conceive of help as prescription in fact reduces it to the level of a control process directed at nothing more radical than adaptive efficiency. It leaves no place for love or joy.

The difficulty of taking help, the demands that accepting help make on a person, does however raise a very important question. What about the person who needs help but does not ask for it? How much ought we to press help on him and what happens to our theories when this has to be done?

We need to distinguish here three kinds of situations. There are first those who are in trouble in relation to some external force, such as the law. Maybe they have been brought to court, or will have to leave school if their grades do not improve. The very fact that they are in such trouble may be a concealed way of asking for help. Offered the help in facing their situation that the court, or the rules provide, they are often capable of putting their need into words and openly accepting help. Even if they are not, help must very plainly be offered, and the alternative, perhaps prison, perhaps loss of parental rights, perhaps having to leave school, must be made very clear. This cannot be done simply by offering the choice of taking or not taking help, alone and without help in coming to this decision. There are too many unknowns. Help is threatening enough to need careful exploring, in terms of what it may and may not involve. While the right to refuse it exists, and in fact it cannot be given unless there is some willingness to risk the refusal of it, it does need to be discussed with understanding of its difficulty. One may need help in accepting help. The helping person may also need to be very clear with him what the alternative is, and how hard it may be.

A remarkable fact is that help given under such circumstances is often most productive. The person to be helped is in a crisis situation; it is in facing alternatives that he has not chosen himself that he finds the power to move.

The second situation is more difficult to define, and, moreover, overlaps both with the first and the third. It is the situation in which a person plainly needs help but is unable to ask for it, and where the failure to get it will inevitably lead to some more or less major disaster—the delinquency of a child, or death from cancer, for example. Here we might feel a strong compulsion to offer help and most of us would certainly try. Sometimes in fact the very offer will make it possible for the other to respond. But all too often the very fact that help has not been asked in so obvious a situation means that the resistance to it is very deep indeed.

Some such resistance may be cultural. Refusal to ask help of official agencies, even those like the school and the welfare agency which are primarily helpful rather than authoritative, is not infrequently found in areas where there is a deep suspicion of all parts of the "establishment," beginning of course with the police.[2] Here a helper may have to be quite persistent and to work quite a long time on the very business of people's fears of taking help. But help can only be forthcoming as these fears are overcome.

In others it has to do with a phenomenon which we shall deal with more fully in chapter 3—that of "choice" and "nonchoice." Briefly, man in his encounter with any threatening piece of reality can and does react in one of four ways. He may accept and use the threat constructively to gain new resolution or clarity. He may struggle against the reality and try to change it in some way. He may try to ward it off by escaping into some fantasy or rationalization. Or he may allow it to paralyze or crush him.

The first two reactions can be spoken of as "choice-reactions." They lead to some action, good or bad. The second two we can call reactions of "nonchoice." They lead to no action.

In the situation of the person facing a crisis and apparently doing nothing about it we do need to consider whether this is a genuine case of "nonchoice" or whether the ill that we foresee for him has been chosen, perhaps in preference to some ill we cannot see, or as a deliberate risk. If it is genuine nonchoice we might try to intervene, not to prescribe what he should do, but to face him with the need for action of some sort.

This is a difficult and a skilled business. If we are going to attempt it we need to have some skill in helping. We need to be sure, too, of the almost objective nature of the disaster that will arise out of not taking help. It is very easy to confuse such a situation with a third kind, which is where the other person's need for help is really a matter of the would-be helper's opinion; where he disapproves, for instance, of the way the other is rearing his children, or where the result of what this person is doing will lead to something the helper does not want but the other for some reason does or is willing to accept. This may occur where, for instance, an elderly person prefers to live alone in rather unsuitable surroundings than go to a nursing home. Indeed, some modern studies warn against forcing help of this kind on the elderly. They suggest that to do so may even accelerate the time of death, and thus produce the very result the helper is trying to prevent.[3]

2. A good description of this kind of situation can be found in Alice Overton's, "Serving Families Who 'Don't Want Help,'" *Social Casework* 34 (July 1953) : 304-9.
3. While this has not actually been proved, studies tend to show that environmental change does hasten death. See an unpublished paper by Margaret

While intervention may be justified and responsible, all too often one's need to intervene is a matter of one's lack of belief in the right of individuals to manage their own lives. It may come, too, from the helping person's conviction that he is right and therefore has the right and responsibility to impose this rightness on others. Many people convince themselves that a person who is on the outside is less involved than the person seeking help and can therefore see things more clearly. To a limited extent this may be true. Sometimes there is a piece of reality which a person in trouble cannot see and which needs to be clarified. But for the most part it is not that the person to be helped does not see the reality, it is that he does not wish to face it, or sees it so plainly that he is overwhelmed by it. He is simply at this time unwilling or unready to accept an alternative course of action, and unless we really do have the right and the responsibility to force him to do so and the skill to do this, we may be simply infringing on his rights to live as he sees fit and in the way he wishes to do so.

It is not hard, however, for a person with a strong moral code of his own, or for one who believes himself to be some kind of expert in psychology or sociology, to find some mandate to intervene in such a situation and to insist that he is acting from a wholly laudable sense of responsibility. Then, when he meets resistance, he attempts to push it aside. Not only does he usually fail to help in such a situation; in a sense he poisons the ground. He controls, rather than helps and forces the person he is helping to throw up all of his defenses against any real change, and he often makes it more difficult for that person ever to take more constructive help.

Actual physical "asking" for help is therefore not necessary, although it is generally helpful and makes a good starting point. One social agency I know uses an application form even for the kind of help one generally thinks of as being wholly unasked, the help offered to a neglecting parent who is facing as an alternative to taking help the removal of his child from his home.[4] The recognition that this is help and that one can refuse it, if only at considerable cost, is a way of coming to terms with its difficulties. But readiness for help before it can be effectively given is a necessity. Help in the long run cannot be given. It can only be made possible.

Blenkner entitled "Environmental Change and the Aging Individual" given at a plenary session of the Seventh International Congress of Gerontology, Vienna, in June, 1966, and such studies as C. Aldrich and E. Mendkoff, "Relocation of the Aged and Disabled," *Journal of the American Geriatric Society* 11 (1963) : 185-94.
  4. The Baltimore Department of Public Welfare.

III. CHOOSING TO DO SOMETHING ABOUT IT

It is perfectly possible, up to a certain point, to control the actions of another. Men can be frightened, browbeaten, tricked, cajoled, gently persuaded, or argued into actions which will make them more acceptable to society. They may thereby become more comfortable for the time being in their daily lives and even apparently more at peace with themselves. Recent accounts of brainwashing and subliminal advertising have made clear how easily opinions and certain kinds of choices can be influenced. Hypnotism makes it clear that this is not entirely a conscious process, although it is generally held that the hypnotist cannot command behavior that is in conflict with what is rather loosely thought of as a man's "essential nature."

Sometimes, perhaps, it may be necessary to cajole, browbeat or gently persuade someone to a course of action that will for the moment ease his situation, or avert an obvious danger, before he can be helped in another way. These situations are, however, rarer than they might seem and often arise not from the real need of the person being helped but from the unwillingness of the helper to bear the helped person's situation or to risk the mistakes his clients may make in the course of his attempts to deal with it.

Nor are commands, suggestions, persuasion, or even punishment entirely ineffectual means of helping a person who is ready to accept them, as we know in the upbringing of children, when the right of the parent to this kind of control has been accepted by the child. It is only when they are relied on in the absence of any "will" (as we have used the word) or readiness to make use of them that they prove to be barren, leading to no lasting change, self-defeating, or actually harmful. It is at this point that we find "backslidings"—the helped person who "behaves beautifully" as long as the helper stays with him but then reverts to his former behavior—as well as the person whose efforts always seem to misfire since unconsciously he is resisting plans made for him, and the person who reacts against what he has been expected to do and ends up in a state of rebellion. To no small extent it is true that:

He who complies against his will
Is of the same opinion still.

To understand why this is so and the need for one or more acts of will on the part of the helped person before help can result in significant growth or change, we need to consider a phenomenon generally accepted in all psychological theory known as ambivalence. Ambivalence, literally "valuing both," means simply that all human emotions are a mixture of pleasure and pain, of positive and negative, of wanting and not wanting.

To say that man is ambivalent is another way of saying that there is always a price to pay for all human experience. Every emotion or desire contains to some degree its opposite. It is not possible, for instance, wholly to love another person without at the same time sometimes feeling angry with him for what this love is costing the lover, a fact that would make a lot of mothers much more comfortable if they would only believe it. Nor is any but the most trivial decision an unhesitating one. There is always the other side to the question, the other possible choice, the other potential advantage lost because we have chosen to do this rather than that.

It is not hard to see this principle operating in almost everything we may do. To go on a vacation, for instance, may seem entirely pleasurable. But the predominant positive feeling is still counterbalanced to some extent by the knowledge of the work accumulating on one's desk, or regret that one will not be involved in some decision that will be made in one's absence.

Normally this mild ambivalence presents little problem. Either the balance is very clearly on one side or the other, and we have little difficulty both in making up our mind and in living with our decision after it has been made; or the depth of emotion involved is trivial, in which case it hardly matters what we decide. Ambivalence is still present but can be easily accepted. But when the issues are large ones and, as they sometimes are, complicated and often nebulous, and the two sides of the question more or less evenly balanced, ambivalence may result in one of two conditions that may inhibit growth. Either one can become paralyzed by one's ambivalence, so that one does nothing at all, or one may try to escape the choice by making a second kind of "nonchoice," a choosing of something that is not there as a way around the problem. The first often gives the impression of stupidity, particularly in its true sense of being in a stupor. One either obstinately continues in a course which will obviously lead to disaster, or one vacillates between the two courses open to one, and, in one's own words, "doesn't know which way to turn." The second leads to a fantasy life which becomes progressively less satisfying and cuts one off from making any constructive choice at all.

One normally thinks of such ambivalence as operating in what might be called "big" decisions, such as whether to enter into or terminate a marriage, or whether to try to overcome a habit that one knows to be injurious. But often the actual decision that has to be made is apparently a small one. It is what the decision symbolizes, the feelings it arouses that produces the paralysis or the escape. I know a woman whose mother once gave her a table not knowing that it was veneered rather than solid wood. I have rarely seen anyone suffer more over an apparently little matter than this woman did for ten days as she decided whether to let her mother know that the table was not what it seemed. On the one hand was a deep reluctance to appear ungrateful and to hurt her mother's feelings, complicated by a feeling that she had not always been as appreciative a daughter as she might have been; on the other was the recognition that she would have to live with the table for the rest of her life and a real reluctance to do so with a sham. This kept her awake for several nights and brought other projects to a standstill until the choice to risk being misunderstood by her mother was made—a choice which resulted, as so many similar ones do, in the solution of the problem, her mother wanting just as much as she did the table to be the real thing.

It is, therefore, out of ambivalence that man needs to choose his way, and it could be said that the whole purpose of a helping relationship is to maximize the chance that this can be done.

In terms of the four reactions we touched on in chapter 2 this means the passing from a condition of nonchoice (evasion of reality or being overwhelmed by the problem) to one of choice (accepting and using a situation or struggling against it) .

Before we accept this statement too literally we need to be very careful that we understand what we mean by the word "choose." It is misunderstanding of the nature of this choice, both on the part of professional helpers and those who observe their practice, which has led to theories of extreme permissiveness both in helping and in education and has convinced many people that those who pretend to expertise in helping others are both unrealistic and amoral. Permissiveness may have its part in helping, particularly when the helped person's experience up to that time has been one of too great restriction, but this is in fact a side issue and has nothing to do with the kind of choice that is necessary in the helping process.

We use the word "choice" in ordinary speech in two different ways. One has to do with the selection of alternatives. I choose to wear a green or a blue tie. I choose to go for a walk or to stay home to read a book. I choose where I will live and the kind of job that I will do.

This kind of freedom to choose is undoubtedly both pleasant and in many respects conducive to a full life. It is the particular pride of democratic countries. In the early days of psychiatrically-oriented social work this belief in freedom of choice was erected into a principle called "client self-determination" which was partly political (a belief that one person did not have the right to control another) and partly theoretical, stemming from Freud's early emphasis on the dangers of repression and a Rousseauistic belief that man's own decisions about his affairs were more likely to be of value than the judgments of society.[1] Psychologically it lived in rather an uneasy relationship with early Freudian psychic determinism. It was thought of as at one and the same time inevitable—Bertha Reynolds once said that "it is no longer a question of whether it is *wrong* to try to make our fellow beings think and feel as we want them to. In the long run it is simply silly. The vital needs of their being will in the end determine what they shall feel and how they shall act"[2]—and, curiously enough, as a right that could be granted or withheld by the helping person.[3]

Recently Helen Harris Perlman has shown that much of this self-determination is an illusion.[4] Man is much too much of a social creature to be able to exercise any significant amount of self-determination. As Mrs. Perlman points out, tradition and culture as well as law limit many of his choices. He is free to choose between ham and sausage for breakfast, but, for practical purposes he cannot elect

1. For a more detailed account of this principle, see my article, "A Critique of the Principle of Client Self-Determination," *Social Work* 8, no. 3 (July 1963) : 66-71.

2. Bertha C. Reynolds, *Re-Thinking Social Case Work* (San Diego, 1938) , p. 15.

3. The only contemporary writer who pointed out this anomaly was, to my knowledge, Grace Marcus, who wrote: "How difficult it is for us to accept this harsh truth is revealed by our distortion of it into the facile concept of 'self-determination,' whereby, we can relapse once more into a comforting dependence on free will and, by talking of self-determination as a 'right,' flatter ourselves that a fact which is often intolerably painful to the individual and to society is still within our power to concede or refuse as a social benefit." "The Status of Social Case Work Today," in *Readings in Social Casework, 1920-38*, ed. Fern Lowry (New York, 1939) , p. 130.

4. Helen Harris Perlman, "Self-Determination: Myth or Reality," *Social Service Review* 39, no. 4 (December 1965) : 410-21.

instead caviar or gin. Yet, she points out, the little bit of self-determination left to man is tremendously important to preserve. It would be intolerable if it were thought right and proper to restrict even further, more than was absolutely necessary and without some showing of one's right to do so, the small amount of self-determination of this kind that man actually enjoys.

The second meaning of choice has to do with much more than the selection of alternatives. It involves the whole of a man's person, his total reaction to a situation and always, includes his willingness to act on the choice that he has made. For this reason I have called it "active and willing" choice.

Possibly the single word which expresses its essential quality most closely is the word "commitment," and yet, although it may involve commitment in its positive aspect, it still remains a choice. Active and willing choice is the choice to get well or to remain ill, to do something constructive or even destructive about one's problem, to come to terms with life or constantly to struggle against it.

There are a number of things to grasp about this kind of choice. First is perhaps that it bears little relationship to the amount of selective choice that is available. A prisoner in jail has little opportunity for selective choice. He cannot choose where to live, what to wear, what to eat, or what work to do. But he does have one very important choice to make. He can decide whether to make use of his imprisonment, which might be by learning a trade or even deciding to act somewhat differently in the future. He can choose to struggle against imprisonment, perhaps by planning to break out or by a resolution to fight society from now on, or he can make a nonchoice and spend his time in daydreaming or be utterly crushed and embittered by the experience. Indeed one of the rather curious qualities of this kind of choice is that it seems to require some limitation of selective choice to become fully operative. Anita Faatz, whose analysis of choice in the casework process first drew attention to its special nature, says: "But to a degree far greater than we are usually willing to admit, and to an extent that we are fearful to concede, the crisis in the helping process is more truthfully described as a process of helping the client achieve a new relation to the *inevitable*, instead of uncovering constantly new sources of choice."[5]

This does not mean, let us hasten to say, that in order to enable "active and willing" choice one needs to restrict the area of alternative

5. Anita Faatz, *The Nature of Choice in Casework Process* (Chapel Hill, N.C., 1953), p. 128.

choice. The normal conditions of life do that quite adequately. And indeed, there is some evidence that in order for anyone to be able to make an active and willing choice (as opposed to a nonchoice) there must have been some experience in making alternative choices. The person with no experience of choosing anything cannot as a rule choose actively and willingly, too. What is not necessary, and indeed is sometimes harmful, is too wide a range of alternative choices without the capacity to make them except impulsively.

There is a relationship between the two kinds of choice that does need to be recognized. Alternative choice may appear often to be morally or emotionally neutral. To wear a green tie or an orange— what does it matter, except to satisfy a whim? But if the orange tie is worn in Dublin on St. Patrick's Day, or is chosen to please one's wife despite being wholly out of fashion, the choice involved may be an active and willing one. It might be said, then, that alternative choice may in some instances be conditioned by active and willing choice, or be symbolic of it. Or it may mean very little at all.

What Miss Faatz is saying is that active and willing choice must be made in real conditions, and not in an unreal world in which there is illusory freedom of choice, or in which choice made will not result in natural consequences. It has also been shown over and over again that it is extremely helpful if the real conditions limiting selective choice— the law, the function of an agency, the "rules" of a service, the authority invested in a teacher or administrator—are explicit and inevitable in the sense that neither the helper nor the helped have the power to change them.

I have used the words "accept and use" to express active and willing choice in its positive aspect. A person "accepts" a situation, in the sense of recognizing its inevitability, and ceases to struggle against it. But if he did this alone, if he simply accepted it as inevitable and made no use of it, he would not be making a choice. Hence the doublet. I prefer the words, however, to the word "yield" which is sometimes used by Rankian social workers, including Miss Faatz. "Yield" can all too easily develop connotations of defeat, although in any coming to terms with a problem there is a yielding of one's own will that does have to take place.

The second characteristic of this kind of choice is that it must really be a choice, in an alternative sense as well as an active and willing one. This may seem to deny all we have said about the difference between these two kinds of choices, but it does seem necessary to state that a choice cannot be a choice unless there are at least two things to choose from. Many writers, and all too many practitioners, appear to be so impressed with the importance of "accepting and using" that they lose sight of the fact that one cannot assert a positive unless it is also possible for one to choose the negative in its stead. There is, and there must be, a choice between accepting and using the situation, and struggling against it, or even resolutely refusing to do anything about it. There must be choice, too, in the ways one accepts and uses or struggles.

We can see this theoretically when we recognize that the one person who cannot sincerely affirm a "Yes" is a "Yes man," because he cannot say "No." We can see it if we realize that to risk something is in a sense to choose the possibility of it happening and then consider the plight of the man who cannot "risk" or "choose" death by putting himself in any situation in which he could possibly be killed. Such a man could not cross a street or drive a car. He would be unable to "live" to any extent. One can only assert a positive if the negative is also possible. The very concept of goodness itself presupposes the possible choice not to be good.

Yet one of the major weaknesses of a great deal of help offered today is that it does not offer a real opportunity for choice. It presupposes the positive, that is, the socially sanctioned or acceptable one, and, by doing so, robs this very answer of much of its strength. The attempt to make someone good, however rationalized in terms of "influence" or "persuasion," is effective only where in actual fact the choice to be good has already been made.

From that point on the character-building agency has much to give. It is often less effective with the child who is not committed to good, which is one of the reasons why those agencies that express conventional middle-class "goods" find such difficulties in the slums.

And let it be said now that to "influence" and to "persuade" (in the sense of appeal to with moral overtones) are just as strong verbs as to "make" or to "command." There seems to be an illusion that somehow a person is left freer to make his own decisions if he is persuaded or influenced rather than "made to" or "commanded," but in fact almost the opposite is true. If I am commanded or made to do something, I can at least identify the force that is being brought to bear. If necessary, I can rebel. But if the force being brought to bear is moral suasion or influence, it has behind it sanctions I am not big enough to challenge. It is no longer a personal battle where I might have a chance of victory, but a struggle with the values and sanctions of a culture. To fight it is like fighting the mist. Persuasion and influence are weapons, useful perhaps at times, in controlling people, but no less forceful than a direct command. They are only rather more subtle and often much more unfair.

The difficulty, of course, with allowing a real choice is that we so much want a person to make what we think of as a positive choice that we do not dare risk the possibility of his making what seems to us a negative one. Even the possibility of his doing so often feels like treason to us. This is particularly so when we are very sure ourselves of what the positive is and much committed to it. Churches perhaps make this mistake more often than any other body, but are not alone in doing so. Schools, juvenile courts, child protective societies, and even other agencies who have learned to value growth and change often cannot bear to see their clients choose wrongly. They feel a responsibility to see that they choose the right.

Sometimes we forget how difficult it is to know what is right for another. It is no disparagement of a general good to say that it may be impossible for another to choose it at this time. It may even be quite inappropriate to his need. This is the frequent mistake made by those who, recognizing, for instance, that probation is "better" than prison or reform school, which is in fact generally so, will not permit a probationer to choose to break his probation. I have seen a teen-age girl commit a serious delinquency for the sole purpose of convincing her wooly-minded and idealistic probation officer to send her somewhere where she would be protected from the impulses she could not handle on probation. In fact to prescribe for another what choices he can or cannot make, except in very general terms or for his immediate protection, is a form of presumption, and this is true whether the criteria used are moral or psychological—whether we tell a person that he is not free to sin or that he may not remain unadjusted.

To identify "positive" with the accepting and using choice and "negative" with the choice to rebel is possible only if these words do not carry an implication that the "positive" choice is always better. While in general this may be so, there are clearly situations in which the opposite is true. If one is sinking in a quagmire, one does not accept the situation. One struggles to get out. Rebels are necessary to society and where there is social injustice or repression, the "negative" choice is much more positive than the "positive." The words should therefore be freed from any moral connotations and should be understood much as they are in electronics, as indicating "moving towards or away from accepting and using the situation."

Many people need to make a negative choice, in perhaps both

meanings of the word, before they can make a positive one. Often the negative has to be tried out first to see, as it were, where it leads one. One of the most successful pieces of helping I have ever seen recorded was of a puritanical, suspicious grandmother, full of fear of her granddaughter's puberty, haunted by the knowledge that her daughter, the child's mother, had gone wrong and inclined to blame her own leniency for this, and yet caught up in her love and pity for the child and a longing to be reconciled with the daughter she could not forgive. This woman ended by recognizing her own part in the story with the rather dramatic statement, "I'm not hardhearted, only hardheaded, I declare" and was able to enter into a much more understanding and warm relationship with both daughter and granddaughter.

Yet, after the first interview, in which she came to understand that no one could or would reform her granddaughter for her, she tried to solve her own problem the next time the child disobeyed her by marching her down to the cellar and taking the carpet beater to her. It was only in reliving this experience with her caseworker that she was able to make the choice to face and to allow to develop her real love and warmth for the child.

Whaling a thirteen-year-old girl for a minor disobedience is not generally thought of as a positive act and was clearly contrary to the values of the child welfare worker who was trying to help this woman. She could quite easily have used the incident to lecture the grandmother, to make her feel guilty, even to give up trying to help her anymore. The result of this, with a woman whose culture approved rigidity rather than leniency, would as likely as not have been even severer beatings, if only to prove the worker's censure wrong. And if they were severe enough, no doubt the beatings would solve the immediate problem of the child's rebellion, although not the grandmother's unhappiness nor the real problem of this relationship. But when the grandmother told the story the worker recognized this as the woman's first real attempt to find a solution for herself and a step towards getting well. Her exploration with her of what the experience meant to her and how desperate she must have felt was what led to her ability to change.

A person who makes a negative choice is much nearer making a positive one than the person who makes none. And this perhaps calls for some clarification of what we mean by a negative choice. A negative choice is never the nonchoice, the decision, if it can be called one, to remain in ambivalence or to escape into fantasy. That kind of nonchoice is utterly defeating. It is incidentally, what a helped person goes through when he is put under pressure to make a positive choice and cannot do so. It is what we mean by failure. It is static and leads nowhere.

Negative choice is, on the other hand, dynamic. It is the resolution to alter the situation, to do without help, "to go it alone," to fight to do things in antisocial and unapproved ways. And if it is real negative choice, and not a blind impulse of rage—though the two are sometimes hard to distinguish—it involves a willingness to accept the consequences of one's acts. When we say that negative choice must be permitted, we do not mean what the "permissivists" so often seem to mean by free choice—that negative acts may be indulged in with some sort of guarantee that they will not result in unpleasantness in return.

Within the helping relationship itself anger, or negative choice, may not carry unpleasant consequences. This is necessary because the helping person must permit it to be experienced. Moreover, if he is concerned with the person he is trying to help, and not with his own feelings, he is not hurt by the helped person's anger or criticism and has no need to retaliate or punish. He may even wish to set up opportunities for the helped person to try out negative feelings in a safe environment, as the play therapist does with the dolls the child is permitted to torture. But where the negative choice is exercised in the real world, the client must take responsibility for his choice. He cannot be protected against the consequences of his act.

What is often not recognized is how close a person who makes a negative choice is to making a positive one. Those who care for children in Children's Homes, for instance, have long discovered that it is the rebellious child who gave them the most trouble who often comes back ten years later to express his sincere gratitude for what was done for him, while the conforming child who does this is rarer. Some of the world's greatest sinners—Saul of Tarsus and Augustine of Hippo—have become the world's greatest saints. The opposite of love is not hate. It is indifference. Hate and love are very close to each other, as we might expect if we understood the ubiquity of ambivalence. As the old popular song has it, "I hate you because I love you, and I love you because I hate you." A large proportion of murders are of persons to whom the murderer is related in a love-hate relationship —husbands, wives, and sweethearts—and to hate someone it is necessary to care about what they do.

The distinction between negative choice and nonchoice can perhaps be seen more clearly when we consider failure. Failure is, as we have said, what happens when one is incapable of making a positive choice. It is also, curiously enough, what happens when we cannot make a negative choice either. I learned this some years ago when I was academic adviser to a girl who had been a brilliant student in high school but was now, in college, inexplicably failing her work. She felt entirely miserable and unable to account for her bad grades. She was working hard but nothing ever seemed to come out right. I feared that she might be ill, either physically or emotionally, and was able to help her decide to go to the student health service. There she talked to a psychologist. A week later she was back in my office with her head held high, obviously quite a different girl. She had decided to quit school and to go back home to be married. She felt this to be the right decision. Previously she had given in to her father's expectation of her, although, as she emphasized, she had agreed and thought that she really wanted a college education and, even, postponement of marriage. Indeed, she said that coming to college had been in part her idea, to escape from her boyfriend's importunity as well as to please her parents. Now she was able to face her parent's disappointment because she had decided that she was now grown up and had a right to run her life.

To her parents, at least at first, this was a negative decision. Many a university teacher would, too, have seen the problem as one of helping the girl succeed in her courses. The psychologist, however, knew that the more important problem was whether she really could or wanted to succeed, and helped her to see that apparent failure was actually a victory for her.

An active and willing choice can only be made by the helped person himself. It is an intensely personal thing and it involves much more than the conscious self. It cannot therefore be brought about by argument, or persuasion, although a logical looking at alternatives may have a small part to play in it. It is sometimes in facing "the logic" of the situation that feeling becomes crystallized; as often, however, logic has nothing to do with it. It often occurs at the darkest, most confused moment when one is faced with apparent defeat, and, as such, is not unlike Kierkegaard's "leap in the dark." But the insistence that it cannot be made by any other than the helped person himself has nothing to do with permissiveness, or with a moral or political theory of self-determination. It is a simple fact.

That to help involves risk, both that help may not be taken and that the outcome may be entirely different from what the helped person planned, is a corollary of this fact. Kenneth Pray once said of the casework process, that the worker, with all his knowledge, cannot determine—cannot even predict—the outcome.[6] There are, of course, ways of both predicting and ensuring limited or temporary goals that have to do more with adaptation than with growth and change, chief of which are careful diagnosis and treatment, but these are control processes which have relevance only in the context of the major choice, and as such are often subjected to strange surprises.

The most unlikely people prove capable of accepting help and doing something about their problems; equally unlikely people who appear destined to succeed unaccountably make a mess of it. The happiest, most poised and competent child I ever met came from a background so disorganized, so loveless and so culturally deprived that it appeared impossible to find any hope or light in it, was herself of low mentality judged by any objective test, and had been subjected to about the worst set of child welfare procedures and placements it is possible to imagine. While it is possible that the many social workers and psychiatrists who at some time worked with the child missed some important diagnostic fact, it must certainly have been one whose significance is as yet unknown to either of these professions. Indeed, if we knew why some people are able to use disaster and suffering to strengthen their hold on life and others respond to the very same stimuli with apathy or evasion, much of our problem would be solved. Possibly there is some factor that we have not identified. Why some young people flourished and others "went into a decline" was not understood until the discovery of Koch's bacillus. Possibly this is the final human mystery to which no answer will ever be found. All we can do at the moment is to create the kind of conditions that have proved on the whole most favorable for victory rather than for defeat.

Some would object that Kierkegaard's "leap in the dark" is as likely to land one in the lap of the devil as it is in the hands of God. In a sense this is true of the kind of choice we are discussing. I do not know how Kierkegaard answered the objection but I presume that he must have considered that it was more likely that man would find God than the devil. The same, I think, has to be assumed about choice. Man, if freed to make willing choices, generally chooses the good. If he did not, helping would be a purposeless business. One does have to assume that man has in him some natural tendency to maturity of some sort, to being able to cope, to coming out on top and solving his problems,

6. Kenneth Pray, "A Restatement of the Generic Principles of Social Casework Practice," in *Social Work in a Revolutionary Age and Other Papers* (Philadelphia, 1949) , p. 250.

just as he obviously has in him a tendency to grow physically and to increase in mental grasp.

There is one more characteristic of what we have called active or willing choice that is worthy of note, and that is its repetitive nature. We have spoken of an act of choice as if it were a single act at a certain moment of time which settled once and for all the helped person's problem, and there is some reason to do so. There is often a moment of crisis at which the decision appears to be made. This "turning point" can be identified with extraordinary preciseness in some situations. In a carefully structured helping process it can almost be predicted as likely to occur at a certain stage in time. Anita Faatz goes so far as to write: "No matter what the service, no matter how it begins, whether voluntarily or otherwise . . . there is but one crucial moment of time that matters, and this is the moment in which the self chooses between growth and refusal of growth, life or the negation of life; when the organism, in short, chooses to live and turns its energies from the negative fight against what is to the vibrant immediacy of what it can do, no matter."[7]

We can recognize the same kind of phenomenon in some religious experiences. But here we have not only learned to mistrust the conversion that is apparently too wholehearted and too complete; we are aware that the decision has to be reaffirmed again and again, and we also recognize genuine conversions that take place more or less imperceptibly. Similarly, in the helping process the decision is made again and again, as Dr. Faatz explains when in her somewhat mystical language she says of the "moment" of which she writes that it is "as well a moment which recurs again and again, never to be wholly settled or determined, but in constant process of becoming, as is the life process itself."[8]

There is also the problem that the initial choice is made in a particular context—in this case the helping situation—but the effects of the decision have to be carried out in a wider or a different field. The person being helped by another must carry out his decision in the wider sphere of all his relationships. There is a constant need both for new affirmations and for reaffirmations which have to do with doing as well as with feeling. Both stem from the original choice but to some extent this choice has to be made again and again. The one thing which we can be sure of is that by virtue of its having been made once it will be more possible the tenth and even the thousandth time.

7. Faatz, *The Nature of Choice*, p. 53.
8. Ibid.

Nothing that we have said, however, should lead us to the conclusion that, because this choice is a highly individual matter and can only be made by the person directly concerned, all the helping person needs to do is to leave the helped person free to make it. Nothing is more cruel or less productive than to tell someone that the choice is his and, so to speak, to tell him to go into a corner and decide. If that were possible, he would have done it long ago. Our job is not to make the choice for him, it is true. We cannot do this in any case. But it is our job to provide him with a medium, a situation, and an experience in which a choice is possible, in which the fears that beset him can to some extent be resolved, in which he can find the courage to commit himself one way or the other, and, maybe, the practical tools that will enable him to put his commitment into action. This medium is what we call "the helping relationship," the major characteristics of which are explored in chapter 4.

IV. THE HELPING RELATIONSHIP

The medium which is offered to a person in trouble through which he is given the opportunity to make choices, both about taking help and the use he will make of it, is a relationship with a helping person. The helper may be a professional or a friend sought out for advice. He may be someone expressly provided for this service, as is a probation officer, or someone in a position of authority which involves functions other than helping, such as a supervisor or parent. He may on the other hand be sought out because of his knowledge or position, as a physician or a minister, or simply be someone believed at the moment to be able to offer something. But in one way or another an encounter takes place and a relationship begins.

This relationship, if it is to be helpful, has as its primary purpose the enabling of what we have called "active and willing" choice, although it may also be directed towards the offering of a specific kind of help—money, or physical assistance, or advice. If it is to do either or both successfully, it must have certain characteristics, some of which will be readily apparent from our discussion up until now. That these concepts overlap will be evident; nevertheless, each is perhaps necessary to understand the whole.

It may seem unnecessary to begin by saying that its most important characteristic is that it is *a mutual and not a one-way relationship*. There are things which the helped person brings to it and things which are brought by the person offering help, and its success or failure may depend as much on the latter as the former. Yet this, as we have seen, is by no means general knowledge and if things go wrong the natural tendency of the helper is to place all the blame on the helped person. While taking help is hard, giving it successfully is also extremely difficult. It requires a quality which is known as self-discipline, the specifics of which will become more apparent as we look at the relationship more closely.

A second characteristic of the helping relationship, which is indeed part of its difficulty, since none of us likes to be anything but loved and respected and often expect to get out of helping something of this feeling, is that this relationship *is not necessarily consistently pleasant or friendly.* While there must be some sense of working together on a problem, and although in the end there is usually something that might be called trust in it, even this is not always so. Sometimes real moving takes place in anger and reaction.

This is well illustrated in Glasser's *Reality Therapy,* where his refusal to accept his delinquent girls' excuses and rationalizations often provoked anger that helped the child come to terms with her problem. It is quite obvious in many child-parent relationships, even in the punishment that "clears the air."

The attempt to keep the relationship on a pleasant level is one of the greatest sources of ineffectual helping known to man. It results in insincerities, in attempts to please the helper, in staying exactly where one is, or deepening a pattern of evasion, in overdependence and in actions taken without any real readiness for them.

A mistaken understanding of the hesitancy with which most people approach an offer of help, coupled, perhaps, with a realization of how powerful a force "liking" and trust are in inducing change once it has really begun, has given rise to the all too common concept that no helping can take place until something called "rapport" has been established. Helpers sometimes spend much time in making friends with people before they get down to business with them. They give children treats or tell them stories "to establish a good relationship" with them. But the kind of relationship that is bought in this way is not the kind of relationship on which true helping is based. It is often nothing more than a protection to the helper from having to take the full impact of the helped person's struggle. The child, for instance, who cheerfully goes with the nice social worker to a foster home all too often is prevented by the worker's very niceness from expressing and coming to grips with his doubt and despair. He has in fact been disarmed, deprived of his natural weapons to deal with his problem. To use a childish word, he has been "snowed" into accepting something for which he is not prepared.

Aristotle once said that if one pursued happiness one was unlikely to find it, a statement that can easily be verified at Miami Beach or any other large resort. Happiness, Aristotle upheld, is the result of what he called a "virtuous" life—that is, an engaged and active participation in affairs. The same can be said about relationship. Seek it as a goal and generally it will elude one. But a relationship will grow wherever one person demonstrates to another both by his actions and his words that he respects the other, that he has concern for him and cares what happens to him, and that he is willing both to listen and to act helpfully. This is the kind of relationship on which helping is based, and it cannot be manufactured. It begins at the moment that any two people meet. It grows as they work together, but it cannot be forced or hurried.

Another effect of the belief that the helping relationship must be a pleasant one is the fear that some helpers have that the relation will be damaged if they are forced in any way to do what the client will not like—reduce his assistance grant, tell him something he does not want to hear, impose any conditions on him, or make an unfavorable report to some other person. This is particularly common where a social worker must bring a client to court. Instead of being honest with the client about what has been found and helping him face what is likely to happen to him, the social worker all too often virtually pretends that he has had nothing to do with the matter, that any unpleasantness is somebody else's fault, even that he is secretly "on the client's side" against the judge, and would, if he could, help the client to evade the court's decree. This is not only plainly dishonest, but encourages the client in a nonchoice and robs him of his ability to do something about his predicament. It is indulging him exactly as one might spoil a child and is moreover treating him like a child. It is also one of the things that gives the impression that helping people are amoral, that they condone bad behavior rather than, as they actually do, feel for the person who has not been able to do what he should but recognize with him clearly that he needs to do something different.

A relationship that can be destroyed when the helping person has to be firm, or honest, or obey the law, or hold the helped person to the real situation as it exists is a relationship built on false premises. It is not worth preserving, and the attempt to do so at the cost of honesty only perpetuates something that is meaningless in the first place. Laws that insist that a social worker's report to a court should be confidential and concealed from the client are based on a false concept of the helping relationship as well as being very bad law, since they deprive the client of his right to know the basis for the decision that is to be made about him.

The search for a good relationship has in it another danger, too. It ignores the fact that relationship begins the moment helped person and helper meet. The helped person begins at once to explore the quality of help he will get. He puts out his problem to find out how the helper will react. He struggles to express himself. But if the helped person's interest is on the relationship he is building and not on what the helped person is saying, he will and does miss much of what is being said. I have seen a child struggle to tell her social worker, in five or six different ways, each more desperate than the last, how unhappy she was in a foster home, and fail to get through because her social worker was so busy "building relationship" that she could not hear the child.

Most helping relationships come in the course of helping to be pleasant and friendly, and full of trust. And they cannot be mean, rigid, sadistic, cold, unfeeling, or unconcerned. Concern for the helped person is, and must be, always present. But this is what the helper brings. He has no right to expect, in return, agreement, gratitude, or liking. He may and probably will find these in the majority of his encounters. But if he goes out seeking these he is seeking something for himself, not for the people he is serving. The desire for "good relationships," rather than for productive ones, can be a major obstacle to one's ability to help.

The relationship is, however, *one of feeling as well as of knowledge.* Some would-be helpers, either uncomfortable with feeling, afraid of being drawn in too deeply into the helped person's problem, or impressed with a false concept of what it means to be a professional, try to maintain a relationship that is detached, cold, "impartial," or objective.

The coldly "objective" person betrays by that very word what it is that he does to people. He treats them as objects in the grammatical sense, people he can study, or manipulate, or make in some way to change. The person who really wants to help is committed to treating people as the subjects, so to speak, of the sentence. They are that part of the operation whose feelings and opinions matter, who will be doing the things which give purpose to it. This is the reason why an objective science *about* people or social conditions can never offer all that is needed to teach how to help people. An objective science works *on* people. The helping process is a method of working *with* them or even being made use of *by* them to find something for themselves. This is what makes it possible for some helping professions to talk of helped people as clients even when the relationship has not been initially sought by them.[1] They truly attempt to serve their client's interests.

The helper, however, who is objective—and this is perhaps a slightly different use of the word—has avoided one obvious pitfall. He has not thrown himself into the situation in a wholly undisciplined way,

1. For an attack on the word "client," see Barbara Wooton, *Social Science and Social Pathology* (London, 1959), p. 289.

becoming swayed by every wind of feeling and taking sides either for or against his client. He is not wholly an amateur as I would be, for instance, if I tried to take part in a game of professional football, not knowing what was going on and being pulled out of position by every move of the ball. I need, however, more than a knowledge of the game to be an effective player. I need skill, strength, a sense of anticipation, an ability to be part of a developing movement. Just not to be pulled out of position is at best a negative virtue.

Helping is always a matter of both knowledge and feeling. One cannot do without either. The true professional is at the same time objective and full of feeling—a paradox, perhaps, but nevertheless one true of any true professional in the arts. It takes rigorous practice and hard objective learning to become a great dancer, but the dancer who does not dance with feeling betrays that fact at once.

A third characteristic of the helping relationship is that *it has a single purpose* which controls everything that happens within it. The defined purpose of this relationship is to help a person, or possibly a group of persons, to make choices about a problem or situation and about the help he or they are willing to take about it. It can be said as simply as that. Yet this is one of the most difficult things to achieve. All too often when we set out to help another we have all sorts of secondary purposes, conscious or unconscious, in mind, such as satisfying our own conscience, proving some theory, advancing some cause or showing our skill in helping.

How intrusive such a second purpose can be is not generally recognized. We can all see the obvious cases. If the helper has a need which the relationship is being asked to satisfy, if he needs to control others, or to feel superior to them, or to have them like him, it is not too hard to see how these needs can distort what happens in the relationship. We can also, if we imagine ourselves to be comparatively free of these needs or to be able to keep them under control, stigmatize them as selfish and therefore see that they can have no part in helping. It is not, however, these rather obvious "second purposes" which are the most difficult to control. It is rather our "good" interests which often get in the way—our desire to be of help, our feeling for justice, our need to try to build a better world, our concern for the honor and dignity of the organization which we represent, even our desire for knowledge about the person we are helping, that distract us from the business at hand. These are the things that prevent us from really listening to what the person we are helping is saying. They all too often shift our concern from the way in which he can come to grips with his problem to what we would like to do about it.

For the past twelve years I have been teaching groups of public welfare workers in short courses in the summer. They have made remarkable progress in learning to help people and in general I have been able to observe each year more clients helped in a way that resulted in a radical change in ability to deal with their problems. Only one year was there a regression. This was in the year in which the 1962 amendments to the Social Security Act were implemented in part by requiring written social summaries of each client's situation.

Although these had a good purpose and undoubtedly helped workers plan more wisely what could be done to help, the centering of the welfare worker's attention on the client's whole situation, on the possible meaning of this and that fact, came between client and worker. The worker became temporarily much less able to hear what the client was telling him about his situation and what he thought he was able to do about it. Opportunities for constructive choice were missed because the helping person's interest was not on what was happening in the here and now, but on some overall picture of the client's total situation. Clients became aware that the worker was no longer responding to what they were trying to tell him but were thinking of something else.

The surprising thing was, however, that when the workers stopped being concerned about their summaries, when they stopped asking questions to try to uncover facts, when they concentrated at the time on what the client was telling them and only tried to compose their summaries after the interview was over, the summaries were fuller and generally much more useful. The clients had actually told them all that they needed to know.

Much the same is true of our concern for justice or morality or for a better world. If we are thinking of these when we are face to face with a person we are trying to help, our attention is on something other than his problem. Unconsciously we are trying to use him to fulfill our purposes and not his. We have abandoned our belief that only he can make a decision that will have real meaning to him. We lose him in our enthusiasm for something which, however important, is not part of his present struggle.

If we can postpone these concerns, at least until he is out of the room, we will in general find that what has happened between him and us has conduced to our other interests, too. If it has not, we are faced with a choice. Which do we really want to do—help this person discover a way of meeting his problem, reform the world, or promote morality? If our interests in the second and third are such that we must restrict our helping to helping that will produce the kind of result we want, then we must recognize that our helping will be of a different kind and perhaps should not be called helping at all. We may, quite justifiably desire all three and work on them in different situations, but in the helping situation the client's need must be the sole focus of our concern.

Even more the same pattern is true of our desire to be of help. This can be a major trap. It can entice us into doing things for people they can and need to do for themselves. It can make us try to force decision before the helped person is ready for it. It cannot allow people to move towards and away from taking help, as all people need to do, and it is, despite its apparent altruism, basically a need of the helper rather than that of the helped person. Just as it could be said that one of the conditions for helping someone come to a positive decision is not to wish it too passionately oneself so it can be said that one of the conditions under which help can be given must be that the helper does not too passionately wish to give it. This does not mean that he is indifferent, or does not care. It means that he cares so much that the help given is real help that he will not insist on it being given when it is inappropriate.

A difficult situation is apparently created when the helping person has, it might seem, a double loyalty; where he is at one and the same time a helping person and an agent of social control. Social workers are often expected to act in this twofold capacity and in some fields, such as child protection or probation, it would appear to be inherent in the job. Indeed there is an increasing tendency, in the United States at least, to emphasize the fact that the social worker is employed by the community and not by the individual, and that all social workers are to some extent involved in enforcing the values of the culture. One writer, for instance, believes what is known as the "hard core" or "multiproblem" family requires in order that any change be made that the worker "sees himself and behaves as the instrument of social control and social change" although not "the personal embodiment of the 'right' attitudes and values." He becomes to his client "the ego-ideal, the personification of the core-culture."[2]

It should be apparent at once that this writer is not concerned so much with a helping process as he is with one of control. Are, then,

2. Kermit Wiltse, "The 'Hopeless' Family," *Social Work* 3, no. 4 (October 1958): 19.

such social agencies instruments, primarily, of control rather than of help? Is there a place in them for the helping process?

There is no doubt that a good deal of most constructive help, as opposed to control, is offered by social workers who work in what might be thought of as "social control" agencies, and, as we have already made clear, the kind of choice with which help is concerned is not dependent on freedom from social restraints. But, if the social worker is also concerned with implementing these restraints, does not the interview have exactly the kind of double purpose we have said that it cannot have?

It would be useless to try to escape this question by asserting that this is a book on helping and not on social casework, since social casework obviously includes a helping function, and our statement is that helping must be the sole purpose of the helper-helped relationship. Nor can we take refuge in the assumption, often made by those who are unhappy about the apparent authority involved in some social casework roles, that a person "really wants," in being helped, to do what society wants of him.[3] While this is sometimes true it is obviously not always so. It also introduces two assumptions that we have been at considerable pains to discount—that there is something that a person "really" wants that is different from what he sees as the solution to his problem in the present, and that the solution to human problems is more or less limited to adaptation to social demands.

It would be even worse to suggest that the help given by an agency with social control functions is in some sense not "real," since by every criterion we can establish for real help—change of attitude, clarity, decisiveness, and ability to translate choice into action—some of the help given by these agencies is the most "real" of all. One of the best helping agencies I happen to know is a woman's prison, another a juvenile court. It might be said, based on experience, that the limitations imposed on the client by the apparent other purposes of these agencies are important factors in the help they give.

Yet to have another purpose in the helping relationship does in fact do all we have said. It does distract. In trying, as it were, to kill two birds with one stone, we all too often miss them both.

3. The best example of this that I know is Annie Lee Davis's comment in *Children Living in Their Own Homes,* U.S. Children's Bureau (Washington, 1953). She states that to bring to neglecting mothers one's demands that she change is not an imposition, since in "an atmosphere that is warm, understanding and non-blaming" they "begin to feel that they too can become better parents, and most parents want to be better parents. It is part of the total culture of the country," p. 34.

The solution to this apparent paradox lies in a more careful examination of to whom this other purpose belongs. It is the law, or the agency empowered in some way to enforce the demands of society, and not the helping person himself who has this purpose and creates, or makes apparent, a reality which is outside both helper and helped. It is not I who demand that you should do this or that. It is the law, or the organization which I represent. I may in fact agree with it and probably do in general, since this is where I work, but this is incidental and my business with you is the undivided one of helping you make decisions in relation to this reality. You may decide to deny it or to struggle against it, but if so there are consequences, which I did not create and which you will have to cope with. Ultimately the choice is yours.

This distinction may be difficult. Yet it is very important. The function of the helper is not to maintain the control, but to help the offender come to terms with the reality of what society expects of him. This is in part what we mean when we say that ours is a rule of law and not of men. It is not I that tell you that you must not neglect your children, or get drunk, or cheat your neighbor. It is the law. Even the moral law is not of my fashioning, however much I accept it as binding on me. It is something outside both of us which as a helper I can help you look at and choose or deny with as much clarity as I can. If you deny it, then there are consequences, which I will try to help you see.

In some situations the same person may be responsible both for helping and for setting the conditions which the law, or some other expectation, will demand of a person. A judge may be in this situation. So may a teacher, who wants to help a student but still must require a certain performance if the course is to be passed. A business executive may want to help a worker, but cannot permit inefficiency. These people are not prevented from offering help, as long as they are able to disassociate their two roles. What the law, or the course, demands must remain a given, a reality which, in his helping role, the very person responsible for its interpretation can help the other look at and accept or struggle against. This can be done.

It is not easy. It requires a willingness on the part of the helper to be undefensive about the authority he has, to admit, even, that he may be wrong, but that this is where he stands in this situation. It may, and sometimes should, include helping the person helped to change the law or the regulation which the helped person represents, to appeal and to present his case. But for the moment this is the law and my interpretation of it. I can understand how hard this may be to you but I cannot do anything else but hold to it at this time.

The importance of identifying one's role as a helper, and disassociating it from other roles, such as preacher, reformer, teacher, researcher, or executive, focuses attention on the helping situation itself—the actual meeting between two persons or groups. One of the important things to realize about it is that it is limited in time and space. Although the helping that takes place in it may affect the helped person's whole life, the helping encounter *takes place in the here and now.*

Two or more people come together, at a certain place, at a certain time, for a certain purpose, and under certain conditions. What they say, or refrain from saying, and still more what they feel, is often as much conditioned by the particular situation as by their wider problems. The person who tells you of his marital problems is as much concerned, at that moment, with how you will react as he is with his struggle at home.

He has, in fact, a double problem. He has to be concerned not only with the problem for which he wants help, but with the problem of getting help. And often the second problem may take precedence, temporarily, over the first. Thus a person in trouble may float "trial balloons," or try flattery, or test the helper out to see if he really means what he said. What he says about himself will almost certainly be distorted, not necessarily deliberately, but by the very fact that he is sharing something with another.

The process is a very natural one. All of us, in all our contacts with people, care about what others think of us. All of us care, indeed, what we think about ourselves. We create what is known in politics or business as an "image." Moreover, we use this image to try to manipulate others. It may be an image of strength or one of helplessness or despair. It may be of rectitude or nonchalance. Whatever it is it is our protection against being fully known by another—that almost ultimate threat—as well as the way we have found to deal with others.

In one sense it could be said that no real helping can take place until the "image" is dispelled and the real self can be shared. But it cannot be abruptly broken. It must be yielded bit by bit, explored, found unnecessary. And always some of it will be there. Indeed the kind of image that a person projects tells us a good deal about the kind of problem he has and how he goes about solving his problems.

This is the way he is trying to get help, or to ward it off, or to limit it to what is acceptable to him. And since in order to be helped one first has to make a decision about taking help at all, what he is saying and doing is, so far from being irrelevant, the very material of which help will have to be built.

It is important, therefore, that the helper is aware of what is happening in the here and now. He cannot accept what the helped person says solely as bits of information to be stored for future use as those who have tried to follow too strict a system of diagnosis and treatment soon found out. Not only what is said is important, but why and when and obviously, how. One of the most neglected questions in helping is, "Why are you telling me this now?" and this question may need three different emphases: Why are you telling *me* this now? Why are you telling me *this* now? and Why are you telling me this *now*?

The same is also true of what the helper says and does. Not only does the helper have his own image to project, but what the helped person says or does not say may be a direct reaction to what the helper says or does. That is why an account of an interview needs to be so much more than a collection of facts about the client or his problem, if it is to be fully understood. It must contain what both helped and helper said and did.

The "here-and-nowness" of the helping relationship means also that it can be separated out of a man's total experience and given special artificial characteristics of its own. In a sense this may seem to be impossible: both helper and helped bring to it the whole of their past life experience simply by being there, and its repercussions may affect the whole of the helped person's life. But it does exist as a special occasion and this gives the helper, or the organization for which he works, the opportunity to set certain conditions that may help both helper and helped focus on what needs to be done.

Among these conditions is time, much used by psychiatrists who offer severely time-limited sessions or time-limited courses of treatment. There is nothing so frightening or debilitating as unlimited time. It is the saving grace of many human experiences, including childhood, formal education, a vacation, and the process of being helped that they will end. If they did not, if one had, for instance, to remain in school until one knew everything there was to know, or be helped until one was entirely well, it would be intolerable and no one in their senses would engage themselves in such a project. Time in the form of a deadline is also extremely useful in helping one concentrate one's efforts on a particular goal. Few students would complete a paper if they had unlimited time in which to do it. Many good helping persons also build into the process times at which a review of progress made to date can be made. This avoids continuing with a situation in a way that is making no progress. It helps pull the process together.

Also important are those factors which limit the scope of the help to be given or the power of the helping person over the person helped. These may be external criteria, such as the law or the regulations under which assistance may be given, which often, as in public assistance in the United States, limit the welfare worker's discretion to refuse or to reduce a grant as much if not more than they restrict the size of the grant he may give. Or they may be in the nature of contracts or agreements—it is this I am asking help for and not this or that, and you have agreed to help me only with this at this time. Being helped is such a frightening thing that some people only find it possible to risk taking help if they are aware, to some extent, of how far the helping person will press them, although the result of being helped in a limited area may turn out to be upsetting to the whole.

All too often, however, especially in such programs as public assistance, before social services and financial assistance were separated, asking for money has meant that the asker has subjected his whole life to the review of the caseworker, who feels compelled to help him in all sorts of ways the client has not envisaged or may not want. Although the helper who would do so is not likely to be a good one, a clear understanding of the conditions of help is helpful both to helper and helped.

Limiting the scope of help may also help the helped person partialize his problem, that is, concentrate on one bit of it instead of trying to handle a "whole sea" of troubles all at once. A partialized problem is quite often one one can do something about when one is helpless before the whole. If one can start work on even a little bit of the whole, one may gain courage to tackle a little more.

This setting of special conditions that exist only for the helping relationship, or for a part of it, is sometimes called "structuring" the relationship. The term can also be used for a single interview. Its rationale is the not unreasonable expectation that the helped person, once having had the experience of finding himself able to handle himself in a protected situation, may gain the confidence in himself or in helping persons to handle his problems in a wider sphere. It is the same rationale that we use when we allow a child, for instance, to manage his own clothing budget in a family setting, where he cannot make too disastrous a mistake, in the expectation that he will thereby be more able to handle a more total budget when he no longer has us behind him.

Another closely allied characteristic of the relationship is that *it must offer something new*. This is obvious. If it did not, there would be no reason for the helped person to make a decision now when he had not been able to do so in many identical situations. But it is not as simple as this. To introduce difference into a situation in such a way that it proves a moving rather than a paralyzing factor requires that there be a good deal of likeness, of shared experience and understanding, on which the difference can be based. Indeed the whole helping process has sometimes been described as a skilled use of likeness and difference. The helping efforts of many untrained or occasional helpers is apt to contain much too much difference in the form of blame, unsolicited advice, commands, or moral precepts. This might be called inappropriate difference.

For many years helping theory has tended to emphasize likeness, rather than difference. Carl Rogers's nondirective counseling does not go this far, but it does put the counselor in a nondiffering position. Popular feeling has to some extent followed this bent. Parents are urged to be "pals" to their children, to minimize the difference of age and responsibility. We deplore "the generation gap." Much has been made of the impossibility of the middle class understanding the feelings of those in poverty, or of whites trying to help blacks. The growth, in American social work, of "indigenous workers" is a sign of this trend.

While there is some truth in the statement that people from widely different cultures or age groups find difficulty in understanding each other, the problem is one of imagination more than it is of similar experience. It is not necessary to have experienced the same problems as the person one is trying to help. Despite the experience of Alcoholics Anonymous, who have built a very successful method of helping on an initial likeness, it is not necessary, obviously, to have had an illegitimate child to help an unmarried mother. It is not even necessary to be a woman. Nor is it necessary to be of the same class or color as the person one in helping. None of these more or less artificial likenesses is necessary to helping. They have to be created when there is in those who normally handle the problem a lack of imagination and respect for the person being helped. What one needs to help a criminal is not to have committed a crime, but to know what it is like to be tempted to do so, or the imagination to feel the tensions and frustrations out of which crime is born.

There is even a danger in having had experiences too much like those of the person being helped. Initially it may be an advantage in establishing what we have called likeness. But there is no more harmful helper than the person who has successfully solved a problem, taken credit for it, and has forgotten what it cost him to overcome it. Such a person often expects other people to solve their problems in the same way as he has done. "I solved it. Why can't you?" Often, too, such a helper is threatened by a helped person's doubts or anger, even by his discussing the problem. If the helper's victory over the problem has been achieved with the help of some repression, he cannot allow the questions he himself had and repressed to become live options again.

Alcoholics Anonymous's apparent reliance on likeness alone as a major factor in helping is perhaps the exception that proves the rule. In my opinion what makes their work both possible and productive is their insistence on the role of a force—divine grace—outside either helper or helped.

We need therefore both likeness and difference. Specific suggestions for the introduction of specific difference into the helping situation will be made in a later chapter.

Again it may seem almost too obvious to mention, but this relationship must be one in which *choice is truly offered;* not, of course, unreal or manufactured choice, or choice stripped of its consequences, but what we have called active and willing choice. This means in practice that the relationship must be one in which negative as well as positive solutions can be examined.

It follows that negative as well as positive feelings must be allowed expression, without the fear that these will lead to blame, or shock, or the withdrawal of the helping person's interest, concern, or esteem.

People generally need more help with their negative feelings than they do with their positive. We can illustrate this statement by likening a person to a car or a trolley with at least a moderate tendency to proceed down a road. Man, we have said, must be presumed to have some innate tendency to grow, to go forward, to make constructive choices in his own interest. But a person in trouble is like a trolley which has stalled.

While it is conceivable that the engine has worn out, there are two much more likely explanations for the trolley's failure to advance. One might be that the road is indeed too rocky or steep, in which case, when we come upon it, the sensible thing to do is to try to remove some of the rocks. It is indeed good sense to be sure, in any situation, that obvious rocks, such as lack of money, or physical illness, or lack of education or skill, are either removed or recognized for what they are and, if possible, a path found around or over them.

In many situations it will be found that although the way appears to be clear, and the engine not seriously damaged, for some reason or other the trolley fails to move. What has actually happened is that the forward motion of the trolley is pressing against a strong spring of negative feelings, that is of fear, guilt, anger, or despair.

We can now draw our diagram thus:

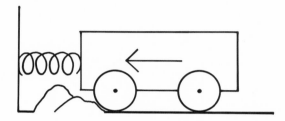

although we will have to admit that the stanchion or post to which the spring is attached (on the left of the diagram) has no real existence. It, and the spring, are actually inside the trolley itself and are preventing not the whole trolley moving but, say, a wheel turning or a piston completing its stroke. Nevertheless, diagrammatically, the figure will serve and the result is the same.

The usual impulse of a helping person, finding such a human "trolley" that appears to be stalled, is to get behind it and push. That is, positive feelings are encouraged, and the person urged or exhorted to move. But the result, if our diagram has any validity, will be a small positive movement, it is true, but at the same time a tightening of the spring, thus:

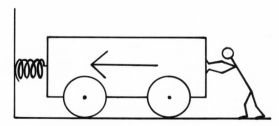

Resistance to help is therefore increased and either the whole mechanism breaks down, which is what happens in mental illnesses of various kinds, or, when the helper stops pushing, the trolley slides back (or backslides).

Any engineer, faced with this model, could tell us that the sensible thing to do is to remove the spring, or, if we cannot do so, to uncoil it in some way so that it no longer holds so much tension in it. This requires looking at it, which, in our analogy, means allowing negatives to be expressed, discussed, and seen for what they are, which is usually far less ominous than they were feared to be.

The analogy is not perfect, but it may help us to see why, in human helping, it is not possible to proceed on a basis of "accentuating the positive and eliminating the negative," despite the popularity of a well-known preacher who recommends exactly this. His very popularity in America explains in fact why it is so often necessary for the helping relationship to deal with negative feelings. The whole of American culture tends to ignore negatives. An optimist is highly regarded, a pessimist somehow thought of as someone who is dissatisfied, or even disloyal. There are hundreds of Optimists Clubs in the United States, and no Pessimists Club, to my knowledge. A person in trouble will find little difficulty in finding people to support his positive feelings, to push his trolley, to tell him to look on the bright side of things, to "snap out of it" or to "be thankful for small mercies." Only the true helping person will be willing to help him with his negative feelings, with the things that are really blocking his progress, which everyone else cheerfully chooses to ignore.

There is a popular fear that to discuss negatives will in some way encourage them; that, if left alone, they will somehow shrivel and die. Negatives would be encouraged if by discussing them we meant sympathizing with them, sharing them to some extent or being sorry for someone on account of them. But, as will become more apparent later when we discuss empathy and sympathy, to discuss something with someone is not to encourage it. It is rather to see it for what it is and cut it down to size.

Psychiatrists, if is true, recommend that one not discuss or "explore" negative feelings with a person suffering from depression but, rather, encourage him, and this may seem like a rather important exception, for how do we know that our apparently "blocked" person may not be a depressive? But this is more a caution against identification with negatives and what might be called "dwelling on them" than it is a recommendation that negatives not be explored. There may, however, be some situations where, contrary to usual experience, a person has had his negative impulses reinforced by friends, relatives, and neighbors, perhaps because he has sought this reinforcement, and whose greater need is to discuss the unseen positive. These are not usually hard to detect. The person seizes on the negative, demands one's agreement with it, displays it, one might almost say, flaunts it. At the same time he is unwilling to consider any realistic discussion of it. He needs it too much.

One cannot say that this type of negative is not a "true" negative, since to ascribe to emotions, truth, or falsehood is to make value judgments one cannot support. But it is true that this kind of negative is somewhat different from the negative feeling that one does need to discuss or explore. Perhaps we should use different words for them. The negative that needs uncovering and discussing is one of which generally the helped person is afraid or ashamed. It may be denied, or even repressed. It is thought to be unacceptable, like having rejecting feelings about one's child, or fearing a necessary operation, or being guilt-ridden for something one has done. The depressive, on the other hand, is using his negative feelings, sheltering behind them to resist getting well, even sometimes what we call "wallowing" in them. We might reserve the term "negative feelings" for the first and call the second "negative projections" to indicate the use that is being made of them. The second category would then include the negatives that form such a part of the paranoid's world, which, also, it is unwise to discuss or explore.

The need, however, to permit the expression of what we have called here "negative feelings" should be apparent. It is one of the reasons why the helping relationship cannot always be pleasant and why the effort to make it so is so often unhelpful. One cannot express negative feelings and keep a relationship pleasant, particularly if one of the negative feelings is anger, and even more particularly, if this anger is directed against the helping person or the organization he represents. Fear, guilt, and despair are all ugly emotions. We tend to discount them or cover them up.

The need to be able to express negative feelings in the helping relationship is also the basis of another characteristic of the relationship as a whole, which is that it must be *nonjudgmental*. This too has often been misunderstood, and thought to mean that the helping person must be willing to condone any kind of behavior. But bad behavior is not condoned by the nonjudgmental person. It is true that it is not punished in the course of a helping relationship, except where the helping person has, as part of his function, this responsibility, and even then such punishment does not, it could be hoped, carry personal reprobation. It becomes more a setting of limits of an exposure to the natural consequence of one's act—just as one might have to say to a child, "I'm not passing judgment on your motives for what you have done. I can even see that you may have had to do it. But in the interest of good order, or fairness to others, or as a reminder that it could lead to real trouble if you did it again, I'll have to punish you for it."

But in the majority of helping situations the helping person is not there to judge. Punishment, or reproof, is left to those whose function it is in our society to administer these sanctions. A judge, or a parent, is empowered to exercise this function, but even then needs to be careful that he does not exceed its bounds.

For the rest of us the tendency to judge, to approve, or disapprove is in general only a way of asserting our superiority over the person with whom we are dealing. While in an imperfect world society finds it necessary to control actions both by punishment and reward and by social approval or disapproval, and I may find myself, most unwillingly, in a position where it is my duty to apply these sanctions, this is no reason why I should take this burden on myself when it is not my responsibility. If I have any knowledge of how hard most decisions are, how little I can know the conditions under which they must be made, and if I am aware that I have never been in exactly the situation which this man has had to experience, common sense might prevent me from wanting to be judgmental. Particularly it might warn me from being judgmental about feelings, for this is a totally fruitless exercise. A man can help, in some instances, what he does about a situation, but not what he feels about it. To tell a man that he ought not to feel "like that" about something is like telling a man with a broken leg that it ought not to hurt and that it is his fault if it does.

Yet this kind of judgmentalism is all too common in our helping. It goes along with the belief that help should be given only to those who are "deserving," whereas it would seem sense to say that it is the "undeserving" who are likely to be in the most trouble and to need help most.

The need of the helped person is to find practical ways of doing differently. He is not helped by a reinforcement of moral judgments of which he is in all probability only too aware. He needs to look at the feelings which led him to act as he did and find out what he can substitute for them, and this is often impossible if his chief preoccupation is his shame or guilt. New beginnings have to be made within the framework of feelings that he already has. He cannot be entirely different from what he has been before. He must be able to look at himself, and this he cannot do if he sees himself as entirely bad.

For this reason alone the helping relationship cannot be that of self-appointed saint with a sinner, or self-appointed judge with an offender, or, its modern equivalent, self-declared adjusted person with the maladjusted. It must be a relationship between two fallible human beings, each of whom could, in the last analysis, have done what the other did if circumstances had been different. It is true that one is probably stronger than the other, or better educated or more intelligent, and we can only hope that this one is the helper. It is also true that one may hold a position which elevates him above the other and gives him some authority over him. These are often useful "difference" factors. But the likeness must come first, and a common humanity and fallibility is the basis of likeness.

These, then, are some at least of the characteristics of a productive helping relationship. For convenience we might list them again. They are eight in number. The helping relationship, if it is indeed to be helpful, must be recognized as being a mutual and not a one-way relationship, is not necessarily consistently pleasant or friendly, must be one of feeling as well as knowledge, must have a single purpose, takes place in the here and now, must offer something new, must be a relationship in which choice is truly offered, and must be nonjudgmental.

The helping relationship is, however, only the medium in which help is offered. It is not help itself. To be able to establish the kind of relationship described here is half the battle, but not all of it. Something more dynamic needs to come into the relationship. One needs to do more than avoid some of the crasser errors of undisciplined helpers. One needs to be able to help. This leads naturally to a discussion of the helping factor itself.

V. THE HELPING FACTOR

There must be something which the helping person brings into the relationship through which help is actually given. The relationship we have discussed cannot do this by itself. We have already described it as a resultant and not something that can be created apart from what goes on between helper and helped. We cannot set up such a relationship and then sit back and expect help to flow from it without some positive action or contribution on our part.

Quite clearly too the helping factor is something more than the material things with which help often deals, such as money, a job, housing, or medical care, although it is a mistake to think that these things are unimportant. It was one of the misapprehensions of many nineteenth century helpers, that to give material things was wrong, or at best a necessary evil, and that all meaningful help was conveyed through psychological reinforcement. Octavia Hill herself believed that all material help to the aged was a mistake.[1] We can read only with some distaste of the early settlement worker who was "as liberal with his sympathy as he was chary of meat and coal tickets."[2]

Yet the psychological factors in helping have had such a hold on the thought of welfare workers in the United States that a false dichotomy has been created in many places between tangible and intangible help, and some states have tended to justify a low standard of material assistance by emphasizing the supposed excellence of their counseling services.

A job, a house, an opportunity are very important to people. They may be completely necessary to the solution of their problems. Yet, there is something more to helping than this. While there are obvious situations in which they are all that are needed, in which case helping would seem to consist solely in their provision, in the majority of

1. Evidence of Miss Octavia Hill before the Royal Commission on the Aged Poor, 1895, excerpted in Gertrude Lubbock, *Some Poor Relief Questions* (London, 1895), p. 275.

2. Edward Dennison, from *Letters and Writings of the Late Edward Dennison M.P. for Newark,* ed. Sir Baldwin Leighton (London, 1872), p. 145.

situations something else has to happen, either in the actual giving or possibly before it, if a person is to make full use of them. And even then their mere provision can be done in such a way that their use is enhanced or limited. The dignity of the application procedure, the concern shown for details, the promptness of their provision, even the setting in which they are given, all contribute to or deduct from their helpfulness.

The problem not of opportunity but of how to use opportunity, may be one of the greatest problems facing such programs as the American "war on poverty." While it is obviously good to create opportunities for those who have never had them, and while a great deal of attention has been given to the problem of ensuring that these opportunities are appropriate and what people "want," both by making use of detailed research and by including in decision-making as many of the potential consumers of these opportunities as possible, the actual readiness of people to make use of what they are given has received rather little attention.[3] Already there are signs in some areas that this may be a crucial factor.

There have been many attempts to isolate or define the primary helping factor. The nineteenth century, by and large, relied on moral exhortation, friendliness, and encouragement, as in the classic nineteenth-century statement: "Let the moral sense be awakened and the moral influence be established in the minds of the improvident, the unfortunate and the depraved. Let them be approached with kindness and an ingenuous concern for their welfare; inspire them with self-respect and encourage their industry and economy. . . . Those are the methods of doing them real and permanent good."[4]

Later a more rationalist approach relied on careful case study and appropriate treatment, which in general meant manipulation of the environment and the supplying of influences which the helped person was thought to lack. Some attention was also paid to the participation of the helped person in plans made for him.

A little later, in the late twenties and early thirties of this century it was believed that listening alone was perhaps the primary helping factor, and American social work went through "the era of the

3. For an excellent statement of this, see Anita Faatz, *Poverty and Social Work,* First Annual Isabelle K. Carter Lecture, School of Social Work, The University of North Carolina (1965).

4. *Annual Report of the Society for the Prevention of Pauperism,* 1818, quoted by Edward Devine, *People and Relief* (New York, 1904). It is interesting how the report lumps the improvident, the unfortunate, and the depraved together as if misfortune were a sin.

mouse."[5] The helper became little more than a mirror against which the helped person projected his concerns. It was thought that if the helped person could verbalize his feelings and his problems he could look at them more rationally. Carl Rogers's "nondirective" counseling became the principal model.

With the advent of psychoanalysis interpretation of unconscious motives was given the first place. It was, and is, believed that the rationality of the conscious brain, brought face to face with the apparently infantile reasoning which the unconscious seems to employ—its tendency, for instance, to identify wholly unlike things— would reject this irrationality in favor of more sensible behavior.

So deeply is this concept ingrained in this generation that many people will uphold that one cannot modify one's behavior unless one knows exactly why one has misbehaved in the first place, which is clearly not always so. Some understanding of one's motives may be very helpful in coming to a decision, but many of man's most fruitful decisions and commitments are made without knowing exactly why. Incidentally, this belief, somewhat misunderstood, has led to one of the least fruitful exercises of the beginning helper, the constant asking of the helped person "why" he did something, or "why" he feels this way, when he either does not know, or is afraid to tell you, or, more likely still, has provided himself with a whole set of rationalizations to prevent himself facing this problem. Anyone who has ever asked a naughty child why he did something and has been greeted with silence or "because . . ." will recognize what happens.

The same belief once caused a class of mine to insist that the purpose of an interview with a delinquent girl we were studying could be no other than to find out "why" she ran away from home. They were quite shocked when I said that this might be quite helpful, if it could ever be known, although I doubted that this would ever tell us more than the precipitating factor. The actual causality would be probably almost infinitely complex and involve many factors outside both theirs and Mary Ann's control, a recognition which is being increasingly made by students of epidemiology. If they were interested in trying to create conditions in the community which would minimize delinquency, such an analysis might have value.

But this was not the purpose of the interview as it was held. It could have only one present purpose. That would be to find out ways by

5. The title of an article in a social work journal which I can no longer identify. Date, ca. 1932.

which Mary Ann would be able to handle her impulse to run away again.

I do not mean that the epidemiological approach, the desire to control or alter conditions so that other Mary Anns might not need to run away, is something with which a social worker should not be concerned. I do mean that to help Mary Ann in the here and now the knowledge of her action's complicated causality is probably not enough. There is always a temptation in helping to think that if one knows why something has occurred one can correct it. But this is simply not so. Even if Mary Ann could say, and even be convinced, that she ran away because of any number of factors, there is still her will, her image of herself, her fears and the reality of her present situation to take into account. Man is not a rational creature, and a fourteen-year-old girl perhaps not always an exemplar of logical thinking.

If Mary Ann were a very sick child, or if her impulse was such that it was uncontrollable by any conscious act on her part even with some change of attitude on the part of her parents, psychotherapy with interpretation might have been necessary. The need for this would have shown up, perhaps, in a more total disorganization than this girl was presenting, or in her failure to make use of the helping process that most people can use to some extent. Even here her problems might have been solved by psychiatric treatment not involving interpretation.

Her particular behavior might be amenable to conditioning or to drug therapy. This would involve a "why" of a sort—knowledge at least that her condition could become manageable if certain tensions were relieved, which is not so much a "why" as a "how." Sometimes by handling one factor in a complex a person may be brought to a condition below, as it were, the critical point at which symptoms appear.

This is, however, very different from the probation officer coming to her diagnosis of why Mary Ann behaved as she did and then interpreting this to her. Of much of this kind of psychosocial diagnosis, especially if not made by a psychiatrist, one can only say, "So what?" It might perhaps help the worker make some suggestions to Mary Ann's parents about how they might treat her to avoid exacerbating her problem. That is, if they were ready for this help.

But it would have done more, or less. A preoccupation with causality would have failed to engage Mary Ann's capacity to face her situation and do something about it herself.

Particularly is this true, as Glasser points out in his book, if the causality of an action becomes an excuse for not doing something about it. It is all very well to know that one behaves badly because one has been rejected or unloved. There is no doubt that to be rejected makes it harder to behave well. But it does not remove the responsibility of a person to do something about his behavior. And this is what Mary Ann needs to struggle with now. To help Mary Ann do this the probation officer must start with the reality of the situation, the fact that she has done something illegal, the possibility that the judge might send her to a correctional school, or let her go home only under supervision, which she might find difficult to bear; even the fact that she might find it impossible not to run away again. In order to decide what she wanted, what she could bear, what use she could make of whatever was decided, and what help she needed to do this, Mary Ann would need to be held to facing these facts and possibilities.

She would also need to be free to discuss and explore her feelings about them, and in fact reassured that her expression of these feelings would not get her into trouble. Part of these feelings might be anger, at her parents, at the judge, or at the probation officer. The last is particularly likely if the officer has done her job in holding Mary Ann to the reality of the situation; but since this anger is something which Mary Ann cannot help feeling about the situation, and since to repress it, or "bottle it up" will only make it more important and harder to deal with, it may need to be expressed.

Lastly, if Mary Ann is to take help in her situation, she must know that the officer will be available to her, will not turn against her when she is troubled, and will provide as far as she can what Mary Ann needs to carry out her decisions.

This situation may serve, despite its particularity, to help us see what it is that the helping person must convey to any person in trouble. What has to be conveyed can be phrased as a "statement" which the helping person makes, although it is much more than this. It is not simply something said. It is something conveyed by words, feeling and action. But in terms of a statement it could be phrased in three sentences, as follows:

"This is it."

"I know that it must hurt."

"I am here to help you if you want me and can use me,"[6] or, more succinctly, "You don't have to face this alone."

6. These sentences were first formulated, with one difference, in my article, "The Nature of the Helping Process," *Christian Scholar* 52 (Summer 1960) : 119-27. The reformulation from "that it hurts" to "that it must hurt" was made at the suggestion of a class of welfare workers in Maine and is obviously more correct.

These three sentences in turn may be expressed in terms of what is actually offered through them. In this form the helping factor is composed of three elements which we may call *reality, empathy* and *support*.

Such an analysis may seem extremely simple. If this is indeed the helping factor and all that a helping person needs to do and be is to be realistic, empathic, and supporting, then it may be thought that there is little to it. Anyone ought to be able to help. The analysis is, however, a very simple way of expressing a very complex matter, and like many simple statements, religious, philosophical, or scientific, it is extremely hard to put into practice. The relationship, too, between its parts is of great importance to the whole.

Yet, these three elements are always necessary in any helping process, and the three together do in fact constitute the helping factor. I know of no piece of helping that cannot be analyzed in these terms, and no piece of unsuccessful helping that does not show a weakness in at least one of these elements. Either reality, or support, or empathy, or more than one of these, has been lacking, misunderstood, or, perhaps more frequently, not fully carried out. Reality has been partial, empathy and support conditional.

Other formulations are, of course, possible. Some friends of mine have suggested, for instance, that encouragement to act on one's own might constitute a fourth element, while I would see it as part of reality (no one can solve this problem but you), of empathy (this is what you want), and of support (I am here to help you, not to control you). Dr. Mahoney's fourfold division into acceptance, listening (both elements of empathy), presence (a major part of support), and information-giving (curiously a very small part of reality and a part of what is meant by support) is not denied but enlarged by this analysis. It remains, in my experience, both the most comprehensive and the most useful conceptualization I have found.

It might be wise to examine first each principle by itself and then try to bring them together. The order in which they are presented here does not necessarily mean that one introduces them, in helping, serially or in this order. One may start with an expression of empathy or even of support, and in any case they are interwoven. One does not stop where another starts. But if there is an order, reality often does come first.

Reality means a number of things, some of which have already been touched on. It means, first of all, not discounting another's problem, not taking it away from him by believing it unimportant. This is a thing we are particularly likely to do to children, whom we cannot believe, for some reason, feel as deeply as we do. How often we say, "Oh, they'll soon forget it," or "They're too young to be affected much," when everything that we really know about them points to the fact that their despair, their fear, and their anger is not only intense but can leave permanent scars. To be real, on the other hand, means to face the problem with someone in all of its ugliness or terror. It means doing him the honor of taking his problem seriously. And, with children, in particular, but with adults also, this is the first requirement if a relationship is to grow. One cannot have a relationship of any depth if one does not take the other person seriously.

Another form of taking away a person's problem is to solve it for him or insulate him from it. We either produce a quick solution or we help him to evade it, to forget it, not to come into contact with it.

Often we do this because we see that the problem is painful. The helped person is disturbed about it. We wish to spare him this disturbance. But, while it might be necessary to allay some forms of disturbance temporarily, disturbance has about it some of the qualities that are now recognized in a fever. It used to be good medical practice to allay all fevers. Now there is growing understanding that a fever is the body's way of fighting an infection.

A child once, in a Children's Home, was very much disturbed by her mother's visits. The social worker suggested solving the problem by refusing to let the mother visit the Home. The child said, "What you don't understand is that this is something I need to get disturbed about."

People need their problems if they are to solve them for themselves. Sometimes they need to be disturbed. Not to permit them to become so, when they are trying to tackle their problems, is to encourage nonchoice.

A common form of nonreality is reassurance. Reassurance, or rather false reassurance, is an attempt to palliate reality by telling the person in trouble that "things will be all right," when there is no reason to think that this will be so, or when the present hurts so much that this is wholly unimportant. We can recognize obvious cases of it. No wise parent today would tell her child that the dentist "won't hurt." He very well may, and the parent be proved a liar. But we still, some of us, will tell a child that he will be happy in a foster home, when this may not be so and when in any case all he can think of at the moment is his pain at leaving his own parents.

We use this kind of reassurance for two reasons. In the first place, we cannot stand his present unhappiness and are willing, although we may not know it, to try to dispel it even at the cost of greater unhappiness later. And, in the second, we are apt to be a little defensive because a foster home, in this case, or some other service, is what we have to offer him and we do not like the idea that he might not like the only thing that we have to give him. It makes us feel very inadequate. I have seen a welfare worker "reassure" a client that the termination of her grant does not really matter, since she ought to be able to get support from a recently located absent husband, when her lights and gas were to be turned off that afternoon. "Pie in the sky" is no substitute for bread in the here and now. False, or unrealistic reassurance, does not strengthen a person's ability to handle his problem. It effectually disarms him and robs him of the anger or despair he may need to deal with it.

One of the reasons for false reassurance is our natural protectiveness towards those we consider vulnerable or lacking in real strength. We feel that the person we are helping would be hurt by coming face to face with the truth. As such it appears to us at the time as a wholly kindly and helpful action. There may be some instances in which the helped person could not possibly face the truth but more often the helping person is only too glad to have a good reason not to face the helped person with the truth. He fears the helped person's reaction and his own inability to deal with it. The genuine cases where the truth is so horrible that it would be more harmful than helpful are rather rare.

To protect someone from the truth is to make a very serious judgment about him. It is to say that he is incapable of being helped with his real problem. As a minister expressed it to me once, it is to deny him his chance for an "abundant life," fully experienced.

The truth, too, is often much less harmful than what the imagination puts in its place. Some years ago I was approached by a teacher who was concerned about a fifteen-year-old boy, the adopted son of an apparently stable and loving family, who had begun to run away. There seemed to be nothing in the home to suggest a need to escape from it and although the boy was adolescent, he did not appear to be particularly rebellious or have a desire to "freak out." The boy was plainly running "to" rather than "from" and when I was told that the town he was running to was his birthplace I was fairly safe in assuming at least tentatively that he was doing what so many children away from their own parents have to do, which was to answer the question, "Why did my parents give me up?"

I therefore asked the teacher why his parents had done so, and was told that the boy was illegitimate. I asked whether the boy knew this, and was met with the rather indignant statement that the teacher was sure that no one had ever mentioned it to him. He thought, I believe, at the moment that I was suggesting that someone had taunted him with his birth and thus caused him to run away.

It was quite hard for him to take when I suggested that if he wanted to help the boy someone had better tell him the truth. It seemed like a horrible thing to do. We wrestled with this for quite a while, acknowledging what it might cost him and the possibility that I was wrong in my belief, and in the end decided that he would at least try telling the truth. This he did, very honestly and bravely.

To his surprise the boy was greatly relieved. As the boy expressed it, "Of course she had to find another home for me." Later the boy confessed that he had been for several years tortured by two alternative fantasies. One, derived from a film, *The Bad Seed*, which is based on the theory that evil is inherited, was that both of his parents had been executed for murder. The other, derived from an advertisement, and comical if it had not been so tragic, was that he had an unbearable odor about which "even your best friends won't tell you." When for a moment he was able to talk himself out of the one fantasy and see it for what it was, the other would rise to plague him. The truth was far less dangerous than the untruths he had imagined.

We are much too ready to assume that another person cannot bear the truth. Only when an untruth has become so necessary to a person that he cannot live without it is it wise not to face the truth. We must remember, however, that reality is only one of the three helping elements. It cannot be introduced without empathy and support.

We sometimes call a piece of reality deliberately introduced into a helping situation a piece of difference. It may be a fact. It can conceivably be an opinion, although we need to be careful that it is not a prejudice or a personal point of view irrelevant to the helped person's need. Unskilled workers are, as we have said, full of inappropriate difference, and introduce pieces of difference in inappropriate ways.

How do we know when it is appropriate? How do we avoid perhaps robbing someone of an illusion that he needs? We do need difference, something new, in the helping relationship. I would suggest at least four criteria.

The first, and perhaps the most important, is that there is sufficient likeness—understanding, common purpose—to assure the helped person that this is not a wayward attack. Perhaps the most successful piece of consultation I ever did was with an agency that had been severely criticized for its practices by a number of authorities, and had become quite defensive about its program. I was asked to its campus as one who understood and shared many of its ideals. The difference I introduced was even more extreme than that of its other critics, but it was difference expressed in the context of common goals, of respect for their efforts, even where misdirected, and of appreciation for the good things they had done. This time the agency listened and changed even faster than anyone could possibly hope. One can, after all, say things to people who know that you love them that you could not possibly say to a stranger.

Secondly, the difference must be expressed in the helped person's terms. In this case I could express my difference in terms of the agency's own goals. I could show them that their methods were not accomplishing what they themselves set out to do. Often the most useful little bits of difference can be expressed by using the helped person's own words.

Thirdly, there is a somewhat elusive quality about the person who is ready to accept difference. There is an element of challenge, of projecting an image and watching to see how you are going to respond to it. This was there in the agency I have mentioned. This is what we are, they seemed to be saying. How does it strike you? Isn't it good? And underneath there was doubt.

This is perhaps the least concrete of our criteria. It is a sense one gets, an understanding of the process of image projection, a knowledge that a projection is being made for a purpose. The helped person is really saying, "Will you buy this image of me?" and if you do you only strengthen the image and make the real self less accessible. I heard a mother once tell a counselor how reasonable she was in her demands on her seventeen-year-old son, and how unreasonable he was. "And he never gets in by nine o'clock." The counselor's quiet statement, "But you know, seventeen-year-olds don't get in by nine o'clock" was a fruitful piece of difference. The mother was able, with its help, to see that she was not making reasonable demands, but was terribly afraid of what her son might be doing at night.

The last criterion has to do with empathy and support. It is briefly that one has no right to introduce difference or reality unless one is prepared to help the other with the shock. Reality by itself is harsh. It can be very destructive. It is only reality approached with empathy and support that is a true helping process. Indeed we might restate the whole method of help as "facing people with reality with empathy and support." To face someone with reality and leave them to handle it alone is cruelty, not help.

The fear of not being able to handle the repercussions is one of the chief obstacles to introducing appropriate difference. I find myself that as I grow older and, if not more confident, then at least practiced enough to know that I can survive, and even be of some help, whatever a helped person's reaction, I grow bolder and more helpful in the introduction of difference. I still have not had the courage to do as one social worker did, and say to a client who was trying to manipulate her or reassure himself by surliness and sarcasm, "You know you are the most unpleasant client I've ever had to deal with."

I would not recommend this much difference to any but the most experienced helper, and not then unless all four criteria were met. Yet in this case it was appropriate and proved a turning point in help. Certainly American helping has, for the last thirty or forty years, suffered from too little difference.

Obviously to tell even a very small percentage of those one was trying to help that they are unpleasant people would be a very poor rule in practice. In most cases it would result in the very reverse of helping. How, then, could this woman risk it? Obviously it could only be done when she was sure that Mr. Smith recognized her desire to help. Just as one can tell "home truths"—in itself an interesting term—to those who are sure of one's love and interest, so one can risk difference with one who trusts one. Again, it had to be true. Mr. Smith had been behaving in an objectively unpleasant way. He had in fact been making a stream of petty but mildly offensive allegations about the whole office staff. But there was a third element present. The worker recognized his unpleasantness not so much to be assumed and therefore false as part of his persona, the projected unreal self which he was using to stifle his doubts. There was an element both of uncertainty and of challenge about what he was doing. It actually demanded an answer, and if the answer had been a placid acceptance, its value as an escape from reality would have been strengthened. This was also true of the mother with the seventeen-year-old son. What she was really asking was, "Is it all right for me to treat him as if he were much younger?"

The ability to distinguish between an unreality of this type and the unreality which the helped person really believes and in fact cannot live without is a matter of some skill. To tell a sufferer from a functional heart disease that his illness is imaginary, which is objectively true, would in most cases be disastrous. He knows that he is ill, cannot prevent himself from being so, and has the same pain and shortness of breath as the person with heart damage. It is largely a matter of listening carefully to the feeling behind what is being said, of catching that element of challenge and doubt, and of being aware that the helped person will always, to some extent, project a persona in his effort to protect himself from you. Sometimes one can pick it up through an inherent contradiction in what the seeker for help may say. A man who came to complain of the care his estranged wife was giving his children said that he deserted his family because he could not bear not to be master in his home. The social worker asked if he felt that quitting had made him any more the master, and this helped him to express his frustration and defeat, of which his complaints were a symptom, and to ask help towards a reconciliation.

Another form of difference which can sometimes be of help, providing again that it is kept within a framework of likeness, consists in the speculative assumption of exactly the opposite of what the helped person is asserting, so that he may gain strength in demolishing your argument. This is in fact the function of the devil's advocate in a canonization procedure. What a devil's advocate says is, in effect, "Have you considered the possibility that we're on the wrong track altogether? Let's look at the possibility." This is a form of difference that can only be used when the helped person is fairly sure of himself; when, in fact, all that he needs is to move from a tentative statement to a forthright claiming of what he knows and believes. It cannot be used when a person is struggling to make sense out of chaos, or when he is searching for an answer. It requires, too, a clear understanding of the helping person's authority and purpose. It is not an argument as much as it is a way of examining and strengthening the basic presuppositions on which one is acting.

Reality also means not being indirect. Helping people, unfortunately, have acquired something of the reputation of being rather "wily birds" who tread like Agag, delicately, and never quite say what they mean. This is sometimes described as "tact" or "consideration," but so easily becomes either evasion or a way of gently manipulating someone else to do what you want him to do and at the same time think that it was his own idea. I have even heard helping described as doing exactly that. But clearly this is far from the kind of helping with which we are concerned. "Tact" may be a good word when it means telling the truth with concern for another's feelings, but all too often when one says, "I told him tactfully that . . . ," one means, "I hinted that it might be so because I was afraid to say so directly." There are some things that cannot be said "tactfully" in the sense of gradually or evasively. They can only be faced for what they are.

One area in which the reality of the situation needs to be very clearly expressed is that of the helping relationship itself. Generally this means what we described in our account of Mary Ann—what will, or may happen, the probable consequences of actions, the authority and rights each person has in the situation, who can tell whom to do what, and the conditions under which help is being offered. Concealed power is both unfair and generally unhelpful. The worker from the juvenile court who minimizes its authority and presents it as **only** wanting to be "of help" without making clear that it will enforce this "help" is trying to buy relationship at the cost of the truth, and will end by having neither.

A further requirement of reality is that it must be presented as it is, without attempts at justification. One of the things we all do when it becomes our duty to present or enforce an unpleasant reality is to try to justify it. "It's for your own good." "We have to be fair to everyone." "I'm sure you'll find out eventually that it is wise." The moment one does this to reality, one robs it of its primary helping value, which is that it exists outside both helper and helped person and is something that they can both look at together, as a fact, and without a predetermined mental attitude towards it. To justify, or to explain, means that one claims the reality as "good" and that the helped person is wrong in being angry at it. While some objective explanation may sometimes have some value if for nothing else than to establish that it really does exist, one has to be sure to stop short of presenting the argument for it, when there are also arguments against. To do so in fact weakens reality. It raises the possibility that it could be different and nearly always ends in a wrangle between the helped and helping person about what might be instead of about what is.

But there is one use of the word "reality" which helpers should avoid. Unfortunately, the word is often used in professional social work literature to mean the social worker's estimate of the client's capabilities. A course of action is seen to be unreal if in the social worker's opinion the client is attempting something beyond his powers. But this, although it may be common sense, is not reality for the client. It is merely a judgment on him. What is real is what such plans would cost him and the very real possibility that he might fail. These need to be discussed. But, as David Soyer points out in a most perceptive article,[7] people have the right to fail and may not in fact be satisfied with a second best until the impossible has been attempted. Sometimes, too, people surprise one. To elevate into reality a diagnosis, however careful, is presumptuous and is in all too many cases a disguised form of protectiveness. The history of art, athletics, and many other fields is full of stories of those who have overcome apparently impossible odds in the pursuit of an idea.

Reality is perhaps the hardest of the three elements to hold to for any sensitive person. None of us likes to be the bearer of bad news. We do not like seeing people hurt, and reality often hurts. Americans in particular find great difficulty with it, since American culture puts a high premium on considerateness and not "hurting people's feelings" which makes plain speaking very difficult. If anyone doubts this—and paradoxically many Americans think of themselves as outspoken—one need only compare American and British book reviews or political comment.

There is a deep tradition in our culture about being "nice." Really to face reality with someone often feels like being "mean," although it can be tremendously helpful. Even professions which have something of a tradition of "toughness" and "no nonsense" about them have apparently developed a need to show themselves gentle and understanding.

I recently had occasion to teach a number of adult probation officers. Before we began I was apprehensive about their reactions to being instructed by a social worker who, a few years before, would have seemed to them "starry-eyed" and a "bleeding heart." I thought they would find my material on empathy very hard to take but that they would have little difficulty with reality. Exactly the reverse was true. These men were willing to go to all lengths to try to understand their probationers, and to do things for them. They counseled with them, found them jobs, obtained medical care for them. The one thing they found it almost impossible to do was to tell them that they were on probation and that if they broke its conditions the judge could and might send them to prison. Yet it was around this fact that they could have given the greatest help; if, that is, they had used this fact not as a threat but as a reality with which the probationer needed help.

In order to help someone else with reality one has to show empathy for him. Empathy is the ability to know, or to imagine, what another

7. David Soyer, "The Right to Fail," *Social Work* 8, no. 3 (July 1963) : 72-78.

person is feeling and, as it were, feel it with him without becoming caught in that feeling and losing one's own perspective. It is not, let us be very clear, a way of softening reality. It is not the jam with the pill, or the praise for part of another's work that enables one to come out with blame or correction where it is neeeded. It is not in any way something "thought up" by the helper but a response on his part to what the helped person is going through.

It needs to be clearly distinguished from two other responses to people in trouble. While words are somewhat difficult here, since we all put connotations on them that make them difficult to define, we shall call these other two responses sympathy and pity.

The three responses have sometimes been described as feeling "like" someone (sympathy), feeling "with" someone (empathy), and feeling "for" someone (pity), but I find these prepositions somewhat difficult. The real difference between them lies in the amount and the kind of difference from the helped person that the helping person maintains.

In sympathy there is little difference. The helping person feels as does the person he is helping. He shares the same feelings, identifies himself with his interests, becomes aligned with him, loves and hates the same things. Empathy on the other hand understands the feelings that the other has about the situation, knows how uncomfortable and even desperate they may be, knows, as we have said, that "it must hurt," but does not claim these feelings itself. In the middle of all his understanding and the feeling this may engender in him, the helping person remains himself, with his own grasp on reality. Pity also retains its difference. It does not get overwhelmed by the troubled person's feelings. It does so, however, only by insisting on the helping person's superior fortune or merit. It puts its emphasis on the difference between them and the likeness, or understanding, is for the most part lost.

The difference between these feelings can perhaps best be illustrated, somewhat facetiously perhaps, if we consider three reactions to someone who has told us that he strongly dislikes his wife. The sympathetic person would say, "Oh, I know exactly how you feel. I can't bear mine, either." The two would then comfort each other but nothing would come of it. The pitying person would commiserate but add that he himself was most happily married. Why didn't the other come to dinner sometime and see what married life could be like? This, in most cases, would only increase the frustration of the unhappy husband and help him to put his problem further outside himself, onto his wife or his lack of good fortune. The empathic person might say something like, "That must be terribly difficult for you. What, do you think might possibly help?" And only the empathic person, of the three, would have said anything that could lead to some change in the situation.

Sympathy, as we have described it, is not entirely useless. There is some value in the precept to "rejoice with those that do rejoice and weep with those who weep." It is good to know that one is not alone and there are others who feel as you do. But this is really a function of support rather than of sympathy, and the empathic person who feels for one in what one is going through is able to give a lot more help than the person who simply shares one's distress. I can remember a social worker who met a client's distress over her son's behavior by saying, "Oh, I know exactly how you feel. I cry myself to sleep every night over mine." The client left angrily saying "She's in as bad a way as I am."

This may seem like an exaggerated sympathy. But this is one of sympathy's problems. One often hears it said that one can have too much sympathy for such and such a person (or such and such a group of persons). This is perfectly true. Sympathy can very easily become a weak emotion, and it can confirm a weak person in his weakness. But the person who, on this account, is suspicious of any attempt to understand others, who sees this as somehow a sign of weakness, has not understood how empathy differs from sympathy. Empathy is both a strong and a strengthening emotion. Because of the difference it retains, it never condones or confirms weakness but enlists the troubled person's feelings in the attempt to overcome it. One cannot have too much empathy. But—and here, perhaps, is the rub—empathy very easily slops over into sympathy. Sympathy is much the easier emotion. It is very easy to get caught in someone else's feeling system and to begin to identify with it. Young and inexperienced helpers find maintaining the distinction one of their hardest tasks.

I have spoken of empathy as an emotion, and purposely so. It is, of course, formally an act, but an act based on feeling. The best description I know of it is an "act of the loving imagination." Both words are important here. While empathy requires imagination and therefore knowledge, and it is possible that the most important contribution of the kind of specialized knowledge of an individual's likely behavior that we call "diagnosis" is to make empathy more likely to be appropriate, empathy is much more than knowing intellectually what another must be feeling. It always involves the ability to enter into this feeling, to experience it and therefore to know its meaning for the other person and the actions that are likely to flow from it.

There is in fact a paradox here which it is very hard to explain in ordinary, rational terms. How can one at the same time feel an emotion and yet remain separate from it, which is what we have said that empathy demands? It is all too easy to do one or the other, but not both; either to give up empathy for sympathy or to rely on knowledge without feeling. Yet both to feel and to know is necessary if the purposes of empathy are to be fulfilled. Nothing carries less conviction, or is likely to fall so wide of the mark, as an attempt at empathy that is purely intellectual. The purpose of empathy is to convey feeling, not knowledge. But because feeling is communicated by so much more than words—by gestures, tone of voice, facial expressions, and bodily posture which are too complex to be capable of dissimulation—an assurance of feeling can only be communicated if this feeling actually exists. We have therefore a plain showing that this kind of genuine feeling and separateness from it are both necessary, but not a purely rational explanation of how they can be combined or how one acquires the ability to combine them.

These difficulties have caused many people to assert that empathy cannot be learned. It must be a natural gift. Or possibly it is something that one only acquires in practice. In my experience, however, the facility can be trained, if not fully taught. While there are certainly people who have a natural empathy for others, there are also those who can release a great deal of loving imagination once they can free themselves from stereotyped reactions to people and once they become aware of their tendency, in some situations, to respond negatively, or sympathetically rather than empathically.

To learn empathy one has to be free from the kind of blocks that are thrown in one's path by liking and disliking people, lining oneself up either for them or against them, instead of just caring about them, whether we like or dislike them. And this comes largely from self-knowledge. It is not so much that we stop liking and disliking as it is that we learn to control the consequences of such feelings.

Empathy also depends on knowledge, and on encounters with people who are quite different from ourselves. Many well-to-do people find it hard to be empathic with the poor, because they never meet them on a social or equal basis. The same is true of whites and blacks. To hear how another feels, expressed frankly and without equivocation, can be a shock but also a reality on which empathy can be built.

Knowledge of social conditions and some of the causes of feeling can also be of help. But some would-be empathizers become overwhelmed with the amount of knowledge they feel that they need before they can empathize at all. They feel that they cannot possibly know exactly how the other person feels, especially if they have never experienced a similar situation. They are quite correct. To think one could do so would be presumption. But empathy does not in fact need to be too precise. There is always something of the tentative about it, an acknowledgment that feeling must be present, and probably within a given range, and an invitation to the helped person to express his feeling more precisely. That is why the statement which we have used to typify empathy is not, "I know how it hurts" but, "I know that it must hurt."

Again, the empathy which is needed, at least in the beginning of a relationship, is largely directed towards the struggle through which the helped person is going, his fear of help, his wanting and not wanting to get well, the frustrations of his efforts to solve his problem by himself, and this is common human experience, although not always recognized as such. Later perhaps one needs to expand to the wider problem, but by that time the person you are helping has usually given you quite a bit on which to proceed. Empathy is not something which the helping person constructs entirely by himself. It comes more by degrees, in a process of dialogue. It is needed in some degree initially, however. At this point it is an unlocking act. In the framework of the trolley diagram we discussed in the last chapter, it is the key which unlocks the casting so many of us have constructed around the spring of our negative feelings.

There are times when one can convey empathy in a subverbal manner, but generally it does need to be expressed. I find that many young helping people can feel empathically, but find it difficult to put their feeling into words. There is, of course, some risk in empathy. Like reality, it may trigger unforeseen reactions, both in the helped person and the helper, since it does deal very directly with feeling. Often it can start on a very simple basis, about a wait, if there has been one, or the difficulty of putting feelings into words.

Often the most immediate and important occasion for empathy has to do with the helping situation itself. This is particularly so when the helping is unsought. One of the first things a protective worker—that is, a social worker who investigates complaints about the neglect of children—has to realize is that it is his presence that constitutes for the moment the client's most immediate problem. It is with the feelings about his visit that he needs to empathize first, even sometimes to insist on, so that these feelings do not get displaced on to the original complainant, where they are much harder to handle. And often it is this initial empathy that literally unlocks a door.

An example of empathy which may illustrate some of its characteristics came to my notice recently in a welfare case. Mrs. Brown, a recent widow, informed her welfare worker that she was withdrawing her application for financial aid for herself and her young daughter since she had accepted the invitation of a Mr. Timms to share his house. She announced this quite aggressively and had a good deal to say about the inadequacies and insecurities of a relief budget. She had clearly braced herself against the argument which she expected to encounter and was presenting her decision as already made. She was taken utterly by surprise at the welfare worker's comment, "That must have been one of the hardest decisions you ever made in your life."

A number of factors contributed to this remark. The worker knew that to argue would result merely in a battle of wills which Mrs. Brown would inevitably win. She knew, too, that from the moment this battle was engaged, Mrs. Brown could never change her mind. To do so would be to admit defeat. She was also aware that Mrs. Brown probably knew all the arguments which the worker could possibly use. If she did not her neighbors would undoubtedly have let her know them.

At the same time she felt, underlying Mrs. Brown's aggressiveness, the need to stifle still existent doubts. The very way that Mrs. Brown cut off argument and denied her need for advice showed her fear, and this process the worker was able to recognize and to feel for. She may, too, have felt that Mrs. Brown was not a person who made an immoral decision easily. But she did respect the fact that Mrs. Brown had come to what Mrs. Brown herself believed to be a firm decision, and she accepted Mrs. Brown's right to be angry about the inadequacy of the relief budget.

She did not allow either her own distaste for Mrs. Brown's decision or her defensiveness about her program to stand between them. And finally she kept her attention on Mrs. Brown's feelings and not on her own wish to see Mrs. Brown choose differently. Thus, respect for Mrs. Brown, an ability to feel for her at this critical time in her life, and a knowledge of some of the dynamics of the helping process combined to produce a very simple statement, at the same time spontaneous and based on an acquired self-discipline, which allowed Mrs. Brown to change.

The statement opened the door to Mrs. Brown's doubts and fears.

She asked to look again at the relief budget. She found it to be rather less rigid than in her anger and disappointment she had thought it to be. She asked questions which she had been too angry to ask before. She herself brought up what her decision would cost her in terms of her own conscience. She said it would cut her off from her church, which was one of the things that she valued. Finally she told the worker that, with the loss of her husband, she had to find something to depend on "and I don't know but that the church and you are a little bit stronger than Mr. Timms."

This instance, although primarily an example of empathy, also begins to illustrate what is meant by support. Empathy opened the door, but both empathy and support, in both of its manifestations, were necessary to complete and sustain the change.

The two forms of support that play a part in helping are the material and the psychological. Material support, the means to accomplish the task, may or may not be present in the helping situation. It is not generally part of either psychotherapy or problem-related counseling. When it does occur in these it takes the form of technical know-how of some kind, whether this be marital techniques or where to find a school for one's son. In some helping it is, however, the most visible part and is thought of by many people as all that there is to help. It is what helping gives, whether this be money, opportunity, or know-how. Nor, as we have said, can it ever be considered unimportant. People need money, opportunity, education, and technical assistance to implement their decisions. If Mrs. Brown's worker had had only as rigid and as niggardly a budget to offer her as Mrs. Brown feared, Mrs. Brown might well have chosen Mr. Timms.

But Mrs. Brown also needed psychological support, a fact she expressed when she included the worker as one thing she could depend on. The quality she found in this worker is what we have tried to express in the statement: "I am here to help you."

The important word here is "here." Support is in fact the assurance that the helper will not give up. He will not be shaken in his desire to be of help, in his concern for the helped person, "no matter what."

Particularly he will not desert the person he is trying to help because that person disappoints him, or makes an unwise or immoral decision. It is true that there are two, or possibly three situations in which this decision or failure may mean an inability on the part of the helping person to go on being the primary helper. One situation occurs when the decision, or some limitation in the helped person, removes him from contact with the particular source of help with which he has been working. A student may fail and be required to leave a school, a child's behavior may be such that for the protection of others he must leave a Home, or a client be no longer eligible for assistance. Or, the nature of the problem may be revealed by a person's act or decision to be such that he needs a kind of help which the original helping source is not equipped to give. The person being helped may need psychiatric care, or a sheltered environment, or some particular form of training or counseling which can only be given elsewhere.

There is also always the possibility that the helped person's problems may be such that no one knows at present how he can be helped. His resistance to help may be so strong or his ability to act so lacking that no skill that we have at present would be enough to provide any help. He may need, for his own protection or that of society, to be institutionalized, or control measures may have to be substituted for help. This decision would, however, have to be made with the greatest reluctance and with the knowledge that the helped person had not so much proved himself unhelpable as we unable to help him.

But even should one of these conditions separate helped person and helper, the principle of support means that the separation is not accompanied by rejection. The helping person still cares. He still respects and is concerned about what happens to the other.

Sometimes indeed it is in this very act of separation that helping really begins. Not long ago I knew a child in a Children's Home. She was a most unfortunate person, fat, dirty, low in intelligence, and from a family whose moral standards were appalling. Attempts to help her had met with little success and most people found her quite repulsive. It was hardly a surprise when she became involved with a man who, because the child was a few months under sixteen, was charged with statutory rape. Nine Homes out of ten would at this point have written off a child whom they had shown that they could not help and, who, since there was some publicity, had also embarrased them. Some even today would have accompanied their rejection with a lecture on her ingratitude, although hopefully not with public disgrace.

The trial was to be held in a city some distance away. Dorothy clearly could not continue to live at the Home, and the normal procedure would have been to discharge her and have her placed in a detention home to await the trial. Her housemother, however, approached the superintendent and said, "My other fifteen children can do without me for a while. Dorothy needs me now as she has never done before." The superintendent, agreeing with her, made arrangements for the housemother to live with the child in a motel during the trial and until Dorothy's subsequent commitment to a correctional school.

It was, not unnaturally, to the housemother who had shown concern for her at her worst that Dorothy turned after she left the training school. It was she whom she consulted over the problems of working and marriage. Six years later Dorothy's younger sister, who had remained at the Home, began to be restless; Dorothy, hearing of this, offered her a home. Investigation showed that Dorothy, although still somewhat fat and lazy, had quite a decent home to offer. Measured in terms of the distance Dorothy had traveled from her own beginnings, the Home had done more for Dorothy than it had for the hundreds of "nice" children it had reared. And it had done it at the point that its efforts had seemed in vain.

It goes without saying that support is also hard to practice. It is very easy to reject those who have let one down especially where this has been accompanied with anger, blame, or ingratitude. One can more-over believe oneself either moral or realistic, according to one's taste, in doing so. Trying to help Dorothy after she had behaved as she had could so easily have been thought of either as condoning her behavior or simply as a waste of time. Her background and her intelligence did not suggest the possibility of her taking help at this point. Some girls might not have done so, but one might still raise the question whether they had been offered so solid a support.

It is extremely difficult for human beings to get away from the idea that to care about a person in trouble is not to condone what he has done. It does not seem sufficient to allow someone to suffer the consequences of his act or take his punishment for it. We seem to need to reinforce societal sanctions by disassociating ourselves from those who have offended against them, instead of seeing them as those who need our help the most. Recently there are some signs of improvement in this, but also a backlash against it.

Part of this is reaction against unrealistic helping. To be concerned about a delinquent is not to approve of delinquency. Nor is it to excuse it, to throw all of the blame onto conditions, or onto society. Poor conditions, poor heredity, undoubtedly make it harder for acceptable decisions to be made, but not all people make such decisions under these strains. The helper whose support is a disguised form of exculpation, who believes that the delinquent had no choice but to act as he did, is being unrealistic. He is indulging, rather than helping.

But in part our unwillingness to try to help rather than punish the delinquent is our fear of ourselves. It is a strange reflection on how delicately balanced our "good" and "bad" decisions must be that we get so angry at the bad ones. This anger has its roots in fear. We fear that we too may be tempted. It has long been known to psychiatrists that those who are most violently opposed to some social ill are often those to whom it is secretly most attractive, and that the faults we see in others are often the ones we are most prone to ourselves.

Support may be indicated in a number of ways. Sometimes the mere fact of being there is sufficient. Sometimes it is indicated by physical contact, particularly with a child. Sometimes it includes a direct offer of help, or making clear that one is available. Sometimes it is a matter of giving someone an introduction, "breaking the ice" for him in facing a new experience. One must, however, remember that the statement is not simply, "I am here to help you" but "I am here to help you if you want me and can use me." Support is not taking over or forcing help on people. It is at its best when it is consistent but unobtrusive.

These, then, are the three elements of the helping factor. They still do not tell us how to help in any given situation, which is perhaps something no one can tell another, but they do give us some idea of how we need to approach the problem. But even here they are not prescriptions. No one can go into a helping situation saying to himself, "I will be real. I will be empathic. I will offer support." The very effort would distract one from listening to the person one wanted to help.

But they do offer a way of looking at our own helping efforts. In every helping situation that has gone wrong, or been less productive than one hoped, it is good to ask oneself three questions. Have I been able to face reality with this person or have I glossed over the truth or offered false reassurance? Have I been able to feel and express real empathy, or has empathy been lacking, or limited ("You can share your feeling with me as long as you don't feel so and so")? Have I offered support or has it been conditional support ("I will continue to try to help you as long as you don't do this or that")? An honest answer to these three questions often shows us what has gone wrong.

All three elements are necessary to each other. Reality without empathy is harsh and unhelpful. Empathy about something that is not real is clearly meaningless and can only lead the client to what we have called nonchoice. Reality and empathy together need support, both material and psychological, if decisions are to be carried out. Support in carrying out unreal plans is obviously a waste of time. The three are in fact triune, and although in any one situation one may seem to be predominant all three need to be present.

VI. THE HELPING PERSON

Before we can discuss specific suggestions or "rules" for helping—the application, that is, of these principles to practice—one of the things we need to pay attention to is the kind of person who will be a successful helper. For it is only a person who can give life to rules and without a person behind them, rules are of very little value.

Much has already been implied about the helping person. We have already eliminated as successful helpers the coldly objective "student of humanity," the person whose major interest is knowing about people rather than working and feeling with them. We have warned, by implication, against those with strong personal needs to control, to satisfy their own conscience, to feel superior, or to be liked. We have also issued, as it were, incidental warnings against confirmed optimists, against those who have solved their own problems and have forgotten what it cost them, those whose own solutions have been precarious or have involved repressions, those whose major interest is in justice or morality rather than in helping, those who are afraid of hurting others' feelings, and quite a number of others. These constitute a powerful accumulation of negatives, and it may be thought that helping can only be done by some sort of extraordinary saint, rigorously denying himself, and at the same time perfectly adjusted.

If this were so we would be even worse off than if we had accepted the doctrine that help should only be offered by those extensively trained in social and psychological diagnosis and treatment. There are probably fewer well-adjusted saints than there are competent diagnosticians. But fortunately we do not have to be a saint to be a competent helper, and indeed the kind of saint most people would envisage from this description would not be a good helper at all. He would lack warmth and spontaneity and might find empathy very difficult.

We do have to recognize that helping is not everyone's métier. There are those whom helping does not interest at all, and there is no particular reason why it should. There is much else to do in the world. The world needs helpers, but it also needs people who are more interested in machines than they are in people, and those whose competence and interest are in research or in pure knowledge. These people are not helpers but they often contribute to our knowledge of help.

There are others who are interested in helping but who harm instead of help. They use helping more or less as an excuse to satisfy quite unrelated needs, such as to control, to be liked, or to feel superior to others. Many of these should not be put into helping positions.

But here I think we have to be careful not to insist that the helping person be utterly selfless. To do so would be most unrealistic. There must be some satisfaction in helping, other than that of the wish to serve.

It would also be dangerous. As Erich Fromm points out in his *Art of Loving*, the person who "does not want anything for himself" or "lives only for others" is often a neurotic. He lacks "self-love," which, as Fromm says, is the opposite of selfishness and alone enables us to "love our neighbor as ourself."[1] There is nothing wrong in getting pleasure out of helping. Indeed one usually does best what one likes doing. At the same time while most of those engaged in helping hopefully have something of a desire to serve, their choice of helping as the form of service they will perform probably means that they have in some measure those very needs which, if carried to excess, would disqualify them from helping. People who want to work with children usually like to be loved by them. A person who tries to help a community organize itself probably gets some pleasure from the changes for which he is responsible and the feeling of power that this gives him. A consultant rarely minds being referred to as an expert and many a good helper has felt that serving others does not do his conscience any harm.

Where then is the difference? Is it simply a matter of degree? I would suggest that it lies rather in the ability to postpone the personal satisfaction in the interest of the person one is helping, to accept it where one finds it, not to insist on it, and not to let one's desire for it get in the way of the primary business. As someone who loves children, and one who loves to be loved by them, I might know that in the course of my work I will find a number of children whom I can love and who may even love me in return. But I can also be aware that in a particular case a child may need to struggle against me or to hate me, and I hope that in such a situation I could postpone or subordinate

1. Erich Fromm, *The Art of Loving* (London, Harper Colophon ed., 1956), pp. 57-63.

my own need to that of the child. This is far from denying that I have this need. The dangerous person is not the one who frankly delights in children, and gets great satisfaction from them. It is the one whose desire to be loved by children makes it impossible for him to face them with an unpleasant reality. It is the one who cannot let the child leave him to go on to another helper, or share the child with other people (including, sometimes, the child's own parents).

A person is much more likely to be able to defer his own need, or to allow it to be met where it reasonably can, if he is aware of it. It does not take him unawares, and he is not afraid of it. Although sometimes it may have considerable force, he knows that he can handle it under most circumstances, which is probably all that we can say of any of our needs. Some needs are more or less obvious. Others, such as the need to control, or to be thought wise and compassionate, we tend to hide from ourselves. Others still we may have repressed and to recognize them may involve us in considerable risk.

Self-knowledge is a necessary part of being a helping person. But self-knowledge in itself is not enough. There has to be as well a quality of not being afraid of oneself. I put it this way, rather than using the term "accepting one's self," which is used by some writers, as this may carry the connotation to those unfamiliar with it of being satisfied with what one is unwilling to try to change. The two things are not the same. One may not particularly like oneself. One may try to change or improve, and yet not be afraid of what one is, accept the fact that at this time this is how one reacts or behaves. The person who is afraid of himself denies what he is; the unafraid recognizes his own lacks.

To be unafraid is the quality of not having to deny one's own feelings, or to prevent their natural expression by keeping a tight control over them. A person who has learned not to be afraid of himself does not have to create an image of himself that denies how he actually feels. He does not present himself, for instance, as the "oversweet" person whom we can usually recognize to be quite hostile underneath, and whom we would really like better if he or she could occasionally get angry or say an unkind word. The person who knows himself and is not afraid of what he knows is not threatened by the anger, the dependency, even the seductiveness of the person he is trying to help. He does not have anything to prove or to protect. He will not find the helped person's problems triggering unexpected and perhaps unwelcomed reactions due to his own repressions.

This suggests one other group for whom helping is not an appropriate type of service. This is those for whom this self-knowledge would cost too much to acquire. All of us, to a certain extent, throw up protections against feelings we do not want to acknowledge. Sometimes these protections are unnecessary, and although it may be at first painful to learn to do without them, one finds that one can do so. But sometimes these protections are necessary to us and to give them up, as one might have to, in order to help others is simply too much to pay.

There is nothing wrong in such a decision. One of the apparently most promising social work students I have known had to make this decision for herself when she found that to discuss with a neglected child his feelings about his parents was too painful for her to bear. It brought up too many memories she had repressed about her own parents. If this was what helping demanded of her, she would have to choose another career, and this is what she most sensibly did. Her repressed feelings about her parents would be no handicap to her in almost any other profession. In a helping profession they were.

And yet it was probably because of this very problem that she chose to work with children in the first place. She was, although she did not know it, unconsciously aligned with children against adults. But to become a helping person with children whose feelings about their parents were ambivalent she would have had to consider both sides of this question. This would have cost her an inordinate price. She was wise not to pay it. What would have been unwise and harmful to those she was trying to help would have been to go on trying to help without being willing to pay the cost that helping entails.

Psychoanalysts have traditionally held that a training analysis is necessary before one begins to practice this specialty. The primary purpose of the analysis is to uncover any distortions of reason which the student may be prone to because of his own unconscious mind. To this extent it is somewhat analogous to the process of becoming unafraid of oneself which all helpers need to do. But, unfortunately, this necessary preliminary has given rise in some circles to a belief that what a helping person needs is to be cured of all of his problems before he can be permitted to help. At the end of the training analysis, so runs this thinking, the student will be "well-adjusted," and thus ready to help.

That this normally happens must be open to doubt. Analysis is a method of solving certain deep-rooted problems, not a general tonic to the personality. Many psychiatrists, skilled in their work, are patently not too well adjusted in themselves, despite a training analysis. The claim, however, is sometimes made, and gives rise to other claims—that the analyzed person sees things clearly, is alone unswayed by an irrational unconscious, and therefore has the right to tell others what to do or to serve as an example for them.

The same is sometimes claimed for other helping persons. Helping people are supposed to need to be perfectly adjusted people, without problems of their own. Otherwise one can turn on them and say, "Physician, heal thyself." But this again misunderstands the role of the helping person. While he obviously cannot have problems of his own so pressing that his major preoccupation is the effort to help himself, he does not heal by example or by reasoning better than the person he is helping, except perhaps in the specific situation the helped person is distorting, which nearly anyone else could do. He is simply someone who, because he does not need to protect himself in a helping relationship, can make available reality, empathy, and support to the person he is helping. Moreover, because these things demand an interchange of feeling which must be felt to be sincere and immediate, spontaneity and ordinary, fallible human emotions are more characteristic of him than controlled, carefully thought out responses.

We wrote earlier of a response which was "at once spontaneous and based on an acquired self-discipline." In doing so we may have left a paradox dangling. It may be hard to see how a helping person can be both disciplined and spontaneous.

Obviously a good helping person does not behave impulsively or even, sometimes, in what we would think of as a natural way. To take but one example, it is normal and natural to reassure an unhappy child and in any casual contact we would not only do so but be insensitive and unnatural if we did not. Yet there are situations in which to reassure a child robs him of his ability to deal with his problem, to express his anger and despair, and to accept our support. I have seen a little girl of five struggle for years with her despair over leaving her mother and with the fear that she had in some way been the cause of the family breakdown, and in this struggle lose for herself eight foster homes in a row, principally because a kindly but not too knowledgeable caseworker reassured her, to stop her sobbing, that she would be loved in a foster home. This happened to be the one thing she could not bear. Love from a stranger only deepened her sense of her mother's lack of love.

How, then, could the response which this worker needed to make, but did not, be thought of as spontaneous? Perhaps an analogy could be drawn from other fields, and this might also help us look at the meaning of true professionalism. The professional dancer, for instance, has acquired a great deal of self-discipline, some of it quite painfully and slowly, and in terms of the normal impulsive gestures an untrained person would make on a dance floor, quite unnatural. But, as she becomes a professional, she does not have to think each move out beforehand. Her dancing, within the framework of the discipline she has acquired, becomes entirely spontaneous and she puts into it, we say, "all of herself."

Much the same happens in helping. The beginning helper is often overwhelmed by the realization that his natural impulse may be to do or to say something that would be harmful. He restrains himself. He strives to be objective or to learn rules and principles. His responses are intellectual rather than feeling ones, and he feels that all the joy, the natural warmheartedness, has been "professionalized" out of helping. Others, still acting impulsively, may observe him and feel the same. At the moment they are right. But as the helper becomes more at home in a helping relationship, as the habit of concentration on another's needs becomes second nature to him, as the knowledge he has acquired about how people take help or deal with their problems becomes his normal and natural way of looking at other people, and as he learns no longer to be afraid of his own feelings, he begins to find a wide area for spontaneity. He is no longer concerned about saying exactly the right thing—a frequent fear of beginning helpers—and knows that if he can stay with the other person in feeling—that is, feel with him but maintain his difference—what he says will be appropriate.

There is a good deal of popular feeling about the professional helper. Although we do not depreciate the teacher, the nurse, the physician, or the minister who has undergone rigorous training in order to be able to serve others, we often feel quite differently about the professional social worker.

There are a number of reasons for this. Helping is something we all like to think we can do without any training. All it needs is a warm heart and common sense. We have a firm belief that helping should be spontaneous, "from the heart," and that to think about it spoils it. We fear the coldness of "organized charity" or tax-supported programs. And somehow we object to people making a living out of helping, although we do not object to the minister, the doctor, or teacher doing the same thing.

Quite why this is so it is hard to say. Part, I think, is due to our own pleasure in helping. We do not want to be denied this pleasure, or to be told that our helping is insufficient or possibly harmful. We resent, as it were, the person with the license to help. Part may be our identification of helping with Christian "love" and our feeling that love ought to be something spontaneous and impulsive, although that is actually the kind of love (eros) that is self-seeking rather than seeking the good of the other (agape). Certainly our culture has put emphasis on irrationality in all types of love. And partly we may have met professional helpers who do seem to us cautious, cold, impersonal, and insensitive. But the "professional" worker who is any of these things is not a true professional. He is someone who knows that all too often both the undisciplined will to help, and the harsh judgment on others, are self-serving emotions. But he has not learned to put anything in their place. He is also the most likely to insist on his own professionalism.

My own experience is quite different. The warmest, the gentlest, the most sensitive helpers have been those who in pursuit of helping have subjected themselves to the most rigorous training, both of their minds and their feelings. They have cared enough to learn.

This raises the whole question of how much training, if any, and of what sort, is necessary in order to become a competent helping person. Part of the purpose of this book is to suggest that much can be learned about helping by the person who does not plan to undergo extensive professional training. And yet as we face the need not only for knowledge of the helping process, which might be supplied in part by this book, and for the acquiring of self-discipline, to say nothing of a disciplined spontaneity, which this book quite clearly cannot provide, there are bound to be some doubts about the matter. Can one hope to acquire self-discipline in the school of experience?

I think I would have to answer that if someone intends to make helping his career, if he hopes to be more than a competent helper, one of the highest class, then he would be advised to take professional training, either in social work or in some other discipline that is concerned with helping the helper look at himself in practice. Without going into detail about what this training should consist of, which is not our purpose here, certain things could be said about it. It should be a continuous structured experience, not an accumulation of little bits of knowledge, and an experience in which the helping person himself experiences a helping relationship with teacher, adviser, or supervisor. One of the principal ways of learning what to give help is like is to be a receiver of help. Indeed it has sometimes been said that as one receives help, so one is likely to give it.[2]

2. This process is outlined in detail in Ruth Gilpin's *Theory and Practice as a Single Reality* (Chapel Hill, N.C., 1963).

Again, such a course of training needs to contain, or even to be built around, a deliberately sensitizing experience, in which the student is enabled to examine his own feelings and his reactions to others. This is usually some kind of group experience. And, thirdly, the whole experience should contain some form of field work, under supervision, not so much to give experience in practice—this can be gained elsewhere—or even to try out theory in practice, but as a chance to try out for oneself, in a setting established for that purpose, how one actually performs in the stresses and strains of the helping relationship.

If this is training for a specific profession, as it most usually is, then a fourth element needs to be added—that of specific knowledge of services and how they work, of social conditions, of normal and abnormal psychology, both individual and in groups. Because we have upheld that specialized knowledge in this field is not an absolute prerequisite to beginning to help at all, it does not mean that it is not an important tool for the professional helper. In some form or other knowledge about people and about society is an important tool in all forms of helping.

Yet this kind of training is not and will not be available for a great number of people in full-time or part-time helping. Some of these may be able to rely in part on good supervision, which may supply the important experience of taking skilled help. Others will not. They may be helped by short-time courses, or even by books such as this, but their chief learning will have to come from experience. It will not come, however, unless this experience is pondered, unless there is an attempt at honest self-appraisal in terms of one's ability to do what is demanded of one and some clarity at least about what needs to be done.

What short courses, in-service training, and books may do is to stimulate the process of self-appraisal, bring in some new ideas which may enable one to look at the process from a fresh point of view, warn against some persistent dangers, and offer the thinking person some framework of theory and some vocabulary in which he can couch his thoughts.

Despite this emphasis on the need for training, however, one does have to admit that there are many people with little or no training who are capable of really skilled helping. Both of the examples we used to illustrate empathy and support in chapter 5 were the work of "untrained" people, although both had had long experience and both had had some short-course and in-service training.

We outlined briefly at the time what may have gone into the skill of the welfare worker whose empathy helped Mrs. Brown reconsider her impulsive decision—a combination of knowledge, acquired self-discipline, and the ability to feel. The houseparent who helped Dorothy in her hour of apparent defeat found the ability to do so in her religious convictions. It was her strong sense both of her own sinfulness and of her having been forgiven that made it possible for her to transcend her shock and disgust and offer Dorothy something of what she herself felt that she had received. Yet quite clearly the same religion, although not perhaps the same implications drawn from it, could have caused in another woman an almost totally opposite response. It could have resulted in an unyielding moralism based on her hatred of sin. There must have been something in this houseparent, as there must have been in Mrs. Brown's worker, which enabled her to make use of her knowledge and her belief. The little training each had received may have sharpened these worker's skills, but they also had something in their temperaments on which this training could build.

Many attempts have been made to describe the qualities of the person who is, or is likely to become, a successful helping person. Most begin with a liking for people and continue with a plethora of human virtues, such as patience, dedication, and flexibility, and end with a sense of humor. They become little more than a description of an ideal human. Therefore I shall select only three characteristics which it seems to me are not usually sufficiently stressed, but which the helping person needs rather more than does the nonhelper.

The first of these qualities is courage. This may sound a little surprising to those who have in their mind somewhere a stereotype of the helping person as somewhat meek and mild and perhaps more feminine than masculine in his temperament. It is true that helping makes use of a number of qualities that are traditionally ascribed to women—sensitivity to feeling, interest in people rather than in things, a willingness to serve rather than to dominate or to control. On the other hand, the desire to control others by psychological rather than physical means has been held by some to be a predominately feminine characteristic, and the helping professions have suffered to some extent from a long line of extremely powerful women. Social workers might like to make up their own lists.

These so-called "feminine" qualities are sometimes a problem to the young man worker. Actually they have little to do with masculinity. One of the most sensitive and indeed one of the most tender helping people I have had anything to do with was a guard on a Big Ten football squad. But there is no doubt that culturally, until quite recently at least, helpers have been thought of as feminine, except, perhaps, in the more technical fields of psychology and psychiatry.

Indeed it might be suggested that the rather insistent claim that many helping professions make about their "scientific base" is in part an attempt to give a masculine aura to a profession traditionally feminine in feeling. Decreasingly, but still frequently social work, for instance, is thought of as predominately a profession for women, and its most immediate helping aspect, social casework, has been something of a feminine enclave. The qualities that helping requires are for many a man a part of himself of which he needs to learn to become unafraid.

Any implication, however, that these qualities do not demand courage of the highest order is very wide of the mark. It takes great courage to share with another the reality of his situation, and it is lack of courage which so often prevents us from doing so. We do not want to face the bitterness of his despair. We would rather do anything than be the person who brings reality to another.

It takes real courage, too, to hold to one's own grasp of reality in the face of a client's pleading—a courage, perhaps of one's own convictions. Especially is this true when the person we are trying to help is an expert manipulator. We can so easily be "snowed" by plausible requests, which, once granted, lead to the weakening of the whole system of reality in which alone help can be forthcoming. It also takes courage not to be defensive of our programs or of ourselves when we are attacked. It takes courage to bear anger and even to court it deliberately, as has to be done sometimes if the anger is to be expressed. None of us enjoys people being angry with us.

It takes courage, too, to take the risks both with oneself and others that helping inevitably demands. The personal risk involved may be that of failure, or being confronted with an emotional situation one has no idea how to handle, or having one's own comfortable world upset, or being blamed or abused. But perhaps the greatest personal risk is that of assuming responsibility for bringing into a situation an element which may help but which also holds within it the possibility of harm.

How a person actually uses help is always unpredictable. What we think may help could conceivably lead to retreat or breakdown and the more we become engaged in what may really change a situation, the greater is the risk involved.

We can see this in the instance of the runaway boy we discussed in the last chapter. To tell this boy of his birth was an obvious risk. It might have resulted in a great deal of pain and hurt with nothing gained, or it might even have destroyed what little confidence he had in himself. We might have been wrong in our belief that this was what he needed to hear or wrong in our estimate of his ability to take help. The teacher was right to be hesitant. The alternative, however, was to leave things as they were, with the child obviously troubled and needing to run away. We had to make the decision to risk doing harm in the hope of doing good, but we could have equally well decided to leave, not so much well alone, but a moderate ill alone, for fear what our intervention would do.

This kind of decision often faces the helping person. There are obviously some risks one does not take. Sometimes, if it is available, one may try to get expert help in appraising the situation. When, for instance, the caseworker had to decide whether to take a child to see a mother she had idealized and was fighting the worker to be with—the same child we have mentioned before whose struggle had cost her eight foster homes in a row—knowing that her feebleminded mother would not even recognize the child, and that this would be a shattering blow, the caseworker sought the aid of a psychiatrist to help estimate Shirley's essential ability to sustain shock. Yet she might not have had this help.

The alternatives in this situation were to risk real trauma for the child or to have her continue a struggle based on her unreal picture of her mother. All attempts to do this by talking, either by the psychiatrist or by her social worker, had failed. In this case the risk was worth taking, although it cost Shirley ten days of desperate sobbing before she could face up to the truth that she could never live at home. She was then able to give up her struggle. But it might not have been so.

Sometimes the risk involved is simply that of relationship. Too often a helping person fears to introduce some piece of difference, or let someone know his position, for fear that this will cost him his relationship with the person he is trying to help. A relationship, however, that cannot bear reality is generally not worth preserving. However pleasant it may be, it is not achieving anything worth while.

Perhaps the best criterion for deciding to take a helping risk, outside expert knowledge of the person's ability to respond to challenge, and the degree of discomfort in the present situation, is the presence or absence of what might be called "drift." Drift is the gradual but consistent worsening of a situation. A boy in a Children's Home gets into a descending spiral of child-adult and peer relationships; a husband and wife drift apart. By not intervening one is not letting the situation alone. It will not stay where it is and a crisis of some sort needs to be precipitated.

Risks in the helping process need to be taken responsibly, with as much weighing of alternatives as is possible, and a full realization of what is at stake when we intervene in such a way. Yet in my experience I have seen much more potentially good helping go to waste through not taking perfectly reasonable risks than I have seen damage done by taking them. This is true even of children, whom we normally think of as unable to face a harsh reality, and whom we naturally want to protect.

Helping people may also sometimes involve one in physical risks, although these are not too common. This does underline, however that what is involved is not the courage of the person who is insensible to danger or insensitive to hurt, but rather the courage of the man who is afraid and yet does what he knows he needs to do.

I began my professional helping career in a children's protective agency, which involved bringing the fact that a complaint had been made about the care of their children to some pretty disturbed parents. To do so is for many people one of the most frightening demands of a helping profession. To stand on someone's doorstep as the bringer of bad news, to face, and sometimes to court anger, to be abused and sometimes threatened, is not an easy thing and many a worker, myself included, has left the office silently praying that no one will be at home and has circled the block two or three times before knocking at the door. A few people, however, find no difficulty in this. They march up "bravely" to the door, state their business, sweep aside and generally manage to nip in the bud the parent's expression of anger. Quite possibly these people are secretly denying their fear, which means that they are actually so afraid of being afraid that they have to act as if no fear were involved. But even if they are wholly unafraid—if indeed anyone can be so—they are so only because they are unable to feel with the person whom they are supposed to help. Their ability to help is small. It is only the person who can be afraid and not be afraid of his fear who is in a position to help.

The second quality the helping person needs to have is humility. The word is of course a difficult one. It has a negative connotation which suggests a lack of self-confidence, a failure to claim what one knows and is. It often suggests a deliberate and hypocritical self-abasement in the manner of Uriah Heep. But it can also mean not claiming what one is not, being content to play one's part rather than insisting on taking the leading role when it has not been assigned to one, and refusing to assert a more or less specious superiority over others or to claim the right to control their lives. As such it is opposed to arrogance and presumption, and is a genuine virtue.

Humility shows itself in a number of ways in helping. Perhaps its most obvious manifestation is what is often called nonjudgmentalism. This is essentially the refusal to set oneself up in a seat of judgment to which one has not been appointed. It does not mean giving up one's power of discrimination between what is good and bad, but it does mean not using this judgment to belittle another person, either directly to his face or in making plans for or about him.

Where judgment becomes dangerous is where it ceases to be a judgment on an act and becomes a judgment on the person who commits it, which involves a claim to know his motives or his character. To say that someone does not deserve to be helped is to make the kind of judgment that no man has the knowledge, or the right, to make about another. And, significantly enough, such judgments are usually made by people who actually know very little about the conditions in which such acts are performed.

It has long been the experience in welfare programs that the same citizen who is most vocal in his belief that clients are lazy, dishonest, or immoral will insist that the client whom he knows well, and who is objectively no more industrious, honest, or moral than the average, is an exception to the general rule, a victim of circumstance, and deserving of help. Moreover the immorality of the remainder will be greatly exaggerated and will be based on a very few instances, as in the general belief in the United States today that relief clients are responsible to a major degree for the increase in the number of illegitimate births, when in actual fact only one in ten illegitimate children ever receives relief.

This crass kind of judgmentalism may not affect the helper too much. It can be written off as the ignorance and the prejudice of the person who is not engaged in helping. Where judgmentalism deeply affects helping is where it obtrudes into the helping relationship; where it results either in a decision to give up the effort, or cuts off expression of feeling or causes the helping person to decide that the helped person is incapable of making decisions for himself and must be coerced or influenced to do what is right.

All these are, in effect, belittling actions. They assume that the helping person knows better or is better than the person he is trying to help, and that this knowledge or superior morality gives him the right to make such decisions. The person who has successfully solved his own problem and forgotten what it cost him is particularly liable to judgmentalism of this kind. He rapidly loses patience with the person who is struggling to do what he believes, now, anyone ought to be able to do and which he himself has done. Also liable are those who have genuinely found it easy to be good, at least in a limited way, because they have never had to face the particular temptations with which the helped person is struggling. On the basis of their ability to withstand lesser strains, they cannot imagine that they would ever give in to greater ones.

Not all judgmentalism is, however, in the moral sphere. There can be a "scientific" judgmentalism that is just as severe and just as inhibiting to the helping process. This is the judgmentalism that arises out of the claim to know what is right or wrong for another and what is wrong with him.

The helpers of the 1920s and 1930s who took up psychoanalytic theory with such vigor reacted against the judgmentalism of the puritan tradition and remained for a time free from scientific judgmentalism because of two factors. One was their belief in psychic determinism which made it, in the words of one of them, not so much wrong as silly to try to control others. The other was their very genuine awe in the face of the newly revealed complexity of human emotions which psychoanalysis revealed. Both of these safeguards have now vanished. It is a danger inherent in the claim to be scientific that one comes to believe in time that one really knows what is right and what is wrong for another person. Awe vanishes in the intoxication of beginning to understand. While what results is scientism rather than true science, there are today as many scientifically judgmental helpers as there are those whose judgmentalism is of a moral cast. These are those who fundamentally consider all their clients ill, who stress their weakness and dysfunction, who are quick with negative diagnoses and who all too readily assume that their knowledge of what should be done gives them the right to take over, to protect their clients by making decisions for them, or to use one or more forms of more or less subtle coercion. When I read, for instance, that "sharper social study methods and increased psychiatric knowledge brings us daily more useful information about the uncontrolled impulsivity, the impairment in capacity to form relationships and the ego and super-ego defectiveness of those whose social and emotional dysfunctioning comes to our attention,"[3] I may be forced to agree that compared to some norm of our culture this may be objectively true, but I cannot help wondering what kind of relationship can exist between two people one of whom feels like this about the other. One might argue that such a statement is simply reality, and avoids the sentimentality of much writing about help. To ascribe it to lack of humility is perhaps a piece of judgmentalism in itself. One cannot possibly know. But the feeling it would appear to convey is not atypical of an attitude of scientific superiority which is the very antithesis of the quality needed in a helper.

Humility means more, however, than eschewing judgmentalism. It is more, even than knowing that the more one knows, the more one ought to be convinced that one knows very little indeed. It is more than knowing that one can very likely be wrong; more than rejecting the assumption that because one knows a little one has either the right or the ability to decide for other people; more even than the ability to say and feel sincerely, "There, but for the Grace of God or good fortune, or environment, or a happy childhood, go I." It is all of these, but it is also the willingness to allow oneself to be used by the helped person as his needs dictate, and not as one's own need to help demands.

We need again to be careful of terms. "To be used" by another person does not mean to be exploited by him. To allow oneself to be exploited is only to make the other person's problem worse, to provide him with an unreal way of solving his difficulties. To allow oneself to be used in this way would be to contradict one of the implications of courage. To "allow oneself to be used" by another "as his needs dictate," however—the whole sentence is important—means the willingness to let the helped person decide to what extent, and under what conditions he is willing to be helped. It does not mean necessarily agreeing to help under these conditions, or even refraining from pointing out that help is not possible under them. Nor does it mean refraining from offering what help is available, or even, if the need be desperate, intervening in an attempt to get help started. But it does mean, ever and always, treating the helped person as the subject of the sentence, serving his interest, allowing him all possible freedom to be what he wants to be.

It means also being willing not to be the primary helping person in

3. It seems invidious to pinpoint this quotation, which appeared in a very competent article in a major social work periodical in 1958. I use it here as an example and not to refute or object to an esteemed colleague's point of view.

the other's life unless it so happens that this is what the other needs. It means being able to release him to another, or to play a minor role in a team effort. It may even mean playing a role that is unpopular or lacking in immediate satisfaction. In trying to help people with certain character disorders, for instance, one helper may have to be the one who deliberately holds the client to reality and stimulates the anxiety, which the person seems to lack, while another gives empathy and support, and, so to speak, "picks up the pieces." Here the triune nature of help is partitioned and the lot of the representative of reality may be hard.

Humility also means giving up pride in a "finished product" of helping and being content with being able to say, "I helped him at such and such a time, or with this little bit of the problem." It certainly means giving up the need to be thanked or recognized.

One of the hardest forms of humility the helping person needs to acquire is the knowledge that it is not he himself who is doing much of the helping. Quite apart from the fact that it is the helped person who has to make the final decisions and who, in the popular phrase, "is helping himself," the helping person is, as it were, the agent of a process rather than the creator of it. It is true that he puts into it reality, empathy, and support, and that these are not easily supplied. It is true that he approaches the helped person and his problem with courage, humility, and concern—not altogether common virtues. It is true that he can quite easily prevent or pervert the process and that there are skilled and unskilled helpers.

But if these things can be done reasonably well, and particularly where the relationship is well-structured—that is, has a purpose, some regularity in time and a clarity about its conditions—help will be forthcoming. The helping person will not have to exercise close control over what happens. He will not have to take the initiative in creating helping situations as much as he will take the opportunities which the helped person offers him. He will not so much assert his personality as respond to the personality of the other. He will rarely do things which he can look back on afterwards and say, even to himself, "This is what I did to help and only I, perhaps, could have done it."

This is what is really meant by "listening" to another and "staying with him in feeling." It does not absolve the helper from the need to respond in an appropriate and even a courageous way. It is not a reason for passivity. It is rather that in helping one becomes aware that as the other person encounters reality, or limits, and as one is able to show empathy for him, and support him, something begins to happen to him, in which one participates as much as one can, but which is not dependent on one's own qualities. Anyone other than oneself could just as well be there. This is quite a humbling experience.

Its main effect in helping is to temper the helped person's need to try to accelerate the process or to force results. As such it is the source of another virtue often ascribed to helping persons—that of patience. It is surprising how often in helping, just as one comes to the conclusion that nothing is happening, the helped person finds help for himself.

The third quality of the good helping person is what might be called concern. I use this term rather than the more usual "liking for people" both because it is more than "liking" and because "liking" is in itself a difficult word.

To "like people" may mean a number of different things. The cheerfully extroverted "good mixer," the person who enjoys crowds, and inconsequential chatter, may be thought of as "liking people," but his relationship with them is a superficial one, and he is rarely a good helper. The man who enjoys working with people to some other end, the salesman or the manipulator, may also "like people" but he enjoys them as objects and not as persons. When we mean by "liking people" that we see only the good in them, that we never get angry at them, and that there are not some whom we cordially dislike, then we are asking of ourselves an unreal sentimentality or a dangerous self-deception. "Like" and "dislike" in this sense are matters of taste and experience. They arise from roots often quite deep in the personality and although they are sometimes irrational they are often not under conscious control. The problem is not so much to change them—one may doubt if this can really be done—as it is to transcend them.

A student of mine recently found herself supervising a woman she thoroughly disliked. This made her quite uncomfortable. She felt that she ought to be able to like her, and tried very hard to do so, looking for her good points, for reasons, and even excuses for the other's behavior. This made her feel so guilty when, in spite of all she could do, she felt waves of dislike for the woman that she soon ceased to be able to hold her to any standards in her job. I had to point out after a while that her efforts to like Mrs. P. were seriously affecting her ability to help her.

It was only when this student could acknowledge and cease to be afraid of her dislike, which, incidentally would seem to have been, if not deserved, at least not unnatural, and yet could assert truthfully that she did want to help, that she came to understand that what the helping person develops is a feeling to which liking and disliking are wholly irrelevant.[4] This is what is meant by concern.[5] It means to care what happens to another person quite apart from whether one finds him attractive or unattractive. The housemother who helped Dorothy did not find the child attractive. She did not like her in any ordinary sense of the word. Yet she had a deep concern which showed up like and dislike for the personal and somewhat selfish emotions that they are.

The quality of concern is sometimes called, quite simply, "love," both by secular philosophers and by theologians. This again is a slippery word and can involve us in quite erroneous concepts. We need the Greek distinction between different kinds of love. The kind we are speaking of is very close to the Greek word agape. Indeed a careful reading of the most famous passage on agape, the thirteenth chapter of Paul's letter to the Church at Corinth, will show that so far from this being a general exhortation to "love" our fellows in some rather vague way, Paul is attempting a precise definition of this quality. Even the Latin word translated in the King James's version as "charity"—caritas—means caring for, or concern.

Some of the qualities Paul ascribes to agape—its not being puffed up, or easily provoked, or insisting on its own way—bring it close to what we have called humility. Others, such as its endurance, are close to what we mean by support. In a more secular context Erich Fromm, in his *Art of Loving*, calls this quality rather surprisingly, "brotherly love" (which tends to equate it with the Greek philia) but catches some of its meaning when he describes it as "the sense of responsibility, care, respect, knowledge of any other human being, the wish to further his life."[6] He makes clear that it transcends differences in talents, intelligence, and knowledge, but he falls short of adding Paul's "love never ends" and ascribes this characteristic to what he calls "motherly love." The mother, he says, makes an "unconditional affirmation" of the child's life and his needs, and this, he points out, instills in the child a love for living and not merely the wish to remain

4. Ruth Ramsey, "Concern, Like and Dislike in the Supervisory Process," unpublished paper included in vol. 3 of *Studies in Social Work Practice*, The University of North Carolina (1965).

5. Mrs. Ramsey and I were unable to find the word "concern" used in social work or related literature. She traced its possible origin as a "helping" word to Erich Fromm and Paul Tillich, both of whom use the word in this sense.

6. Fromm, *The Art of Loving*, p. 47.

alive. This is close to what underlies the whole theory of helping: that love, or concern, stimulates to some degree the capacity for love and concern in the helping person.[7] Where Fromm's definitions may mislead us is that he equates "motherly love" with inequality, so that his "motherly love" always includes some element of superiority and protectiveness. This may be true of "motherly love" but not of the love, or concern, that the helping person needs.

It may seem that we are requiring of the helping person a kind of "freeing love" which is a high spiritual quality unlikely to be possessed by a normally fallible human being. In one sense this is true. It is only this kind of concern and the empathy which springs from it which brings the apparently impossible command to love one's enemies within the realm of practicability. It is only by transcending like and dislike that one could possibly "love" those one "dislikes."

We do not do this by changing "dislike" into "like." We are not asked to like our enemies, but to be concerned for them. Unnecessary disliking is a pity, and, when that dislike is based on moral judgmentalism, it is destructive to helping. But we should distinguish between disapproval and dislike. That "there is so much good in the worst of us and so much bad in the best of us that it ill behooves any of us to find fault with the rest of us" is good sense. To say that we ought to like everybody is not.

Yet I do not believe that concern, as we have used the word, is outside the range of any person who has learned not to be afraid of himself and who has some measure of humility. He does not, as we have shown, have to be self-denying. Nor does the helper have to achieve an idealistic liking for people. He can and will retain his natural taste and discrimination, but in his helping he must not so much forget them as become so concerned about the person he is helping that they no longer have the power to sway him.

Nevertheless, he may sometimes have to take them into account if even only to remind himself of their irrelevance. And here "like" can be quite as dangerous as "dislike." The people one likes most are those one is most likely to protect, to want to have like one in return. Sometimes therefore they become the hardest people to help. I personally find it hardest to help, professionally, the kind of little girl that particularly appeals to me and as I look back on my practice I have made more serious mistakes with this group than with any other. I can fill their need for empathy and support, quite easily, but my

7. Ibid., p. 49.

sense of reality, my willingness to let them fight their own battles, tends to flag unless I watch it very carefully. I tend to reassure or indulge them, and this does not help them at all.

People one dislikes are also sometimes very hard to help, because, for the opposite reason, one also tends to indulge them to make up for the empathy one feels that one might lack in their situation. Or empathy may simply be missing. Often, too, the person one dislikes is the one who has the characteristics one has overcome and suppressed in oneself. It becomes dangerous to be empathic with them. Sometimes, too, they remind us of people who have hurt us in the past. I sometimes have to remind myself that this controlling, sanctimonious woman is not my great aunt, but someone quite different who has no power to hurt me.

Concern is, in the final analysis, a much more enduring and stable emotion than either liking or disliking. It is more honest, because it does not have to conceal dislike. It is also more inclusive. One does not have to like a person to help him.

Courage, humility, and concern may then give us some characterization of the helping person. Other qualities such as dependability, patience, integrity, or a sense of humor are of course also desirable, or perhaps simply facets of these. Intelligence and imagination can be of help. But the helping person is an essentially human being, with many of the faults that all of us share. There is nothing ascetic or infallible about him or about his knowledge. He is disciplined but no automaton, sensitive but no seer, knowledgeable but not necessarily intellectual, unselfish but not self-denying, long suffering but no martyr. When we meet him we will probably like him but not, perhaps, be too impressed.

VII. SUGGESTIONS FOR PRACTICE

The suggestions made in this chapter may appear to constitute a set of rules or techniques for the practice of successful helping. In one sense that is what they are. They can be listed and numbered; even, if necessary, memorized; and the helper who has followed the argument of this book so far, and who has acquired some of the qualities of a helper and some of his self-discipline, may be a better helper if he remembers some of them.

The objection to calling them rules or techniques is that they do not guarantee, by themselves or apart from an understanding of the whole, any measure of success, if indeed this can ever be guaranteed in the helping process. They cannot be put into practice without the feeling and the attitudes from which they are derived. They are meaningless outside a relationship that is realistic, empathic, and supportive, and without such qualities as courage, humility, and concern. Nor do they offer a blueprint of how an interview should be conducted, point by point. An interview based on rules and techniques would become a mechanical thing, devoid of the very element of feeling that makes it of help.

Yet they are all important things to do and to remember, and are offered as such. Their numeration and the emphasis given to each in the text is a recognition of this fact. They do, of course, overlap sometimes, and lead one to the other, but this is only natural. Some of them, too, may be repetitive, and yet there also seems some value in putting them together here. I have tried, too, in most cases to give examples that may show how the suggestion may work in practice. Most of these examples, although not all, are drawn from the practice of social work, since it is here that my experience lies, but are equally applicable to other methods or settings of helping.

Seen in this light these suggestions, rules, or techniques can be listed as follows:

1. *Start with the request as it comes to you.* As we all know, what is requested may not be what the helped person eventually may come to want. It is, however, at the moment his evaluation of it—either what

he wants at this time, or what he is willing at this time to discuss with you. It is what he is putting out for you to take hold of and his first definition of the kind and type of help which he both expects and is willing to take from you. Although eventually he may alter his request, or you may help him define it differently through the introduction of new ideas or difference, this can only be done in the context of your having looked at and listened to his original request.

To infer that the original request is not a real one is to show disrespect for the asking person. The only exception to this rule would be when the request is, by its very nature, patently either an invitation to pursue the asker's reasons for his request, or some kind of "trial balloon" to see how one will react. Thus, if someone asked me if I knew a good way of committing a murder I would probably tell him no, and at least wonder why he felt impelled to ask this of me. The same might be true of statements which are really concealed requests for help, like an apparently unconnected statement that women are not to be trusted, which obviously conceals feeling about something that is troubling the speaker. Here I would say something like, "some woman must have let you down," as a way of bringing the problem down to the particular.

Conversely, it is important to recognize the point at which an answer to the problem presented no longer is what the helped person wants.

A woman, obviously troubled about her relationship with her granddaughter, asked for financial help for her. But when a budget was worked out it was obvious that the grandmother was willing and able to supply all the child's needs except those that had to do with her granddaughter's beginning adolescence—cosmetics, clothes, sanitary appliances. Only then could the grandmother come to see that it was not finances that really bothered her, but the child's becoming nubile. She feared that the grandchild would repeat the daughter's (her mother's) pattern, which the grandmother had been unable to control. Yet, when this was implied earlier in the interview, the grandmother rejected it out of hand.

Often the shift is not arrived at by this process of reason but becomes apparent in the asking person's dissatisfaction with the answer apparently arrived at. In the example above, for instance, it was the grandmother's reaction to the smallness of the amount the agency could offer, due to her desire to help the child, that enabled her to move on and discuss her deeper fears.

2. *Respond to feeling rather than to literal content.* This may

sound rather contradictory, after we have insisted that one must accept the terms on which help is asked, but it explains the exceptions we noted. One starts with the request for help and with the person's feeling about it. In the exceptions noted above it is the feeling behind the request which helps us to see that the request means more than its literal word form.

The response to feeling rather than to the literal content of words is perhaps what most clearly distinguishes helping interviewing from social conversation. It does not mean that one ignores what the person in front of one is saying, but it does mean that one's interest is centered first and foremost on what he is trying to convey to you, and that this is as often conveyed by tones of voice, gestures, hesitancies, and the like as it is by the actual logic of words. Words are often used to protect oneself from saying what one feels. Sometimes what needs picking up and responding to is the very difference between what a person says and how he is saying it. One often needs to say something like, "you are telling me this as if it were good, but you don't sound as if you liked it," or to respond to what literally is a simple statement with, "that seems to trouble you."

In a social conversation the interest is almost entirely on words. A word reminds someone of a story or sets up a new train of thought. What ties one comment to another is the literal content of what is said. The consistency of a helping interview is, on the other hand, that of feeling. An interruption in a helping interview is not so much a change of sense as it is a failure to follow feeling. A child said aggressively to her social worker, "I nearly telephoned you today." The social worker, intent at that moment on getting a "good" relationship with the child, and perhaps a little taken aback by the implied blame in the child's voice, answered, "My, but you must be a big girl to know how to use the telephone." In a social conversation this would be perfectly allowable. They were discussing telephones, and it did enable the social worker to pay the child a compliment. But from a helping point of view this was an interruption. There was no suggestion that the child was asking for praise. She was expressing anger and a need for the social worker's help.

The importance of listening to feeling and responding to it is of particular importance when we consider what use the helped person is making of what he tells you. What he says about himself is rarely dispassionate appraisal. It is part of the image of himself that he needs to project, not perhaps to the whole world, but to you, at this moment.

And, as we have said, the question, "Why do you tell me this now?" may be of real importance.

A failure to see this and an insistence on the literal content of what is said, instead of on the meaning it has in the relationship, may lead one far astray.

What it does lead to, only too often, is a simple battle of wills. This is what happens when the helping person expresses an apparent wish to do something that the helped person suggests or wants, "if only" certain difficulties could be overcome. Maybe it is to go to a doctor. But there is no transportation. I will drive you, then. But I can't go at the time you are free, and even if you adapt your schedule the doctor doesn't see patients then. If this is somehow overcome, there is the matter of payment, and if this be wangled somehow, then we find that the patient does not trust this particular doctor, or, on thinking it over, is not convinced that he is ill. So the argument proceeds, with the helped person finding more and more reasons why such an action is impossible and the helping person using even more and more ingenuity in overcoming these reasons.

Very early in such an exchange some recognition of the helped person's fear of doctors would have avoided the fruitless struggle. Yet it is surprising how often we fall into this sort of struggle with logic. It is almost as if we have a need to prove the other person illogical or uncooperative and so excuse our failure to help him.

This suggests a third "rule":

3. *Recognize likely feelings, even before they are expressed.* Although each person's feelings are his own and you may, as it were, "guess wrong," there are certain feelings which are so natural and inherent a part of the process that the helper can safely bring them out in the open even when they are not expressed. He may be wrong. If he is he has usually lost nothing and has in fact done nothing but made a courteous allowance for what the other is likely to feel, as one does when one apologizes for troubling another with a request even though the other is glad to grant it. But often one is right. This happens most often when what one recognizes is in some way the difficulty of taking help, or anger in having to face reality. The neglecting parent, for instance, faced with the protective worker or officer, is much more likely to be able to discuss his situation with someone who expresses some understanding of how unwelcome and threatening his visit must seem than he is with someone who, by his silence or his casual manner, appears not to understand. Tact, in the sense of ignoring unpleasant feelings or situations, is one of the

helper's worst enemies. Instead of reducing likely feeling it leaves it as a wall between the helper and the helped. Sometimes the effect of quite a tentative little piece of empathy of this sort can be most dramatic.

A man, who had long lived as a lodger with a family, took over the parental role for the thirteen-year-old daughter when both parents were killed in an accident. It was, as far as anyone could judge, a purely avuncular relationship with some provision for chaperonage and when the girl was reported for truancy the court, seeking the "uncle's" cooperation, accepted him fully as *in loco parentis*. It was not until a sensitive worker said to him musingly one day, "You know, you must wonder what we all think of you and Jane," that the man broke down and confessed his terror of the whole situation and the blackmail the girl had used, based on some childish familiarity, to force him to allow her more freedom than he thought good for her. He said, "If she gets into trouble, I wouldn't stand a chance in the world." As long as the court had treated him tactfully, trying to convey by their attitude that they saw nothing wrong in the relationship, he could not admit to them his fear of where it might lead.

Possibly in this case the probation officer had sensed the man's underlying fear, but even if she had not, a little "loving imagination" would have suggested that he would naturally be concerned with what the court thought of him and the child.

The fourth rule that has to do with feeling I would formulate as follows:

4. *When dealing with an angry or rejecting person, keep your attention on his feeling and do not attempt to defend what he is feeling about.* This is one of the hardest things to do in all helping, and one of the most essential. It stems from the understanding that an angry or a rejecting person is a person in need. He expresses his anger to you because, in fact, he needs help with it. But we often deny him this help because the thing he attacks is something dear to us, which we feel a need to protect. It may be our program, or our belief, or a person whom we know to be in trouble and to need sympathy rather than criticism. But the moment one tries to defend whatever it is the person you are facing is angry about one lines oneself up against him. One tells him that he is somehow in the wrong to get so angry. If he only understood or had a little more compassion he would not feel like this at all.

This only makes it harder for him to give up his point of view. Even that favorite word of teachers and child welfare workers, "interpretation" of a child's needs, subtly tells the angry person that his anger is unfounded. It also makes clear that one's interest is not in the person to whom one is talking. It is in whatever he is attacking. A mother complained bitterly to a counselor how her child apparently wantonly failed in school because "he didn't care" although she was sure that he had enough brains to pass. The counselor patiently explained that the child tested dull normal, that he had become discouraged, that if no fuss were made about grades the chances were that he could do, not brilliantly, but sufficiently well to pass and that what was needed for his good was for everyone to relax. He illustrated the method he had used in his interviews to reassure the child and help him achieve on tasks the boy believed to be too difficult and encouraged the mother to let him develop his undoubted manual skill. The mother accepted the explanation with some skepticism and covert indignation but promised to try. She was back next week saying that taking off the pressure only seemed to make things worse. Now she knew he was lazy and not stupid. He must not have tried in the test. Twice in the week he had scamped his homework, although she knew that it wasn't too hard for him. Did the counselor really believe that she shouldn't see that he at least did the work?

It was at that point that the counselor saw what he had done. He said that it must be hard to feel so badly let down by one's child. The mother at this began to tell him of her own quitting school despite good grades to marry a man who had no education but was, she agreed, a capable workman. She told of her family's bitter disapproval and insistence that she had lowered herself, of her determination that her child prove a success and confute them, of her fear that he was temperamentally more like her husband's family than hers and of her attempt to prove that it was not so. Only as she began to consider what all this had meant to her could she say, as she finally did, "It isn't fair to him to make him fight that old battle of mine."

The lesson, and it is a hard one, that one has to learn is that by defending what one feels to be unjustly attacked one usually only does it harm, but by refusing to defend it, and trying instead to help the attacker, the chances are that the attack will be turned into help. Yet not to defend is tremendously difficult, particularly when one feels the attack to be unjustified or inspired by unworthy motives. Perhaps the most difficult situation of all is when the attacked thing is oneself. But the rule still holds and if the interest in the other is genuine, not just assumed, it works in the great majority of situations.

The frailty of explanations leads us to a fifth suggestion:

5. *Listen, rather than explain or instruct.* Although it is not true to say that helping consists solely of listening, it is probably true to say that a helping interview can often be judged roughly by the proportion of words spoken by the helping and the helped person. Good helping demands the introduction of reality and difference. It requires expressions of empathy and assurance of support. Sometimes the helping person must intervene or channel a stream of thought or feeling. But for the most part these interventions are short and to the point. The most effective single statement I have seen in practice was made to a neglecting mother who was pouring out her anger against her unfaithful husband and in the process losing sight of what the interview was about, which was the neglect of her daughter. It consisted of four words, interjected into the stream of the mother's complaints, "And meanwhile Barbara suffers," and it resulted in the mother really beginning to face her problem. Much also can be conveyed by what one might call "encouraging noises" or gestures which convey empathy or support.

Sometimes explanation and even instruction is necessary. Sometimes a person actually needs to know how to do something—how to apply for social security, or where to write for a birth cerficiate. But this is not the kind of explanation and instruction many inexperienced helpers tend to give to those they are helping. All too often what we get there is a long explanation of why something is so, which is often an indication that the helper is not sure that it should be so, or a reasoned exhortation showing that such and such a course is the desirable one. It is true that occasionally one may find a person who genuinely does not know how he should behave or what to do in a situation, but this is not man's most common predicament. Generally he knows quite well, but what he cannot do is to do it. Paul of Tarsus, who had considerable insight into human difficulties, put his finger on the problem when he said that he did not do what he wanted, but did the very thing he hated.

Listening means a total concentration of what the other person is saying and feeling. It is what is so easily lost if we allow other considerations to enter into the interview. Other goals, however worthy, other concerns such as our need to succeed, or be liked, or even to help inevitably dissipate listening. But to listen does not mean to be totally nondirective. Nor does it mean, as it has sometimes been held to mean, acting simply as a mirror and turning back on the helped person all decisions. To reply, as some helpers tend to, almost routinely to any request with, "What do you think?" is a technique that can most easily be overused. Sometimes it only has the effect of pushing the helped person away. It says, in effect, that one cannot help. And while clarity can come from the mere act of expressing one's thoughts to another, to rely solely on this process can greatly limit one's ability to help.

A girl sought advice about enrolling in nursing school. She had worked at one time as a nurse's aid and, as she said, "loved the work." Yet she had left it to become a librarian for reasons which were no longer valid. To all objective questions about a nursing career she could give positive answers. Yet she hesitated to enroll.

The interviewer listened. She shared with the girl that there was apparently some reason that held her back they had not discussed. The girl said, yes, but she could not place it. Going over what she had said the interviewer remembered the words "I loved it." Yet the girl had given it up. She asked, "Did you perhaps love it too much?" The girl nodded. "You felt it a kind of self-indulgence?" This brought out all the girl's feelings about her dedication to helping and her fear that she was in fact satisfying her own needs rather than those of her patients. It ended with the interviewer saying "I love my work, too and I think it's all right to love it. It helps me do a better job." "Then if it's all right, how soon can I enroll?"

Here the girl could not risk her fear of indulgence until the teacher broke through, as it were, and fastened on the one statement in what she had said that seemed to carry meaning.

"Nondirective" counseling arose from an understanding of the need of the helped person to make his own decisions, but it underestimated the help that he might need in doing so. It does stand as a warning not to take over the helped person's life. To do so is so obviously fruitless that a warning against doing so would hardly seem worth listing were it not for another curious paradox, which is that to take over is very often the result of having been taken over. Our sixth rule is then:

6. *Hold fast to your function as a helper. Do not take over the helped person's decisions, but do not allow him to control the conditions of help.* The question in a helping relationship is not how much helper and helped control the other, or refrain from doing so. It is what each controls. The helper must not and cannot control the use which the helped person makes of the relationship. At the same time the helped person cannot and must not be allowed to control the helping actions of the helper or the conditions of help itself.

The request of the seeker for help that the helping person "do" something about his problem, make concrete suggestions, tell him what to do is a common phenomenon. It will generally be noticed, too, that when the helping person does this, and requires of the helped person some involvement in it, what the helping person has done proves to be inappropriate. How often does one not hear helpers say, "But I thought you wanted me to. . . ." Yes and no. He wanted you to take the responsibility for this decision, but he did not want to have to live with it once it was made.

What is perhaps not always recognized is how hard the person being helped works to control the situation, to get the helping person to do what he wants him to do. He uses the very same psychological tricks that the manipulative helper so often tries to use on him—disarming him, shaming him, challenging him, and appealing to him. But these efforts are not a sign of the helped person's strength or his ability to make decisions for himself. They are exactly the opposite. They are a sign of a refusal to face up to what is needed. One of the characteristics of those people whom we say are suffering from a character disorder and are the hardest of all to help because they have developed infinite ways of disclaiming responsibility is that their first request of any helping person, even a probation officer, is to ask his help in getting them out of some scrape.

We need to reemphasize here that a belief in the client's need to choose does not include his right to use you to further a nonchoice or to escape reality. You are there to be used, but to be used does not mean to indulge. Paradoxical as it may seem, the helping person must be a servant but he cannot allow himself to be mastered. He must hold fast to what he can properly do, what he is willing to do, and what is realistic and sensible for him to do. Anita Faatz puts it even more strongly. She says that ". . . in every helping process where something does indeed take place, there comes a time when all the strength of the client is gathered into one mighty effort to overcome the strength of the helping person; and if he succeeds, his movement is defeated, and if he does not succeed, he may have won new life."[1]

This is indeed a situation where the desire to help another can prevent one from helping him. It is very easy to be caught in the demands of the person who appeals to us and to start doing things for him instead of helping him do things for himself.

It is this situation which has given rise, in some social work circles to the insistence of many caseworkers on the function of the agency as

1. Anita Faatz, *The Nature of Choice in Casework Process* (Chapel Hill, N.C., 1953), p. 105.

something that bounds and limits what the helper can and is willing to do. Although this can be carried too far and become a way of denying people the help they need, there is validity in the concept.

A child who was having difficulty with his friends in a Children's Home asked the social worker, first, to talk to the older children to tell them to play with him. When the social worker said that he could not create friends for him he begged the social worker to be his friend— "Come and play ball with me." It was only when the social worker stuck to his function—that he was here to help the boy find out how to make use of living in a group—that Tom was able to say that what he really needed help with was his anger at boys who didn't seem to care about having to be in a Home at all. "I'm afraid I'll become like them." This opened up a discussion which ended in the boy's resolution to make the best of what had happened to him, which was his having to be in the Home.

The usual argument for not holding to a function is that one should meet need where one sees it. It might be that the boy needed a friend to play ball with. But who should this be? Not an all-purpose social worker, but a playmate. It was only in facing the fact that no one could create a friend for him that the boy was able to face what was preventing him from making friends.

The lone helper, the one without a clear function or responsibility, is somewhat at a disadvantage in knowing what role he needs to hold to. He does not have an agency or an organization with clear lines of responsibility to rely on. What he must rely on is his grasp of reality, what he knows that he can do and his willingness to do it. He has to find this strength in himself and in the principles in which he has come to believe.

There are, however, some things that the helping person can do to give the helping process some form and set some limits around it. These have already been noted, not quite in this form, in an earlier discussion of structuring the relationship, in chapter 4, and they constitute our next series of rules for action.

7. *Make clear, as soon as possible, both the conditions of service and the authority and role of everyone concerned.* The need to make clear what authority anyone has was discussed in an earlier chapter. It is the first step in establishing reality. The helped person needs to know what you can do to him. He needs to understand the consequences of his likely struggle with you, and just how far this can go. He needs to know, also, if you have no authority at all. He needs to know how far you are willing to go, what you will do for him and

what you will not, and what responsibilities this will involve him in. In a formal helping situation I have a strong inclination to insist that this be reduced to writing, in some sort of agreement, not because such an agreement is binding in law, or can compel anyone to do what he does not want to do, but as a way of defining a common endeavor, and as something to come back to if the relationship seems to be going astray. It is much easier to say, "This is apparently what we saw that we would do together. How has it changed?" than to point out that the other person is making working together difficult.

In private, personal helping and in more informal situations written agreements would be something of a burden. Nevertheless, written or spoken, detailed or rather general, some such agreement has to be there. Sometimes it will not emerge at first. One may need to explore quite fully what help is being asked before one can begin to think of the role helper and helped will play. In others the situation may be pretty well determined already, by legal requirements or by generally understood more or less formal relationships, such as those of teacher and student, minister and church member, or doctor and patient, but will still need to be made explicit and its implications considered.

Included in such an agreement should be the question of confidentiality. It is not always possible to promise someone absolute confidentiality. A priest may be able to do so, but even a doctor may feel compelled to share information with a relative. Particularly in dealing with children one needs to be sure that one really means it before one can promise not to tell anyone when one may have responsibility of which one cannot divest oneself.

A child, about to be returned by a court to her father's custody, told her housemother in confidence that her father continued to molest her sexually, on her visits home. The housemother felt herself bound by the promise of confidentiality she had solemnly given the child. Yet she could not see the child returned to the father. Fortunately she was able to help the child tell this herself to the judge. Otherwise she might have been forced to break her word. In this situation the child's fear of the father made this possible. In some way she may have hoped that her confidence would be broken. The same situation can arise, however, when the helped person is planning something dangerous, or illegal, which no one who knows it can let him do. One may have to tell people that there are some things they cannot tell you in confidence.

A particular kind of condition, which some would-be helpers find repugnant, is that of payment for service. While most service is free, and clearly ought to be so, there is no reason why counseling, or consultation, or other kinds of formal helping, should not be paid for. Not only are there those who have developed real skill in helping and have undertaken expensive education to increase their skill, who may work independently of any formal agency, but there is often advantage to the helped person if he makes payment. To do so can help him struggle with his feeling of helplessness. Where so much is out of his control this is something he can control. It may also help him resolve the kind of guilt one can develop just for having been helped.

The freedom that having paid for something brings is particularly obvious in some adoption situations, where being given a child one was not able to bear oneself sometimes ties an adoptive parent in a net of impossible gratitude to the agency which gave him a child. Some less ethical agencies have not been slow to exploit this guilt. To have paid for service can make this unnecessary and, incidentally, cost much less.

8. *If possible, set limits, particularly in time.* This too has been discussed earlier in this book. It is perhaps only necessary to say here that a known period of time is both far less threatening and gives one an often very helpful deadline with which to work, particularly in matters where there is a very important single decision to make, such as the giving up of a child or separation from a spouse. Here the nonchoice is so attractive that if unlimited time is given things begin to drift. It is also true that in most helping, if there is not significant change in, say, six months, probably something different is needed. Time also permits one to construct certain checkpoints along the way, at which both helper and helped can look at what is happening. The setting of a limit in time has been found very useful in helping an unmarried mother make a decision about giving up, or keeping, her baby, in working with neglectful parents, and in tackling particular problems that a child may have. In one Children's Home the use of a skilled caseworker was greatly enhanced when it became known that her services would be available on a selective basis for ten children only at any one time, and for six months only, with a checkpoint after three. Children began to use her in a much more purposeful way, saying, "I need to get down to things, because we don't have too much time." Defenses tended to be maintained for less time. The child was able earlier to make up his mind to risk sharing his problem.

In much informal helping, the use of time may not seem appropriate, or indeed necessary, except where the relationship is likely to be of some duration, in tutoring, for example, or in premarital counseling. Yet, if the relationship extends over more than one or two contacts and help is still being asked, the setting of time limits may be wise. It is sometimes good to say, "We've discussed this three times, now. Let's concentrate on the problem for a week (or a month) and see if anything happens. We may find you need some other kind of help."

9. *Help the helped person express what he wants and then work with him towards how much of it he can have.* This is a rather important principle when people ask for more than you can give. The natural tendency is to try to persuade the other person that what you do have is good, even if it is not quite so good as what he is asking for. Or, some helpers will carefully avoid discussion of what they do not have to give, seeing this as fruitless and likely to lead to disappointment. Why discuss the impossible? To take either of these positions is to avoid the kind of reality with which helping has to do. The helped person wants the whole. He cannot have it. But his wanting it is reality just as his not being able to have it is a piece of reality, too.

What will really help him is to face this double reality and make what adjustments to it he must. If it is you, rather than he, who adjusts one piece of reality (his wants) to the other, he will not gain the experience of meeting the real situation and he will have, in addition, an unmade decision in terms of his ultimate desire. He will inevitably feel that you did not understand, that perhaps you could have stretched the limits if you had wanted to or had known how deeply he really felt. To say, "This is then what you are saying you really want. Now let's see how much of that is possible," is, in any case, much more encouraging than to throw doubt on what he wants.

A child had reacted to foster-home care with a determined effort to get sent home to a hopelessly feebleminded mother. She came to resent any kindness on the part of foster parents, seeing this as an attempt to keep her away from home. She rejected all efforts to love her. It was only when a foster parent could recognize with her how much she wanted to go home, but how impossible this was, that she was able to say, one day, "Well, if I can't go home, will you be next thing to a mother to me?"

What was done here required of the foster mother a great deal of courage and humility (in the sense that we have used the term). She had to give up pretending that what she, as a foster mother, could give was in any way the equivalent of what a real mother could give. It was not what the child wanted. Yet the child could use it when it was presented honestly as a necessary second-best.

Along with this goes a principle which is very closely allied to it.

10. *Do not defend a reality that you cannot or do not intend to change.* So often when a person is faced with an unpleasant reality the helper tries to soften the blow by explaining that there is a good reason why it is so. I have heard many a welfare worker tell his client that his grant is so low "because we must share with everyone equally," or excuse, to a child, his parent not visiting him by explaining that the mother has been very busy lately. Sometimes what may be at stake may be one's own decision—a permission refused, or a grade given.

While the other person may be helped by knowing the grounds on which a decision is made, or an action taken, one needs to be very careful that such explanation does not become a justification. For if one is there to help a person, through empathy and support, to face a piece of reality, to insist, however subtly, that this reality is good is to say to the other person that his feelings about it are wrong, and this makes empathy impossible.

The moment one defends a reality one raises the question that it can, or at least, ought to be different. One removes it from the status of a reality. One gets into endless arguments about whether it is just, or fair. What results is not two people, standing on the same side of reality, trying to figure out how one of them can face it, thus:

but two people on opposite sides of reality, arguing about it:

This problem often confronts the probation officer, with whom the probationer wants to argue either his innocence, or the justice of the sentence. Neither is usually productive. What probationer and probation officer need to face together is the reality of probation, which neither of them can change.

In saying this, however, we do have to be careful that the reality we are talking of is a reality that we, or the client, really cannot do anything about. It may be, for instance, that the probationer is really innocent, or the grant something the client either ought to protest about, through a welfare rights organization or by appealing the welfare worker's decision. It may be that our decison was hasty. But in order to help someone change reality in this way it is even more important that we stand on the same side of reality as the person we are helping—looking at it, as it were, as it is, changeable or unchangeable, without an attempt to justify it.

Social workers are often accused of helping people adjust to reality, rather than working to help them change it, or working to do so themselves. Sometimes, I would suggest, one has to do both, on a different time scale. However much one may feel that conditions are unjust, however much one may want to change them or help others to do so, for the time being this is reality, and it has to be handled. The important thing is not to become so identified with what is that we deny others the right to protest or act to change it.

11. *Allow the person you are helping to fail if he wants to.* This perhaps is simply a warning against overprotection, which has been implicit in all that we have said, but the problem needs restating in this form. It has two thrusts. First, it is a plea not to try to prevent someone from attempting what may seem to you the impossible, which can arise from your lack of faith in what he can achieve if he really wants to as well as a wish to protect him from an experience that may be very poignant for him.[2] And secondly, it is a reminder that when a person is in the process of failing to do something, it may be because he wants to fail. To help him not fail is then to defeat what he actually wants the most. One of the worst pieces of helping I have ever perpetrated personally had to do with a student in whom I had a great deal of faith and whom I was determined to help become a social worker. But, for some reason, this was not what he wanted to do. When this wish began to show up in poor work, I found myself making allowances for him, grading him a little better than his performance warranted and refusing to allow him either to withdraw or fail. It took him over a year to come to the point at which he could say, "I'm tired of trying to help people" and choose another profession—a year that my refusal to permit him to fail had taken from his life.

12. *Formulate the helped person's problem, from time to time, as*

2. See David Soyer, "The Right to Fail," *Social Work* 8, no. 3 (July 1963) : 72-78.

you see it. This may be more of a device than a rule, and yet it is very helpful. When the helped person has been trying, in one way or another, to get you to understand, clarity can sometimes come if you will say to him, "It seems to me that you are saying. . . ." You may have misunderstood him, or you may essentially be right. Sometimes, too, this gives the helper the chance to introduce a little difference into the situation, by stating the problem in a slightly different light. The person seeking help may reject this difference, or he may find that it helps him to look at it differently himself.

Such a formulation is always a tentative one. It never says, "I know what your problem is," but, "This is my understanding of what you are saying to me. Am I on the right track?" As such it has some of the characteristics of tentative empathy, but is much more specific.

In the situation we discussed earlier of the girl who wanted, and yet couldn't quite decide, to go to nursing school, the helper, after listening to one reason after another why the girl could not go to school at this time—lack of money, home obligations, being tired of "learning," all of which the girl herself disposed of as soon as they were challenged—said to her, "I think you are saying that you want to go to school very much, but there's something you can't identify holding you back." This proved very helpful because it cut short a fruitless exploration of objective "reasons" and centered them both on looking for a deeper feeling that the girl could not put into words.

Sometimes it is good to recapitulate agreements. "It seems to me that we have agreed that your problem looks at the moment like this," or "Let me see. You're asking me if I can help you do this, or that."

The whole point here is to keep contact, to test out one's understanding and to try different formulations of it, so that helper and helped do not go off in different directions.

13. *Partialize the problem.* This is sometimes objected to by those who are quite rightly convinced that all of a person's problems are interconnected, that his failure to earn his living, his disagreement with his wife, his fits of dizziness are part of the same underlying pattern. Yet, unless the person is willing to admit total defeat or turn, perhaps to a psychiatrist to help him remodel his whole personality, he has to work on one thing at a time. Nor can you really help him with a whole reorganization of his life without working on specific things. The hope is, of course, that by managing to change some small part of the total problem the helped person will find that little bit of extra courage or clarity that will enable him to do something about something else.

Often what one needs to discuss is simply the next step in the proceeding, what you and the helped person can do in today's conference. Other things may have to wait. A human being is capable of tackling only so much at any one time. The grandmother whom we used as an example of starting with the actual request, found herself facing a sea of troubles—her granddaughter's rebelliousness, her own feelings about the child's mother, whom she had cut out of her life when she had married unsuitably, her husband's lack of support for her efforts to control the girl (she had whipped her and only made matters worse), her own feelings of inadequacy as a parent and grandparent, her status in the community and her struggle with her feelings about morality. The caseworker suggested that all they could do, perhaps, at this time was decide what she would do if the child came home late that night. Yet on considering that one action the grandmother was able to face her guilt for what she had done to her daughter years before and to restore her relationship with daughter, husband, and granddaughter.

Movement often begins with one foot on the ladder. To have come to some decision often means that the next one is not so difficult.

This prompts another suggestion:

14. *End the interview at a point where a decision has been made.* This is, of course, not always possible. No decision may have been made, or there may be a time set aside for the interview which for some reason may have to be used. But, if there is real movement of any kind in an interview, even if it is of the slightest, there will come a time when the helped person commits himself to something new. It may be the decision to try something he has not quite dared try before, or the decision to risk taking help with it at least in a limited way. Whatever it is, it needs consolidating—sleeping on, perhaps, or actually trying out. Although it has been verbalized, it is not yet something with which one is at ease, or familiar. If the helping person at this point tries to capitalize on it, pushes the helped person to go beyond it or to elaborate on it, its original clarity and determination is often weakened or confused. The process is somewhat akin to that of writing a short story. The story must have a beginning, a middle, and an end, but if the writer continues after the punch line, the story loses its point. Many helpers have made difficulties for themselves and for the people they are helping by going on too long in an attempt either to gather more information or to reinforce a decision they believe to have been half made. It is wiser to leave at this point. Most decisions, in any case, are only foreshadowed in the actual interview. They are

consolidated outside it. At the point that the helped person says
something like, "You know, that might work," it might be wiser to say,
"Why don't you think about it, and try it if it seems good," rather than
to try to reinforce it at the time.

In a protective interview a young girl who was in deep marital
trouble and, in consequence, neglecting her baby, had reached the
point of seeing the court worker's visit as helpful rather than threatening. She began to unfold her marital difficulties, and asked the worker
if he would talk to her husband. This the worker agreed to do. He
would talk with them both. But he would not, at this time, go into
details with the wife. She needed to discuss with her husband their
need for help, and the part the worker might play in it, before he
became involved with one party to the dispute.

As a result, when he came back, he found the couple had begun to
identify some of their problems and to start working on them. If he
had continued with the girl, he would have involved her in possible
solutions, instead of the immediate problem, which was their joint
ability to ask for help.

To end an interview at the point of a decision is closely related to
another problem which helpers sometimes meet. In their eagerness to
come to grips with a problem, they discuss all aspects of it in a first
interview. This does two things. It commits one to rediscuss next time
something on which one has already, more or less, covered the
essential points, and it makes little allowance for the kind of growth
that occurs between interviews. A second interview in this case is often
rambling and repetitive.

This ties in very closely with a question that we have not answered,
and which may well be confusing the reader at this point. We
mentioned a few pages back the dangers in a too facile non-
directiveness and a turning back to the client of all decisions, however
small. We have at the same time cautioned the helper against the too
frequent use of explanation and instruction. We have said that he
must not take over, either as a result of being taken over, or on his
own account. We have insisted that the final decision must always be
the helped person's. We have warned against a battle of wills, yet
spoken of the need to introduce difference. It may be hard for the
helper to know, beset with all these statements, just how active he
should be and what he should leave to the person he is helping.

There is, of course, no absolute rule that can be constructed on this
subject. Too many factors are involved. The helped person's ability to

tackle things for himself, the depth of his need to have us do it for him, the actual possibility of his being able to think or do the thing that is needed, all have to be taken into account. Generally, though, unless one is working with a person who is primarily a thinker, I would suggest that both what one consciously allows to the person one is trying to help and what in any case he will take for himself are actions and not ideas. It is this opportunity to act on a decision that we actually leave for next time. It may be a request to think about something we have said, or to try something out, but it involves doing something that will either confirm or deny the movement that seemed in the interview to have been taking place. Therefore, we might suggest as a rule:

15. *Leave something to work on for next time.* It is often in action that we discover, and the helped person may discover, that movement is or is not real. In the situation just related, it was the girl's sharing with her husband their need for help and arranging a joint appointment for them both that indicated the genuineness of her own ability to do something about her problem. An adoptive applicant, on the other hand, while asserting his desperate need for a child, shared with the adoptive worker the blueprints for the house he was building. No child's bedroom had been included. A man, however, who left an office full of doubts of the wisdom of giving up his relief check for a course of vocational rehabilitation arrived next day with a detailed list of the tools that he would need and a self-addressed envelope so that the counselor could let him know at once that they were available. Trains are missed, appointments forgotten, or someone takes some action that commits him to something new—writes a letter, burns his pipes, or resigns his job.

It might be said, in fact, that the whole process of helping is one of trying out new commitments and finding out whether this will indeed help. But there is more to it even than this. It could be said that in trying out the decisions that one arrives at in being helped, directed to certain ends, and with the helper holding him to reality, understanding his difficulty and giving him his support, someone is actually trying out in a protected situation a way of life that later he can live by himself. The helping situation then becomes a kind of laboratory for testing out ways of doing things, and, indeed, for finding out whether one can or wants to do them. This is perhaps the most significant knowledge that one gains about people in the process of helping them—the knowledge of how they tackle a problem, what they want to or can do, how steadfast they can be, what are their thresholds of being able to maintain what they have begun. The client, too, learns this about himself.

A belief in this kind of knowledge of people, gained through active participation with them in a process of trying out decisions, does not deny the usefulness of a more formal diagnosis based on the pattern of past behavior. Rather it supplements it, and sometimes draws attention to its limitations, which lie chiefly in the fact that a helped and an unhelped person are not necessarily the same. Because this person was not able to handle his problem in the past, alone and without help, does not necsesarily mean that he cannot do so in the future if he is offered help. It is this which makes the negative diagnosis so dangerous, and often so unfair. There is always the possibility that man, once he is genuinely offered help, can discover strength in himself that no one, much less himself, could possibly know that he had.

In terms of suggestions for practice this means that one often consciously requires of the person being helped that he take certain action before one moves on to the next step. This is not to deny him help if the action cannot be taken, but a way of making clear both to himself and to you how ready he is to go on further, or whether the decision that seems to have been arrived at needs further rethinking and perhaps further testing out. The parent who is asking someone to care for his child perhaps needs to bring the child physically to the agency, rather than have the worker take the initiative by going to the home. We might put this as a rule:

16. *Test out decisions through requiring action to confirm them.* Closely allied to this principle is one that concerns giving advice. Advice has, in much modern counseling, gained a negative connotation. The reason for this is in part the need to move away from a former concept of helping, in which it was believed that what man principally needed was knowledge about how to do things, and which had little knowledge of the part which feelings play in the giving of help. To acknowledge, however, that man must make his own final decisions does not mean that advice cannot still be a useful thing. In casual or emotionally neutral situations it is often used. Where it causes difficulty is where it has something of the nature of a command, where it is backed with either formal or informal authority or where the person giving advice presumes without evidence that he knows much more about the specific situation than the person asking for help.

It is exactly this assumption that is often so wrongly made. The advice-giver, the expert, knows more, it is true, about the general situation. He knows what usually works or how others have solved this problem. He knows less than the asker, however, about the particular situation. He knows rather little about the asker's ability and desire to take certain courses of action, and he is not always aware of particular elements that might make one course of action unwise or another more desirable. This is a fact often forgotten by supervisors in various fields and by experts or consultants. They are the generalists, but the worker, the person on the firing line, the person whose problem is under study, always knows more about the particular.

Detailed advice which allows for no modification in terms of the particular is often either useless or harmful. I can remember a consultant who advised an institution, quite properly as far as expert knowledge is concerned, that the Board of a Children's Home should include men as well as women. What he did not know was that this particular board saw for itself no function other than purchasing groceries, sewing and decorating. When the Home, wishing to take the advice it was given, replaced half its women with men, the men found no work for them and there were not enough women to do the job. The consultant's general knowledge needed in this situation to take into account a most individual particularity.

A rule may therefore be formulated:

17. *In offering advice, leave room for modification.* Indeed one way of giving advice, and one moreover that both makes allowance for the particular and engages the helping person in action is what one might call "alternative advice." In this it is assumed that the particular is not known. Advice is given on this premise: that if you find A to be true, then perhaps X is what you should do. But if, in considering carefully the situation as you see it, you believe B to be true, then Y is worth trying. This can be expanded to C and Z if needed. Its major value is that it engages the person being helped in trying to fit his particular into the general. It also makes more difficult that resistance to taking advice that we have noted, where the value of the advice is counteracted by following it too literally. A housemother recently was approached by a boy who was in real trouble with his girl. She gave him plentiful advice about what girls wanted from boys, including, in this case, a pretty abject apology, all of which he said gratefully he would follow. But when she asked him a day or two later whether her advice had worked he shook his head. He said that on further thought he had come to the conclusion that his relationship with this girl was unhealthy; that what she was doing was not objecting to his behavior but seeing to what extent he would abase himself before her. What he

really wanted was advice on how to stand up to her and continue to be himself. The housemother's assumption that he must want to get back in the girl's good graces had prevented him from getting the advice he wanted.

While we are still concerned with action as testing out purpose, it might be pointed out that actions can sometimes be used in another way. Put in the form of a suggestion it might be said:

18. *Where important decisions are made, use if possible physical movement or action to symbolize what is happening.* The value of this is something we recognize when we seal an agreement with a handshake, or as children, with a kiss. We have physically come together, and this fact is remembered long after the actual words have been forgotten. The physical movement carries with it more of a sense of what is actually transpiring than anything that is said. It makes a great deal of difference, for instance, whether an unmarried mother physically gives you her child for adoption or whether you go to the nursery and take the child away. In the first instance she gave you the child; in the second you took it. The actual decisions may have been the same, but the feeling around it, especially after a lapse of time, is entirely different.

The same kind of symbolization can come through the signing of an agreement, or through the very fact that something is written down. It can come through the actual wording of an agreement or an application. It behooves us also to do more to study the effects of the physical arrangements of where we give our help. If we use an office, are we, for instance, separated from the person asking help by a desk, or by a trick of lighting? Are we too close?

This is a subject about which we probably know too little at this time, although some work has been done, in industry and in teaching, on the effects of room arrangement, lighting, and color. For a careful study of the symbolism that confirms or denies decision, it might not be unwise for helpers to ask help from organizations which have studied ritual, such as churches or government, particularly of a monarchical kind. It is a fascinating field and although it is not perhaps essential to helping—good helping has occurred in the most unlikely places and where the symbolism was probably all wrong—this kind of "outward and visible sign" means a lot to people.

Two more things perhaps need to be said about decision, action, and movement:

19. *Start each separate contact where the helped person is at that time.* What is meant here is really a warning that human progress is

not consistent. What was done last time may have to be done again. There will be regression as well as going forward, and much may have happened for good or ill since the last time the two of you met. One thing, for instance, that often disturbs a helping person is that the person asking for help may have told you too much last time. He may have come too near his problem, or exposed himself too much. At the time he may have felt that this was safe. He had you to support him. But thinking it over, he is afraid. He may withdraw for a while until he is sure of you again, or try to control you as he has not done before. While it is often good practice to try to sum up at a new meeting your understanding of what has gone before, this has to be offered in a most tentative way. "This was, I think, where we were. Are we still at that point? How does it look to you today?"

To go back again, to reinforce, to put up with the disappointment when someone who has appeared to share so much suddenly shuts up like a clam, requires in the helper that trust in the process we discussed in chapter 6. Only as one does not have to be the person who succeeds in helping this person; only as one can play one's part, confident that if one does, the other person will find all the help that he is able to find in his situation, will this actually come true. To be sure of this, though, takes both courage and humility.

The introduction of difference, and criteria for it, were discussed in some detail in chapter 5. As a reminder, however, they might be expressed as two principles, in the following form.

20. *Introduce difference where*
    (a) *there is a firm base of empathy and support;*
    (b) *the difference is an important part of the helped person's current reality;*
    (c) *there is an element of challenge, searching, or a patent contradiction, in the picture being presented;*
    (d) *you are prepared to help the client with his reaction to it.*

21. *Express difference, where possible, in the client's own terms.*

In addition to these twenty-one points, which have been presented mostly in a positive form, there have been a number of cautions suggested in the course of the book to date which warn the helper against practices that are all too common mistakes in helping. Some of these are very general and will naturally be avoided, as far as possible, by those who have grasped the essential nature of helping. Such are warnings against trying to establish a "good" relationship apart from the helping process, against false reassurance, protectiveness, or indulgence, sympathy rather than empathy, and too insistent a desire to help. These are so much part of the whole theory that they have little part in a list of suggestions for practice. Two, however, which might be included because they are somewhat specific and might be recalled at the moment that the temptation arises are:

22. *Avoid trying to justify reality,* discussed more fully in chapter 5 (p. 78).

23. *Be chary of using the question, "Why?"* discussed in the same chapter (pp. 68-69). Not only is "why" an unproductive question, it is by its very nature accusatory and it is backward rather than forward looking. Recently, in making a study of a Children's Home, I asked for lots to be drawn for a panel of adolescents with whom I might confer. One child so chosen was Ruth, who, I was told, "could not talk to men" and would be useless on such a panel. Yet no child I have ever talked with tried harder to express to me her feelings about the Home. When I reported this I was met with amazement, as if I had worked a miracle and somehow dissipated this child's fear of my sex. But sex was not the problem at all. What men had always asked Ruth was, "Ruthie, why do you behave as you do?" whereas my question had been, "Ruth, do you think that you can stand it here?"

A third, which may need further discussion is

24. *Use careful discrimination in the giving of praise.* Praise is a device used by many would-be helpers. It is thought of as a way of showing appreciation of another, and encouraging him to greater effort. To the extent that it remains this and nothing more it is a helpful thing. But it is very easy to make something else of it.[3] It can become a way of purchasing a relationship on insufficient grounds. It is often a form of false reassurance: "I'm sure you can do it," when in fact one cannot. Its most serious consequence is, however, when it implies an expectation of another which he feels to be unrealistic. Nothing is more frightening than to be praised above what one knows to be one's capabilities or deserts.

To praise another may be also a subtle way of underlining one's superiority to him. The right to apportion praise or blame is the right of a superior. We therefore perhaps need to distinguish between "praise" as an act of condescension and praise as appreciation for another's skills and efforts given as between equals. This is, perhaps, a rather difficult line to draw. Perhaps the best way of looking at it is to ask oneself what one hopes to gain by praising another. Is it simply to

3. For an excellent treatment of this, see Jessie Taft, "The 'Catch' in Praise," *Child Study* 7, no. 5 (February 1930) : 133-35, 150.

show one's natural appreciation, as perhaps when one praises a little girl who is attractively dressed? Is it a way of conveying one's real liking and respect, as when one compliments someone on a meaningful speech or a cook on a good dinner? Or is it a subtle way of trying to control another, to get him to repeat an action, or to disarm or placate him? Do you expect from praise something specific or only that this other person feel your liking and support?

Two last pieces of advice perhaps ought to be given to all those who attempt to help. The first is

25. *Know enough about the obvious signs of severe mental illness either to refer to a doctor, or to keep out of the situation.* This needs saying with some caution. Any person who is in trouble is in a sense mentally disturbed, and even people who are admittedly mentally ill can very often be helped with that part of their problem about which they can reason and feel quite rationally. But a person in a severe depression, or one who suffers from marked hallucinations or obsessions, or who is plainly living in a world far removed from reality, probably needs a kind of help which the ordinary helping person does not have the means to provide. One does not have to be a psychiatrist or to diagnose the illness to get a sense that this may be so. A failure to respond to any difference or reality, an excessive rationalization of highly illogical acts, an apparently fairly total disorganization may be signs about which advice needs to be sought.

It is perhaps particularly important to recognize the signs of one kind of mental illness, paranoia. This is not only because the paranoid is often perfectly rational except in relation to his one obsession, but because it can be extremely dangerous to become part of his fantasy. The paranoid is one who feels so hostile towards the world that to justify his hostility he must believe that he is being persecuted, or that the people he hates are committing terrible crimes. The danger is that he often comes to the conclusion that he has a right, and sometimes a mandate directly from God, to avenge himself or to vindicate the right, and the helping person who holds firm or will not let him have his own way is sometimes included in those against whom he must seek revenge.

One need not, I think spend one's time suspecting paranoia in the people one is helping. In more than thirty years of helping I have come across only three whose disturbance was deep enough to cause me to take precautions. It might be wise to do so when someone dwells at great length on the injuries done him or when he uses in doing so physically aggressive terms such as "a knife in the back," but we need to remember that mental illness is only an exaggeration of an escape from reality to which all of us are prone. We are all a little paranoid.

The last piece of advice is the following:

26. *Don't expect quick results with problems involving long established habits.* This has particular reference to drinking, or drug taking, or certain forms of sexuality. These have the nature of an illness, even though one might want to dispute the literal correctness of describing them as such. They are often associated with a kind of character that is perhaps in our present state of knowledge less amenable to help than any other. This very character is in itself full of traps for the helper. It is often very charming, apparently very frank, and full of promises that look like the beginning of movement. Such people can be helped, as Alcoholics Anonymous has shown, and can be helped by the kind of methods described in this book, especially with their related problems, but a great deal of what they do is only tenuously within their power to change.

These twenty-six suggestions, then, are presented for what they are worth to the helping person. They are not an exhaustive list and any practiced helper would have others he would suggest and perhaps some he would modify or leave out. For the convenience of the student they are listed here in one list:

—Start with the request as it comes to you.

—Respond to feeling rather than to literal content.

—Recognize likely feelings even before they are expressed.

—When dealing with an angry or rejecting person, keep your attention on his feeling and do not attempt to defend what he is feeling about.

—Listen rather than explain or instruct.

—Hold fast to your function as a helper. Do not take over the helped person's decisions, but do not allow him to control the conditions of help.

—Make clear, as soon as possible, both the conditions of service and authority and roles of everyone concerned.

—If possible, set limits, particularly in time.

—Help the helped person express what he wants and then work with him toward how much of it he can have.

—Allow the person you are helping to fail if he wants to.

—Do not defend a reality that you cannot or do not intend to change.

—Formulate the helped person's problem from time to time as you see it.

—Partialize the problem.

—End the interview at the point where a decision has been made.

—Leave something to work on for next time.

—Test out decisions through requiring action to confirm them.

—In offering advice, leave room for modifications.

—Where important decisions are made, use, if possible, physical movement or action to symbolize what is happening.

—Start each separate contact where the helped person is at that time.

—Introduce differences where

    —there is a firm base of empathy and support.

    —the difference is an important part of the helped person's reality.

    —there is an element of challenge or a patent contradiction in the picture being presented.

    —you are prepared to help the client with his reaction to it.

—Express difference, where possible, in the client's own terms.

—Avoid trying to justify reality.

—Be chary of using the question, "Why?"

—Use careful discrimination in the giving of praise.

—Know enough about the obvious signs of severe mental illness either to refer to a doctor, or keep out of the situation.

—Don't expect quick results with problems involving long-established habits.

VIII. HELPING AND CURRENT VALUE-SYSTEMS

In describing help in this book we have made a number of value judgments some of which are:

—that people should be free to choose;

—that the individual matters, and that his interests cannot be wholly subjected to those of the community;

—that man has neither the right nor the ability to judge his fellows in terms of what they deserve;

—that helping people find their own way is better than controlling them, however subtly;

—that feelings, and personal relationships, matter;

—that people should be treated as "subjects" and not as "objects."

Not everyone would, or does agree with these values. One could equally well uphold that the ability to get along in life, avoid stress or trouble, and acquire adaptive skills was what really mattered, that choice is unimportant, that the well-being of the community is much more worth attaining than any individual goal and that people, on the whole, like a measure of control.[1]

It would not be easy to prove this matter one way or the other, even by the most careful research. The nearest we could come to it would be to say that most people wanted one thing or another, and we know enough about the difficulty of the word "want" to question its validity as a unit of measurement. Outside this we could only say that making certain assumptions about man does or does not lead to certain results.

These results would have to be measured in turn in terms of value judgments that are in themselves unprovable. The only situation in which this kind of research would be valuable to us would be where it could show that belief in one assumption led to a conclusion that violated a value we hold or was inconsistent with itself. If we believed, for instance, both that man operated best in an atmosphere of permissiveness, which would be an assumption about him, and that

1. The classic study of this desire is Erich Fromm's *Escape from Freedom* (New York, 1941).

creativity was good, which would be a value judgment and it could be shown that permissiveness led to a loss of creativity, we would have objective reason to abandon one or the other.

All we can say then is that these values are necessary to the kind of help that this book describes. We then begin arguing in circles. For clearly, unless one holds these values the kind of help described in this book will not make sense. We will want to do something different— perhaps to condition, or to control, or to discount relationship. We could argue most cogently for our point of view and invoke both our experience and our observation of what people are like and how they behave. We could bring scientific theory to our aid. I read recently in a short editorial in one of those science-fiction magazines that takes seriously the extrapolation of present trends a most convincing application of the theory of evolution to society, with the suggestion that man as an individual could be likened to a single cell, such as amoeba, who was developing, on a vast evolutionary scale, into a colony or society, such as volvox, but would eventually discover, in becoming a specialized part of an organism, access to powers and consciousness hitherto undreamed. Although this is an extreme and imaginative example, many social scientists today appear to be moving in something of the same direction.

There is no point in attempting, even if one should want to do so, to refute such conclusions. In the end it comes down to the question of what one believes the universe, and man, and society are all about, whether they have a purpose and what this might be. In one sense this is a personal matter, and values such as we have suggested can be thought of as wholly individual results of any one man's experience. On the other hand most of our values can be seen to be products of certain common sets of assumptions about the nature of man and society which we have learned and grown up with. We may sometimes react against these, but in general we do even this within the framework of certain common value assumptions.

Because these systems of thought have such a strong influence on us, and because they are systems, having some inner logical consistency, rather than being mere accretions of disconnected value-judgments, it seems important to recognize the effect they have on helping. We may not realize, as we begin to act, that we do so largely in response to one or another of these systems, but to the extent that our values are anything more than idiosyncratic and have any base beyond purely personal preference—to the extent, that is, that our values have any roots—we are apt to be influenced by them.

There are in our culture three such more or less logical systems. There are variations on these, and perversions of them, which may be held by some to be distinct belief systems, but for the purposes of this discussion these three may be sufficient.

The first such system, and possibly the most powerful among people as a whole might be called capitalist-puritan or CP for short. Its basic assumptions might be summarized as follows:

(1)   Man is responsible for his own success or failure.
(2)   Human nature is basically evil, but can be overcome by an act of will.
(3)   Man's primary purpose is the acquisition of material prosperity, which he achieves through hard work.
(4)   The primary purpose of society is the maintenance of law and order in which this acquisition is possible.
(5)   The unsuccessful, or deviant, person is not deserving of help, although efforts should be made, up to a point, to rehabilitate him or to spur him to greater efforts on his own behalf.
(6)   The primary incentives to change are to be found in economic or physical rewards and punishments.

The prevalence of these assumptions needs no emphasis at this time. The 1968 election in the United States is ample evidence of it. It is the creed popularly thought of as "American" or even common sense, and as such is part of the heritage of most of us.

Where the system is overtly puritan rather than capitalist, it is officially God, not man, who determines man's success or failure. Although, philosophically, this might seem to make a big difference, in practice it does not. For one thing, few CP's really believe it, or act as if they do. So closely have God's favor and worldly success become identified that the successful are thought of as "good" and the unsuccessful as "bad" or inferior. Man takes over what was originally God's prerogatives of judgment and chastisement and those who do not exercise sufficient ambition or will are shamed, exhorted, punished, or left to the workings of the economic system.

Where the CP system of beliefs is associated with certain other religious values it has strong ethical content, in which success and failure to achieve certain ethical goals is thought of in almost exactly the same way as are material achievement and its opposite. The two systems meet in the matter of work, which has both a material and an ethical value and in statements applying ethical standards to business enterprise, such as the statement, "Honesty is the best policy," or emphasis on the "service" motive in business.

Where the system is associated with religious or ethical concepts of man's responsibility to his neighbor, the result may be a real compassion for the unfortunate, such as the orphan or the widow, who have not overtly at least contributed to their own misfortune. The relationship created is normally one of condescension, however, and often demands gratitude or unusual virtue in the person receiving help.

Because the system has a religious base it is thought of by some as representing the total religious point of view. Herbert Bisno, in his *Philosophy of Social Work*[2] for instance, takes issue with what he considers basic Protestant or Catholic dogma in each of the first six principles of social work philosophy he enunciates. Yet all six of the principles he rejects are not so much religious principles as derivations from a particular theology that have become absorbed into the CP system of belief.

The CP system of belief has been secularized to the point that many people believe in it with no religious consciousness. Others profess religious belief concurrent with it, as it were, or use religious statements to support what is essentially a doctrine of man necessary to laissez-faire capitalism. Max Weber, R. B. Perry, R. H. Tawney and others have traced this development and have given a number of reasons for it, which are not specifically relevant to this discussion.[3]

Almost diametrically opposed to this system is the one that can be called humanist-positivist-utopian, or HPU for short. This is the belief of most social scientists and many liberals, but is also held to some degree by people who profess CP views and by many religious people, despite some inherent contradiction. Summarized its basic assumptions can be presented as follows:

(1) The primary purpose of society is to fulfill man's needs both material and emotional.

(2) If man's needs were fulfilled, then he would attain a state that is variously described, according to the vocabulary used by the specific HPU system, as that of goodness, maturity, adjustment, or productivity, in which most of his and society's problems would be solved.

(3) What hampers him from attaining this state is external circumstance, not in general under his individual control. This, in

2. Herbert Bisno, *The Philosophy of Social Work* (Washington, 1953), pp. 5-24.

3. Max Weber, *The Protestant Ethic and the Rise of Capitalism* (London, 1930); R. B. Perry, *Puritanism and Democracy* (New York, 1944); R. H. Tawney, *Religion and the Rise of Capitalism* (London, 1926). See also a nontheological rejoinder to Weber, nearer to my thought here, H. M. Robertson's *The Rise of Economic Individualism* (Cambridge, England, 1933).

various HPU systems, has been ascribed to lack of education, economic circumstance, his childhood relationships, and his social environment.

(4) These circumstances are subject to manipulation by those possessed of sufficient technical and scientific knowledge, using, in general, what is known as "the scientific method," and consequently

(5) man, and society, are ultimately perfectible.[4]

HPU-ism is perhaps difficult to see as a unitary theory, since many of its devotees have relied on a single specific for creating the utopia it envisages. Dewey, for instance, a strong HPU-ist, saw education as the answer; Marx, reform of the economic system, and Freud, the early Freud at least, the removal of repressions. Erich Voegelin in his *New Science of Politics*[5] calls these the "modern gnostics," each of whom has his own way of creating the Kingdom of Heaven. Yet the underlying assumptions of each of these writers is the same. They differ only in the specific remedy they prescribe and in the degree to which they are primarily positivist or humanist in temper.

The sources of this system are to be found in the Enlightenment and its first prophets were Rousseau and Comte. Today it is most obvious in the Poverty program, but many of its assumptions are inherent in modern materialism, at which point it joins hands with and lives somewhat uneasily with CP thought.

Behind, and yet parallel with these two systems is a third, for which it is harder to find a name. Perhaps the best that can be devised is the familiar "Judeo-Christian" tradition. "Biblical" might be more accurate, but has connotations suggesting literal acceptance of proof texts on all sorts of unrelated matters and an absolute authority. CP thought also claims that it is biblical.

Yet the system is essentially the system of assumptions about man and the universe that are inherent in the Jewish and Christian Scriptures, and is accepted, at least officially, although not always acted upon by the mainstream religious bodies, Catholic, Protestant, and Jewish.

Summarizing its basic assumptions in the same way as we have done for the CP and HPU systems these might be presented as follows:

4. This formulation (my own) first appears in my essay, "Psychiatry and the Care of the Poor," in Helmut Schoeck and James W. Wiggins, eds., *Psychiatry and Responsibility* (New York, 1959) .

5. Erich Voegelin, *The New Science of Politics* (Chicago, 1952) , p. 129.

(1) man is a created being one of whose major problems is that he acts as if he were not and tries to be autonomous;

(2) man is fallible, but at the same time capable of acts of great courage or unselfishness;

(3) the difference between men, in terms of good and bad, is insignificant compared with the standard demand by their creator, and, as a consequence, man cannot judge his fellow in such terms;

(4) man's greatest good lies in terms of his relationship with his fellows and with his creator;

(5) man is capable of choice, in the "active and willing" sense, but may need help in making this choice;

(6) love is always the ultimate victor over force.

The position of this ethic vis-à-vis the others is a complicated one. In one sense it lies parallel to them and is a viable alternative, or a middle ground, especially in item (2), its recognition of man's simultaneous fallibility and potential. In another, it lies behind them and makes both of them possible.

This may be much easier to see in relation to CP thought than it is to HPU. CP thought is a particular and perverted form of this doctrine. But much HPU thought has denied any concept of a creator and has specifically denied item (1)—man's dependence on any purpose or direction outside himself. Yet much of the actual value system practiced by humanists has its roots in Judeo-Christian concepts, including nonjudgmentalism, emphasized very strongly in early Christian writers such as Chrysostom in the fourth century,[6] and man as a choosing being, inherent in Jewish and Christian thought since the myth of the Fall. Justice in the sense of equality of opportunity and a fair share of this world's goods is originally a Hebrew concept; so is the ultimate worth and dignity of all men, not just of an elite.

That these values have been adopted by HPU thought, particularly in its humanistic aspect, is indubitable. But in having been so adopted, they have been cut off from their roots. There is nothing in HPU thought that makes them an utter necessity, to which HPU thought can return if they should be temporarily lost. They are inherited values not essential to a strictly scientific view of the world or of society. Judeo-Christian values can therefore be seen as in some cases an alternative, in some a progenitor, and in some a check or critique of the values of the social scientist.

6. See, for instance, his *Fourteenth Homily on the Book of Romans.*

Beyond the three major sets of assumptions we have outlined there are a number of others that are possible. Existentialism emphasizes man's choice and encounter with reality. Except in its more nihilistic form it can, however, reinforce certain aspects of the Judeo-Christian system and certainly does not contradict it. The system of natural law emphasizes man's power of reason. There is a Thomistic school of helping theory,[7] just as there is an existentialist,[8] but these are more variants of other belief systems than fully-developed systems of their own.

Probably most people are influenced to some extent by all three of these sets of assumptions. All have some value and it is not so much a matter of saying that one is good and another bad as it is of taking a position nearer or further from one or another extreme. Yet we do need to explore which set of assumptions is more likely to preserve the kind of values we see as important in helping, and which is most compatible with what we can observe in the process of helping as we know it.

Quite obviously the CP position is in general the least likely to lead to help. If man is totally responsible for his own actions, if he can better his condition by an act of will, if he can be induced to change by punishment or reward, then helping becomes a simple matter of us arranging the appropriate rewards and punishments. There is no room for relationship, or concern for another, except in a highly condescending and judgmental way.

This is the view of man that created the workhouse and the pauper's oath, which demands of children in Children's Homes or welfare clients that they work harder and behave better than other people, and which is terrified of any welfare measure that would make the receipt of relief in any way bearable or dignified. It assumes without question that welfare clients will "naturally" lie, cheat, or steal if given the chance, prefer laziness to work, and feign sickness in order to shirk working. And typically it is much more concerned to punish the few who may do such things than help the many who do not.

Yet it is not without some positive features. It does at least recognize that it is the person in trouble who must bear the final responsibility for his own betterment, and as such it has moderated some of the

7. See, for example, Mary J. McCormick, *Diagnostic Casework in the Thomistic Pattern* (New York, 1954) .

8. See, for instance, John J. Stretch, "Existentialism: A Proposed Philosophical Orientation for Social Work," *Social Work* 12 (October 1967) : 97-102.

extreme implications of the HPU set of assumptions which, for many helping people, have appeared to supersede it.

In its initial impact on helping theory and practice HPU thought produced a tremendous outpouring of love and understanding. The helped person was freed from the total responsibility he had borne up till then for his own condition. He was no longer a second-class citizen, judged by his fellows. He was valued for his own sake. The particular social science which became the model for helping in the 1930s—analytical psychology—also stressed certain thing which, if not strictly HPU—and indeed I shall argue that they are basically Judeo-Christian and not HPU at all—were at least acceptable to those who claimed to be humanists and utopians. These were in general:

1. A sense of man's common vulnerability. There were, and this is one of Freud's greatest contributions to helping, no longer "sick" and "well" people, but people who were in greater or less difficulty with problems that trouble us all;

2. A habit of looking at problems from the point of view of the helped person rather than from the outside, that is, treating him as subject rather than as object;

3. An emphasis on relationship as the principal means of help;

4. At least in the earlier stages a degree of awe in the face of new knowledge of a somewhat mysterious nature.

But these, which are philosophical rather than scientific statements, were in a sense incidental to rather than part and parcel of HPU-ism's basic assumptions about man. For HPU-ism makes other assumptions which are more questionable. Among these, culled from Herbert Bisno's attempt, in 1952, to discover a common "philosophy" of social work, are that all human suffering is undesirable, and should be prevented, or at least alleviated, that all human behavior is the result of interrelationship between the biological organism and its environment and that the scientific method is basic to an understanding of man.[9]

Let us look at the first of these in terms of what we know about helping. Bisno makes this statement as a reaction against the so-called religious, but actually CP, belief that suffering is either a consequence of sin or is in some way in itself ennobling.

There are of course kinds of apparently purposeless suffering which one would hasten to alleviate wherever they were found. But it is also true that some suffering is a necessary preliminary or an accompani-

9. Bisno, *The Philosophy of Social Work*, pp. 5, 6, and 72.

ment to growth. Sometimes one has to come up against despair or pain in order to move forward to a new organization of oneself.[10] If one's emphasis is on the pain or suffering, then one tends to forego the growth that can ensue from a painful struggle. This may be obvious from our former discussion of the importance of not taking away a person's problem, but the tendency to try to relieve pain on any and all occasions is one of the strongest temptations a helping person can meet.

The desire to avoid pain at the cost of growth can be seen perhaps most clearly in many people's attitudes towards unmarried mothers. Reacting perhaps from a moralistic stance, doctors and social workers identify so strongly with the pain of giving up a child the mother may love, that if she cannot keep her child they make of the whole experience an unreal fantasy in which she never really has a baby at all, so quickly is it whisked away to be placed for adoption. She has little chance to come to terms with what has happened, and so little chance not to repeat the experience. She has little chance to make her decision out of love rather than fear or to abide with it once made. The results are all too often recidivism, an inability to mature, or a deep sense of guilt for having given up her child. The painless way of doing something is sometimes the least productive.

Perhaps this is a semantic problem. Perhaps we need here to make a distinction and even find different words for two very different things. One is needless or meaningless suffering, which weakens or leaves scars, to which we might give the name trauma, and the other that temporary pain that would appear to accompany any meaningful change and is indeed the cost of it, which we might call the pain of growth. It should not be forgotten, too, that some people may deliberately choose to suffer in order to reach a greater goal. Mahatma Gandhi would be a good modern example.

Confusion between these two different kinds of pain is particularly apparent when the pain suffered is that of loss. Tennyson once said that it was better to have loved and lost then never to have loved at all. But, in modern psychology, so much emphasis has been placed on the pain of loss that this equation is often reversed. It is better, in many people's minds, not to love in case one has to give up. One finds this argument used in discussing foster homes for children, and not so long ago after a painful removal of a child from a home where he was

10. See, for instance, Marian R. Gennaria, *Pain: A Factor in Growth and Development* (New York, 1943).

not loved too much but loved too possessively, a responsible newspaper suggested that foster children should be moved routinely every few months for fear of such attachments developing.

Yet separation and loss are part of all human experience. We could not in fact do without them. The greatest separation of all occurs almost at the beginning, with the act of birth itself. The child progressively separates himself from his parents, by going to school, to college, and eventually by becoming independent. All these separations are at the time painful, but not traumatic. We grow through them. The often-made assertion that all separation is traumatic, which has become almost an article of belief in those who work with dependent children, is simply not true. Painful, yes, but not traumatic. What is traumatic is not the separation itself but the feelings that so often accompany it—the shock, the knowledge of rejection, the anger, and the sense of one's own badness when one suddenly loses a home.

The helping person will then assert that love and concern and relationship are more important than their loss. He will, to return for a moment to the unmarried mother, want her to give her child up, if that is what she plans to do, out of love for him and not out of a fear that she might love him. He will not, unless she forces him to it, shelter her from the pain of loving and giving up. He may suffer with her in the process—and indeed helping can be both painful and utterly exhausting—but if he really wants to help her he will not deny her this experience. Nor, if we really have love and concern for others, do we deny them their struggles. To protect someone from reality inevitably means that we have some lack of respect for him.

Bisno's second assertion, that all human behavior is the result of interaction between the biological organism and the environment, commits us to a belief that man is a mechanical being, however complicated, and this is directly contrary to any assumption that man is a choosing being, in the active or willing sense. It denies him any part in his own development. He can only be manipulated, or possibly liberated, supposing one to hold also the general HPU belief in the essential healthiness of the mechanism. It therefore provides us with the basis of a control process, but not one of help, and is one of the reasons why social scientists appear to be turning more and more to control rather than to helping procedures.[11]

11. This trend has been apparent for a number of years. I first noted it in an article called "The Political Theory Implicit in Social Casework Theory," *American Political Science Review* 47 (December 1953) : 1076-90, in which, however, I believe I was too sanguine about the ability of a particular theory of social casework to resist

The same danger is inherent in the belief that the scientific method is basic to an understanding of man. As long as the science that was relied on was analytical psychology, there were the other values stressed on which we have commented—man's common vulnerability, a viewpoint that treated him as subject and not as object, a belief in relationship, even an awe in the contemplation of an internal, subconscious world.

But analytical psychology is not the only social science, and it is scientifically one that is considerably suspect, particularly in its inability to produce certain kinds of social results. Professional helpers, particularly those who are concerned chiefly with helping people adapt to their culture, are turning more and more to the external sciences, such as sociology, for the solution of social problems. These sciences have no use for the philosophical emphases that analytical psychology contributed to helping. They look at man from the outside, from the viewpoint of society, rather than from his own. They care little for relationship and have little sense of awe.

These factors are, in fact, more in the Judeo-Christian tradition than they are in the HPU. Man's common vulnerability is, as Norman Brown points out, a secular formulation of the doctrine of original sin.[12] The question of man as object or subject has been discussed more fully by theologians like Buber and Berdyaev than it has been explored by scientists, and both relationship and awe lie at the heart of the Judeo-Christian tradition.

Paul Halmos, in his *Faith of the Counsellors*, points to a further limitation.[13] Although, he points out, psychoanalysts who claim to be wholly scientific, held, or have held, a theory of man's total ambivalence, a balance between love and hate, between life and death wishes, all helping people tacitly believe in the eventual victory of "love" over hate. "Love" he defines in a rather inclusive way, to include what we have called sympathy as well as empathy and simple friendliness or warmth.

Halmos sees this as a paradox and on this basis he constructs an interesting but somewhat mystical theory on the importance of para-

the trend. The actual change is pinpointed in my "Self-Determination and the Changing Role of the Social Worker," in *Values in Social Work: A Re-examination,* Monograph IX, in the series sponsored by the Regional Institute Program of the National Association of Social Workers (1967) , pp. 84-97.

12. Norman O. Brown, *Life Against Death: The Psychoanalytic Meaning of History* (New York, 1959) , p. 6.

13. Paul Halmos, *The Faith of the Counsellors: A Study in the Theory and Practice of Social Casework and Psychotherapy* (London, 1965) , pp. 74-90.

dox. No one would deny that paradoxes exist in all human operations, and we have already encountered a major example in the nature of empathy. But one might wonder if all that is being said here is that strictly mechanical and measurable "scientific" theory of man is simply not compatible with what we know happens in the helping process. Man simply does not move entirely in terms of stimuli, insight, environmental strain, or stress. There is something more to him that responds to such immeasurable things as empathy, concern, challenge, the personality of the helper, and this all good helpers know.

But the most serious difficulty with a strictly HPU system of beliefs arises from the assumption that man is naturally good, and that given opportunity he will demonstrate this. This, a humanist belief that we owe in the first place to Rousseau, is hardly scientific. It sounds a most hopeful theory and is certainly more productive than its CP opposite, that man is basically evil. But it does not stand up to examination. Man is not a rational creature, most of the time, and he does not always choose the good. He is often petty or selfish, shortsighted, defensive, although he can be generous, loving, imaginative, or kind. He is rarely entirely one or the other. To believe in his perfectibility or his natural goodness leads inevitably to disappointment.

And disappointment, unfortunately, leads to the necessity to take increasing measures to ensure that he does not fail one. This is the lesson, and the paradox, of many humanistic movements, that they begin with an unreasonable estimate of man's nature which he cannot possibly live up to, and then, when he fails to fulfill these expectations, either make more and more exceptions to the general rule, or assume that some outside force is intervening that must be combatted.

Eventually the exception becomes the rule and more and more people are protected from their own weakness by a smaller and smaller elite. A belief in the natural goodness of man leads to its own absolute opposite. The process can be seen clearly in the course of the Russian Revolution from 1917 to today. Lenin believed that once the economic system has been righted there would be no need for a state. Man would collaborate naturally. Yet the final result has been one of the most pervasive and intrusive states the world has ever seen.

Much the same sort of thing has happened to the overoptimistic estimate of man's nature that was current in the social philosophy of the 1930s. Social work, in America at least, can be shown, during the 1950s and 1960s to have turned more and more to methods of control, although this has recently been challenged by younger social workers and indeed by much of social work's clientele. Yet, where it exists, and it does so quite strongly, this emphasis has been accelerated by the belief in the absolute nature of the scientific method. For it is a demonstrable fact that man analyzed objectively in terms of his adaptability, social relationships, etc., is a bungling, capricious creature who often does not know his own best interests. It is very easy to pass from this to a belief that he needs controlling for his own good. What, then, is the alternative? It seems to me that it needs to be to accept the enlightenment that HPU thought has brought, but to recognize its limitations and to check some of its secondary values against the Judeo-Christian tradition.

This does not mean, let me hasten to say, that one must assent to certain theological doctrines or be a "believer" to be a helping person. Many of the greatest helpers have been secular humanists—in fact the record of humanists is far better than that of Christians, although perhaps not of Jews in what they have contributed to helping and in their personal exercise of it.

It may be suggested that some of these humanists shared many of the assumptions of the Judeo-Christian tradition but hesitated to make this explicit because the CP set of assumptions claims a religious base. This has caused a revulsion against any helping theory couched in religious terms. Many church-related persons are basically CP in their assumptions.

What does seem clear is that neither the CP assumptions nor the HPU are in themselves enough without this tradition. Both offer certain insights—in the case of HPU thought some very valuable ones—without which modern helping would not have developed. But both break down as absolute systems. We need many of their insights but we need something more.

One of the most important insights of the Judeo-Christian tradition is the nature of man himself. He is neither the evil being of capitalist-puritan belief, nor is he as good as many HPU-ists believe. But it is not so much a matter of steering between an over- and an underestimation of his nature as it is of recognizing two different factors in his make-up. The first is his fallibility and the second his ability, in certain circumstances, to work out for himself something somewhat better than his fallibility would suggest. This is far from saying that he has in him a potential which needs only some triggering, or some favorable circumstance, to tap. It means rather that with help, or where he is put to it, or from the depths of despair, he can sometimes transcend his own fallibility. Moreover this ability is found in the most unlikely places. It is often demonstrated by those whom objectively one would be forced to believe are unequipped or incapable. This is the constant surprise one comes up against in helping. Not infrequently it tends to have the air of the miraculous about it.

This tradition has some other things to say to the matter of helping. It is concerned with choosing, in the active and willing sense. But again, perhaps we need to make clear that to believe in the necessity of man choosing for himself is not a statement that he knows best what is good for him or will always choose the right. To believe that would be sentimentality. That he "knows what is best for himself" is true only in a special sense: only he knows what he can live with, and only he can put himself into living the kind of life he chooses or is chosen for him. Unless then he chooses to live this life he will for the most part only go through the motions of living. He will be living at second hand, which is exactly what the believer in his wholly mechanical or biological nature believes that he does in any case.

Nor are we concerned here with what social workers have called, rather loosely, the "right to self-determination." This has to do more with selective choice than with active and willing choice, and if held too absolutely can lead to protecting people from the consequences of their choice, which is the real problem of permissiveness.

As a political and social question, such a right has many obvious limitations, such as the law, the right of others, and perhaps, to some extent, one's own good, although we have to be very careful here to distinguish between some clear and more or less objective disaster with which one cannot cope and what some other person thinks would be good for one. The distinction is not easy, and it would seem, should generally be submitted to law, or political process, rather than the personal decision of the would-be helper.

From the point of view of helping, the question is all too often asked the wrong way round. It is not that the helping person has in his power the granting or withholding of this right. This is usually determined by society, law, or the culture. The question is rather whether the helper has the right, in the name of help, to limit or try to constrain this right beyond these limits. The use of assumed power, based on some assumed authority of skill, knowledge, or supported responsibility, is a dangerous weapon however benevolently it is exercised.

Most of us have a preference for a social and political system in which people are as free as possible to make their own decisions, but none of us imagines that this can be absolutely so. It is therefore very difficult to enunciate a belief in a right to self-determination in any realistic terms, though not so hard, perhaps, to determine how much one, as an individual or a member of a profession, believes oneself authorized to intervene.

The Judeo-Christian tradition also emphasizes relationship, non-judgmentalism, the importance of personal as well as societal problems, and the importance of feelings which some forms of HPU-ism deny. It is also committed to the understanding that pride, or the desire to act as master rather than servant, is the primary sin. It is in this particular that it can be perhaps the greatest moderating force on useful and enlightening scientific discovery. For science, unfortunately, has no built-in protection against pride. While many scientists are humble it is only too easy for the man who has some knowledge to believe that this very knowledge gives him the right to control or dominate others.

IX. EXCEPTIONS AND ALTERNATIVES

The method of helping described in this book is one which has been found helpful in a large range of situations. Although the claim has been made that it is based to some extent on certain universal principles, no claim has been made that it can help to solve all of man's problems, or indeed help every man, or that alternative theories cannot or have not been devised. Nor of course is it in any way a finished product. There is much about helping that we do not know, and much obviously to be discovered. Many of the people whom at the moment we think of as unhelpable may be discovered not to be so, and some of these will be found helpable perhaps through a refinement of our present methods rather than through something entirely different.

Quite early in the book a distinction was made between "helping" and "control." It was recognized there that there are certain situations in which some measure of control may be necessary, and that in some situations a measure of control may be a needed preliminary to taking help. How often this is the case, and how differently such people or such situations need to be handled is clearly a question of some importance to the helper, if only to help him know what he should not attempt himself and where his efforts to try to help on his own may only delay a sick person getting the treatment he needs. A helping person may also want to know where the methods described in this book, which for brevity's sake I shall refer to, with no implication of its universality, as "the helping process," are inapplicable, if they are, and what else he or someone else might do.

While we might discount those who believe, however sincerely, that men in general are so controlled by their own experiences that some form of treatment or reeducation is necessary wherever there are problems to solve, we do need to pay respectful attention to those whose experiences suggest that this is far more common than this book would seem to imply. There are, so they contend, so many people who are crippled by their intrapsychic problems, so limited by their lack of intelligence, or so handicapped by their lack of normal human experiences and stimulation, that to believe that even a majority of men are capable of arriving at decisions, or can respond to reality, is an illusion. Many people require, in their view, a pretty complete reeducation of some sort even to begin a process of amelioration, and in this the helping person must be much more active than we have suggested and must make many more decisions about and for the other person than we have allowed him. To them the view of man as a decision-making creature, capable of finding solutions of his own even with the help of another, is as unrealistic as is the belief that he would be able to manage his own affairs simply if he were given the material means to do so.

Let us be clear at the beginning that there are people who are in need of something more than is contained in the helping process. They are in need of medication, of a carefully organized environment, and in some form or other of a complete reeducation. There are also some people whom we do not at the moment know how to help, either through the helping process or through any other method. But who they are, and how common they are, and to what extent their condition makes the helping process inapplicable is another matter.

The first group of people one naturally thinks of are the mentally ill. Undoubtedly many of these need both medication and a specialized environment. Some need an interpretative form of psychotherapy. And obviously if one is too far removed from reality one is, in certain parts of one's life at least, unamenable to a form of help in which the presentation of reality with empathy and support is the guiding principle.

This very principle has, however, recently been challenged by Melvin Glasser in his book, *Reality Therapy*,[1] and although it is difficult to accept his whole thesis, his work certainly suggests that there are groups of those who were previously thought to be in need of interpretative analysis who can be helped by holding them to reality with sufficient understanding and support. There is also some question whether Glasser's main success has not been in relation to what is known professionally as character disorders rather than psychosis and severe neurosis.

At the same time it should be said that certain forms of more conventional psychotherapeutic treatment rely exactly on this process, the difference being that the reality concerned is dependent on the therapist's specialized knowledge of the meaning of irrational thoughts and behavior. In these cases it is not that the theory does not apply but

1. See reference to this book on p. 16.

that this kind of treatment requires a special knowledge of reality to be applicable.

And, although a mentally sick person may need specialized treatment for certain problems, he is often most capable of making other decisions for himself. It is as if he had two parts, a sick part and a well, and although the sick part of him may be large, he rarely entirely gives up the well. A person with even minimal knowledge of his sickness can often help him with realistic plans for himself or for his family, while his more basic problems are getting the treatment that they need. But the two forms of help, or "help" and "treatment," need to go together. This is what makes it possible for social workers who disclaim therapeutic goals, ministers, and many other helpers to have a real role in the mental hospital.

A second group that is generally thought of as incapable of playing the role of the decision-making helped person is the feebleminded, but here we need to be very careful about whom we include. Obviously the ament or the idiot who cannot express himself at all or is incapable of any kind of reason cannot be helped by the kind of methods we have described. But to believe that the merely retarded or "subnormal" cannot respond to the elements of the process would be very far off the mark.

Helping depends very little on intelligence in this sense. It is too closely allied to feeling, and the equation between feeling and the power to conceptualize it or to reason about it is an entirely false one, as we have long since discovered in our work with children. Just as the effective age at which we can help a child come to some decision about himself has been pushed back as we have learned to relate more closely to his often intense feelings, so that in some cases help has been given on a preverbal basis and to children as young as three or four months' old,[2] so some of the best examples of helping a person cope with his environment have been found, in my experience, in work with the mentally retarded.

I can remember in particular a girl of very low intelligence whose

2. See, for instance, Marion Gennaria, "Helping the Very Young Child to Participate in Placement," *Journal of Social Work Process* 3, no. 1 (1939) : 29-59, and the School of Social Work of the University of Pennsylvania's *Role of the Baby in the Placement Process* (Philadelphia, 1946). Some psychiatrists, however, question the reality of such help. Dr. Ner Littner, for example, in his *Primary Needs of Children—A One-to-One Relationship* (New York, 1959), has attacked Miss Gennaria's work and assigns the baby a much more passive role. The question of whether something real has taken place is a very difficult one to determine. In my experience it has and does.

reaction to the unreal expectations of her family had led her to neurotic self-mutilation and to a distrust of all authority being helped by a counselor to assert her determination to find a job consistent with her limitations and to plan realistically for it. This girl was able to come to a most realistic appraisal of her own capabilities, with no sense of self-pity, but in the course of her being helped had to come to some very serious decisions about her relationships to her family. While intelligence is of use in solving one's problems, especially those of a complex nature that require careful analysis, the basic problem of man is his inability to accept and to act on what he knows very well to be so.

Mention of children makes it perhaps necessary to discuss them specifically in relation to helping. Since many of the examples of helping given in this book are concerned with children, it is plain that both the theory and method apply to them, and at quite an early age. Yet children are incapable of making many decisions about their lives, about where they will live, for instance, and, according to their age, what they will eat, or wear, or do for a large part of the day. Indeed to force these decisions on them is often to put on them more than they can properly manage.

Perhaps no clearer example exists between the two kinds of choice than it does with children. Yet to consider them incapable of the kind of choice that helping requires is to fly in the face of the evidence. Children can and do feel deeply and they can and do decide what use they will make of a situation. Inez Baker has used the term "the recalcitrant strength of a child"[3] to describe a child's resistance to a situation he does not accept or understand, and the phrase is by no means too strong. Any child welfare worker who has seen a small infant either accept or refuse new parents, or any other change, will be aware of the strength of their resolution.

Although it will be recognized that children also need measures of control, particularly in the form of limits that do not apply to the adult population, they also require, by definition, a "parenting" type of relationship, in which influence, the setting of example and decision-making by others are natural elements.

This they presumably receive from their parents, or parent-substitutes, or surrogates, such as teachers. There has been much recognition lately of the problems that arise when such parenting is absent, or weak in quality. But there is another side to this coin. Much

3. Inez Baker, "Special Needs of Children," *Public Welfare* 4 (August 1946) : 178.

damage can be done to children if their ability to make decisions, to face reality, is not recognized. This has particularly come to light in dealing with children separated from their parents, where to protect them from the reality of their situation, to assume that what they need is parenting rather than help in facing reality, leads almost inevitably to despair, to detachment, or to unreal fantasy. Indeed most adults, in trying to help children who are not their own, fail because of their inability to treat children as capable of making decisions. They try to be surrogate parents rather than to help.

The senile are another group for whom the question of help or control inevitably arises. Undoubtedly some senile persons do need parenting or protection. Often this arises over the matter of living arrangements. An older person may be living alone. We think he ought to be in a nursing home or some such facility.

A group of public welfare workers dealing largely with the aged attempted recently to come up with some criteria for action on their part.[4] Their statement seems to me, with perhaps some interpretation, the best guidelines that could be developed. They begin by saying that "in some situations it may be necessary for the department to take the initiative to act on a client's behalf and may make plans for him contrary to his expressed will or without his full co-operation," which is simple realism. But, they add,

such action should be taken only when *all* (emphasis mine) of the following criteria are met:

(a) The danger to the client's life or health is imminent and either obvious or established by medical diagnosis (in other words, they are not going to decide on their own that this person is in need of care except on pretty good evidence).

(b) The client is unable to recognize the danger or to make plans on his own behalf. Except in emergency this should not be assumed unless
  (i) attempts have been made to plan with the client
  (ii) the reality of the situation has been presented to him with empathy and support (in other words, attempts have been made to help him) or
  (iii) the client's condition is such that to present reality to him would be patently useless or harmful.

Here they stopped to make sure that the client who knows what he is doing, who "prefers to live in a situation which he knows to be dangerous rather than seek security in less congenial circumstances"

4. Draft Manual Material on Services, Division of Adult Services, Department of Health and Welfare, State of Maine (1969), mimeographed, pp. 5-6.

should not be thought to have failed to make plans or to come to terms with reality.

They had in mind two specific situations. In one an old man, a logger by trade, old and feeble, lived alone in a shack in the woods. There was obvious danger to him. He had rigged up a signal system to call for help if he should be in trouble, but if he should happen to break a leg he might be unable to reach this, which he recognized. Nevertheless he was willing to take the risk, would be very unhappy away from the woods in which he was reared and told his social worker, with a twinkle in his eye, that he expected some day to leave his home in a pine box, but not by any other conveyance. In fact he found the social worker's concern amusing.

The other was an old lady, somewhat disoriented, living in a similar situation, but also amidst confusion and filth, to whom a boarding home had often been suggested, but who could never take the first steps towards a move or even agree to it, and who, because of the worker's failure to insist, eventually froze to death when her stove failed to function.

The group here clearly recognized the old man to be in a state of choice, the old woman to be in one of "nonchoice." Incidentally, or perhaps not so incidentally, there is some evidence that the old man's life-expectancy might be greater, even with the chance of accident, in his own shack than in a boarding home. Recent studies tend to suggest that to separate someone from his natural environment tends to accelerate death.

The group continued by requiring that

(c) no person having greater authority or responsibility—e.g. relatives or the police—are willing and able to take this responsibility.

(d) the need to take responsibility has been communicated to the client and the specific action outlined.

They suggest that such protective services should be accomplished through "persuasion, insistence, cajoling" (all recognized parenting or control techniques) but warn "even where the client cannot make major decisions necessary to his health or life he should be given the opportunity to make as many minor decisions as he possibly can."

Closely related to these situations is the right to die happy rather than have life artificially prolonged. Perhaps we should include the dying among those who are often denied help in favor of control.

A group that is often held not to be able to use help, in the sense that we are using the word, are those often labeled as suffering from character disorders. These are principally those who, although they have not lost all touch with reality and are not mentally ill in any medical sense, have become so wholly self-centered that all their energies are directed towards their own immediate advantage. They are those who appear to have grown up without a conscience and often with a very imperfect sense of the consequence of their acts. They trust to their ability to manipulate others to avoid trouble. Many people believe them to be essentially spoiled children whose parents have protected them from reality and excused or condoned their faults.

It is from this group that many criminals come. Indeed to be a criminal, rather than one who has committed a crime, is a form of character disorder.

These are perhaps the hardest people of all to help, by counseling, psychotherapy, or any other method. They lack what might seem the beginning desire to change since they have all too successfully insulated themselves against a belief that there is anything wrong or that their actions will result to their disadvantage. And there is no question but that they present the helper with his greatest challenge, particularly in view of the fact that the number of people who could be described in these terms appears to be increasing. Indeed it is not untrue to say that while in the first half of this century the majority of those who were in serious psychological trouble were psychotics and neurotics, in the second half the less approachable and often, for a time at least, socially more successful psychopath or character disorder may become the greatest problem.

The best that society, for the present, can do with some of these people is to protect society from them, and sometimes from themselves, by institutionalization. Where treatment is attempted, however, its principles are those of the helping process in a somewhat extreme form. Successful treatment of this group has been attempted by a somewhat remorseless holding to reality, and sometimes even the creation of deliberately harsh conditions, in the hope that anxiety may be raised and the patient be willing to take help. One device sometimes used is to divide the elements of the process, with a probation officer, a policeman, or a teacher doing the holding to reality and psychiatrist or psychologist standing ready to give empathy and support when any discomfort is seen. Where this is not possible a firm holding to reality is perhaps the first necessity. And here again we must speak relatively. Many people with so-called character disorders can be helped. It is only the more extreme example who eludes us.

The four groups discussed here—the seriously mentally ill, the truly feeble-minded, the senile, and the character disorder that is extremely well established—are perhaps what could be described as the recognizably sick part of the population. Although, in varying degrees, they can be helped through the helping process, this may either be very difficult or may need to be associated with some other form of treatment. As each group shades off, however, into a more normal relationship to reality, they prove helpable and in time we may find them increasingly so.

There remain certain other groups whom some people hold to be unable to use the process, or better helped in another way, and these are far more significant for any unified helping theory. They are those whose life experience, and in particular their experience of the parent-child relationship, has been so meager, or so twisted, that in the opinion of many who work with them the most helpful thing one can do is try to give them a better, if belated, experience of being loved and cared for, in a parental way. The helper becomes the "good" mother (or father), at least for a while, in the eventual hope, however, that the helped person will "grow up" and become able to conduct his own affairs.

The first group in our society to be recognized professionally as possibly needing this kind of "parenting" help was, in America at least, the unmarried mother.[5] Here the rationale was in keeping with current psychological theory. It has long been known that unmarried motherhood has a close relationship to unsatisfactory mother-daughter relationship, and, indeed, is much more common, apart from its occurence in segments of society where it is culturally more or less acceptable, where this relationship has been confining, moralistic, rivalrous, or distant. Unmarried mothers, too, are often, although by no means always, youngsters, to whom it is natural to offer a quasi-parental relationship. Professional thinking has also been swayed by a feeling of responsibility for the baby, which has made it important to some, at least, that the mother's decision should be a "right one."

The same divided responsibility may have been in part the reason why many social workers turned next to the neglecting parent as the subject of "parenting."[6] When a mother obviously does not know the

5. See Dorothy Hutchinson's "A Re-Examination of Some Aspects of Casework Practice in Adoption," *Child Welfare* 25, no. 9 (November 1946) : 4-7, 14.

6. The genesis of the parenting theory in relation to the neglecting parent is a complicated one, much involved with difficulty about the problem of self-determination and the growth of "aggressive" or "assertive" casework. I would trace it through articles such as Lionel Lane's "The 'Aggressive' Approach in Preventive Casework with Children's Problems," *Social Casework* 33 (February 1952) : 61-66;

first things about caring for children, when she is irresponsible, dirty, confused, and lacking in imagination, it is very easy to believe that the best possible thing to do is to take her under one's wing, to teach her, to set her a good example, to supervise her expenditures and in fact treat her as a child. It may be indeed that it is the lack of loving instruction from her own mother, the lack of someone with whom she could identify, that is the root cause of her present inability. And meanwhile there are children to consider. This line of thought has been carried out in a number of programs and social experiments, such as certain uses of the homemaker in the United States, and the hostels for inadequate families in Great Britain. It also appears in much of the literature on protective services, alongside literature on the same subject that emphasizes reality and choice.

Recently, however, this concept has been much enlarged, first to the so-called "hard-core" families on the relief rolls,[7] and then, by implication at least, to large segments of the poor, the "culturally deprived" or "socially disadvantaged." This has come, in America, with the rather alarming discovery that there is a "culture" of poverty, quite different from that of the middle classes. It has become clear that many assumptions that have been made about people and their capabilities were illusory, that there were hundreds and thousands of people in the United States who had not acquired the simplest living skills and were, as well, almost incapable of communicating their wants. In particular the assistance program, Aid to Families with Dependent Children, which had been based on a belief that if the means were given to them, families would find a way to live in decency and health and become independent was apparently resulting instead, in all too many cases, in successive generations of marginal, dependent living.

Various experiments seemed to bear out this thesis.[8] Where social workers had much smaller caseloads, where many things were done for people, where workers took more initiative in making decisions, where

---

Annie Lee Davis's *Children Living in Their Own Homes,* Washington, U.S. Children's Bureau (1953); and Lorena Scherer's "Protective Casework Service," *Children* 3, no. 1 (January-February 1956).

7. See Kermit Wiltse, "The 'Hopeless' Family," *Social Work* 3, no. 4 (October 1958).

8. Notably the "Contra Costa Experiment" described in Kermit Wiltse's "Social Casework Services in the Aid to Dependent Children Program," *Social Service Review* 28 (July 1954): 173-85, and programs in Washington, D.C., and the Southwest described in reports of the U.S. Department of Health, Education, and Welfare in the mid-1950s.

homemakers were used to instruct, families did get along better. Gradually, over the past ten years, therefore, the system has become considerably more paternalistic.

Let it be said, however, that this growing paternalism in public helping is not a reaction to the failure of the helping process. Except in isolated areas, and then with severe limitations, a helping process has not been practiced in public assistance.

The underlying assumption about man in the original program was that people could make wise decisions about their lives if given support. Nothing was said, and very little practiced, in the realms of reality and empathy. This was in fact a humanistic overvaluation of man's ability to manage without being helped to change or grow. It coincided, too, with a great deal of permissiveness, in the guise of self-determination.[9] Empathy was certainly lacking, both because of shortage of staff and because the program never attained its own goal of treating the person on relief as someone who had a right to his grant and to manage it in his own way. The dignity of the relief client was never established either in the public mind or in the mind of the great majority of those who administered the program. The one thing which might have made the difference and which was the rationale for the entire program—adequate means for health and decency—was never provided.

"Parenting" has in fact developed as a theory of helping an increasing number of people not in reaction to any failure to help through the helping process but as an alternative to unrealistic, or poor helping. Many professionals who do not deny the ability of many people to use the helping process have turned to "parenting" in the belief that there are many others who are not capable of so doing. It is suggested, however, that these are in general those who do not fully understand what the helping process involves, and who have confused it either with unreal permissiveness or, equally mistakenly, with too rigid a demand for conscious choice.

As long as the goal of parenting is the eventual growth and independence of the person being helped, and this is at least its announced purpose, one cannot make a clear distinction between the two theories on the grounds that parenting requires that the helped person give up his independence at the point of taking help. As we have seen, the taking of help always involves a measure of "yielding"

9. See, for instance, Ernest Witte, "Who Speaks Now for the Child on Public Assistance?" *Child Welfare* 33, no. 3 (March 1954) : 9-12.

to the process, and of giving up one's determination to have things one's own way. But the two methods differ radically in their concept of what one yields to, how one does it, and to some extent for how long.

Of these the "what" is perhaps the most important. In the helping process, what the helped person must come to "accept and use"—the phrase we preferred to the word "yield"—is the reality of the situation and the difference in his concept of it introduced by the helping person. He does not yield to the helping person himself, except as this person represents the process of taking help. There is no suggestion that the helping person is generally wiser or indeed more adequate than the person seeking help. He is simply a person offering help, either as a representative of an agency or by virtue of his specialized knowledge in some particular aspect of life.

But in parenting what the helped person yields to is the personality of the helping person, both as a loving person and as a representative of what is believed to be good. As Kermit Wiltse says in his article on the "hard-core" family, the parenting person must not be afraid of becoming an "ego-ideal" to the person he is helping, and also will be to him the embodiment of "the core values of our culture."[10] The difference he introduces is not the difference between things as the helped person presents or sees them and what is demonstrably so, but rather the difference between the helped person's ways of doing things and what the culture has approved as good.

The "how" is also quite different. In the helping process the helping person helps his client come to terms with reality and choose to change. Although there are many unknowns about it, and a great deal of risk that the helped person will not choose, or will choose wrongly, it could also be said that the helped person knows to some extent what he is doing, even if he knows only that he is taking a risk. In parenting, on the other hand, his yielding is much more unconscious and gradual. He never actually makes the choice, but gradually finds himself assenting to change. Help is indeed smuggled to him.

The parenting method of giving help is enormously attractive to many would-be helpers. It avoids much of the pain of helping, both for helper and helped person. It is certainly effective, at least for short-time goals, and there is actually no evidence that certain long-term goals are not attained. It is true that the goals may not include the kind of capability for discriminating feeling, for love and joy, that we see as perhaps the ultimate product of the helping

10. Wiltse, "The 'Hopeless' Family," p. 19.

process, but these in any case are rarely fully reached and there is no doubt that people who have been helped through parenting can be much more content with life and a good deal more productive.

Perhaps this is all that we can ask. The motive behind this helping is certainly kindly. It may not be to love another as oneself, but it is certainly to love him. It appeals greatly to those who are in tune with their culture, and those who believe themselves in the right or to be possessed of it. Although to be really successful at it may require a good deal of knowledge of social conditions, a willingness to listen, tact, persuasiveness, and sensitivity, these are easier to acquire than the courage and the humility that the helping process requires.

Parenting is, in fact, only a more sophisticated and more knowledgeable application of a method of helping that has been practiced for generations, by the feudal aristocracy, by the plantation owner, by the colonial administrator, by ministers with their flocks, and by parents with their children. The only difference it can claim from these age-old relationships is that where it is entered into by a professional helper it is supposedly based on a careful diagnosis of the client's need for such treatment and given by a person with wide social and psychological knowledge.[11] Even its claim to be only a stage in the helping process is not unique. This has to some extent been the announced purpose of most colonialism—to make decisions for others until they are mature enough to make decisions for themselves.

The danger of this kind of helping being attempted by any other than the most knowledgeable (and I would not include the majority of those even employed in social service agencies in this category) lies primarily in its seductiveness. Because it avoids so much pain, and is often accompanied by protestations of gratitude to the "good parent," it is easy to enter into and hard to give up. History shows few examples of the voluntary giving up of a paternalistic role. Even where this has appeared to happen, it has usually occurred largely in the face of signs of rebellion, and this rebellion, in its turn, often forces a giving up at a time at which the dependent has, in fact, become so dependent that his ability to make constructive choices is vitiated. The history of some African countries is ample evidence of that.

Again, because parenting inevitably implies a superior and an

11. This claim to be able to revert to practices that the profession had rejected as infringing the rights of people because "the elite of responsibility is set within a framework of knowledge and skills unknown to those who worked many years before us" was made as early as 1954 by Jeanette Regensburg in her "Reaching Children Before the Crisis Comes," *Social Casework* 25 (March 1954) : 106.

inferior, it is apt, except in the most disciplined hands, to lead quite quickly to judgmentalism and rejection. Not only do beginning struggles to be independent disappoint or affront those who have a need to have others look up to them and need them, but even more seriously, the parenting relationship nearly always leads to some downgrading of the person being helped in the eyes of the helper. One cannot really be fair to or respect the rights of someone one considers one's inferior. A diminution of rights inevitably follows a diminution of status or stature, which is one of the reasons why the "separate but equal" philosophy in racial matters nearly always ends in injustice.

There is also the question of the appropriateness of this kind of treatment to the individual situation. It does take considerable knowledge to know who is in need of such treatment. Ambivalence can, for instance, very easily be mistaken for cultural deprivation. So can mere difference in culture. It is also very easy for the less knowledgeable helper to be impressed by the apparent desire on the part of the person needing help for a dependent relationship and find himself carrying the whole burden for the other without him doing anything about it himself, or to be caught in the manipulations of a person with an advanced character disorder and play into his pattern of avoiding responsibility. Thus the possibility of doing harm is rather great.

But perhaps the strongest reason for not recommending the less skilled helper to attempt to help others by being a "good parent" to them is the effect on the helped person himself. To assume the role of a superior to another, except insofar as the role is inherent, such as between teacher and pupil or child and adult, and sometimes even then, is a great temptation to pride and to the exercise of unwarranted power. While some people may be able to resist this temptation, any tendency that one has in this direction is fed by such a relationship. The relationship also attracts those who consciously or unconsciously enjoy power over others. One has to be very sure of the purity of one's motives, and very sure of one's own rightness, before one attempts a method of helping in which the major responsibility lies not with the helped person but with oneself.

Professional workers often claim that their scientific knowledge, their ability to determine who is in fact in need of such care, their responsibility as agents of government and the community, their belief in the right of people to self-determination as soon as this is practicable, and the training they have received in self-discipline and self-knowledge are sufficient safeguards against these dangers, and in view of the apparent success of some of their efforts it might seem doctrinaire to raise any serious objections. Yet it seems to me that certain questions should be asked.

The primary one has to do with the uses to which this kind of helping could be put. While it has been presented as an action taken wholly for the client's good, skillful parenting could become a potent weapon for social control and, indeed, indoctrination. This is not to say that it has ever done so as yet but that there lies at its base a tacit assumption that would make this possible. This is that a person's good can more or less be equated with his acceptance of his culture. Diagnosis therefore becomes not so much an objective statement of a person's absolute need for this kind of help as a measure of his ability to conform or at least adjust to the prevailing culture and its values, good or bad. While there is truth in the statement that a man must conform in certain ways to his culture to be happy and successful in it, once this is held to too strongly as a principle on which help is to be given, it provides the rationale for all totalitarian regimes.

Indeed the political implications of a widespread use of parenting as a method of help are somewht appalling. For parenting, as we have seen, cannot avoid the implication of a superior-inferior relationship. It envisages a class of people who are to be treated as children and another class of those who take upon themselves the right to make this judgment. As long as this judgment is sound and arises from real necessity, perhaps we are all right. Such judgments do have to be made, although in a democracy they are usually reserved for the process of law. But can we be sure of this soundness?

It is here that we must rely on the safeguards which we enumerated. Yet, how sound in fact are these? One, the fact that the person making the judgment and in fact doing the parenting holds a formal or informal position of authority, appears at least to be two-edged. While such a person may have some sort of right to represent the consensus of the community about, say, the minimally acceptable standards of child care, and thus can put into words what might otherwise be a rather nebulous or a personalized reality, the very fact of his authority makes it more possible for him to impose either his own prejudices or the interests of a ruling caste.

His devotion to true science may seem the answer to this, but here, as we have seen, the only science he can resort to is based on a number of value judgments derived from that very culture he represents, and if this culture begins to shift in its values, these new values are what he must represent. Is then his belief in self-determination or his self-knowledge and self-discipline—that is, his cultivated commitment to the interests of his client, his conscious use of himself for that purpose and that alone—sufficient to ensure that his client will truly be served? Can he, for instance, deliberately use a relationship of superior to inferior, conscious of the implications that this has for society and of its ultimate undesirability, in order to arrive at a point when he can sincerely respect the person he has been helping and accept him as an equal?

Certainly some people can do so. A psychiatrist, for instance, sometimes has to go through such a stage with a patient, and there are social workers who are undoubtedly able to use themselves in this disciplined way. There are also many who cannot. One of the problems of such a theory is that it has no limits on it. Virtually anyone can decide that another is in need of parenting. There are no standards by which we can say that so-and-so's performance is sufficiently below the normal that he ought to be helped in this way, and no limits to the amount of control that can be exercised, for the client's or society's good. Where this can be determined by law, as, for instance, in probation, such limits do exist, but practitioners of parenting argue that to limit the situations in which they can operate, or the nature of the decisions which they can make denies a useful service to many in need of it. They feel that they must be free to use it wherever they see the need.

Moreover what one person can do safely and successfully may be dangerous in another. An article in a professional paper may describe a successful experiment, carried out by workers with the finest professional skills and exquisite self-discipline, and the theory enunciated in it is put into practice by a group of workers who are in fact hungry for control and frustrated because their clients are unresponsive to their efforts to help. This, unfortunately, often happens when theories are promulgated that seem to offer ways of helping that appeal to man's pride in his knowledge and rightness and his desire to control.

Nor, because a social worker or any other professional has been "trained" or has a degree in social science is this factor eliminated. All too many professionals have difficulty with their desire to control, and all perhaps would like to think their knowledge gives them the right to make decisions an untrained person should not make.

One would feel easier in fact if the number of people in our society for whom a parenting kind of help was being suggested was decreasing instead of increasing, if this reversion to a former method of helping, however fortified with knowledge, were not so typical of the pattern that humanism seems all too often to follow when it loses its first unrealistic belief in man, and if social workers were not increasingly talking of social control instead of helping.

While social control may be a proper function for a social worker, perhaps somewhat distinct from helping, when the two become as entangled as they have been, and social control is presented almost as a method of helping, one cannot but wonder how much its extension will weaken the concept of helping in our society. To help and to control are different processes, however much their goals may seem to be similar. Their practice requires different disciplines and indeed one of the first lessons a helper needs to learn is that he must not control. If he feels himself free sometimes to help and sometimes to control, he may never entirely learn to do one or the other.

There are many good arguments for this kind of "helping." One can instance the plight of many who have not been helped in other ways, its obvious success at least to a limited degree, and its logicality as an extension of the process that does take place in childhood, especially at a time when our culture is extending at least the learning aspects of childhood into young adulthood. In view of these, its dangers may appear to be minimal and to be risked in the interest of those who appear to need this help. Indeed to suggest that they are not is to open oneself to the charge of demanding middle-class abilities of a group incapable of them.

It is therefore with some trepidation that I make the statement more as an article of faith than as a provable fact, and with no desire to discredit those whose experience has been different, that all too often this kind of help is given because the helper either does not know how or has not the courage or the humility to help in a more self-disciplined way. This is not to deny that it may occasionally be necessary, although I would like more safeguards than are presently put around the practice. Nor is it to minimize the need of many people for instruction in what may seem to be the simplest skills. But it is to say that my experience tends to show that when a person is approached with genuine reality, empathy, and support, when he is truly treated as an adult with responsibility, the chances are that he will respond, and that this is true of many people whom it is all too easy to see as in need of a parental kind of care.

Indeed it seems to me that the resort to parenting is all too often a kind of desperation or a form of compromise between one's belief in people's potential and what they seem to be able to produce. And let us be clear that such people cannot be helped by anything else than good helping. Sympathy rather than empathy, reality that is glozed over, or conditional support will make the need for parenting more likely to be assumed.

Yet there are situations in which "parenting" and the helping process may seem to come very close together. There are situations, for instance, where there is need for support through a difficult experience, and even the taking over of some material decisions, as for instance with a child or someone who is clearly sick. There are also situations where reality for the helped person is the authority of the helper— either what he will allow or the culture will allow him to allow. Reality may lie also in the helping person's knowledge, as with a doctor, so that it may be sometimes quite difficult to distinguish between a reality that is personal and one that exists externally. A teacher, a consultant, a minister, a policeman all have authority of a sort that is inherent in their position but might also have personal elements. Their authority in part depends on how well they know their job.

There is no escaping this kind of authority. The question is rather what part it plays in the process. There have been, in the history of helping in this century, various theories of authority. At first there was the tendency to minimize it, which was wholly unrealistic. Formal authority became later recognized as an important part of the client's reality. Inherent authority began to be recognized as a factor.[12] The first reaction of helping people was to guard against it. An early writer on public assistance, for instance, says that the worker "must foresee the client's defenselessness and be very careful not to take unconscious advantage of him."[13]

But later writers progressively claimed inherent authority as right and proper, deriving it first from community assent and then progressively through the responsibility of their profession and their knowledge and skill, till a more recent writer can speak of the exercise of authority as a "specialized use of influence"[14] and a valuable helping method. This, it seems to me, is open to the same kind of question as

12. This was first recognized specifically by Karl and Elizabeth de Schweinitz in their "The Place of Authority in the Protective Function of the Public Welfare Agency," *Child Welfare* 25, no. 7 (September 1946) : 51-56, reprinted ibid. 43, no. 6 (June 1964) : 286-91, 315. I am not sure, however, that they foresaw the use that would be made of this concept.

13. Eda Houwink, *The Place of Casework in the Public Assistance Program* (Chicago, 1941) , pp. 8-9.

14. Elliott Studt, "An Outline for Study of Social Authority Factors in Casework," *Social Casework* 35 (June 1954) : 232.

those we have raised about "parenting" and calls into play the concept of a personal superiority which is used to change another, more or less unconsciously on his part.

Sometimes this really does exist in a particular situation in an identifiable way. To say that one treats another as an equal does not mean that he and you are equal in every respect. It simply means that you do not claim a general moral or psychological superiority over him that gives you the right to judge or to decide matters that are his to decide and act on. Humility does not mean disclaiming the knowledge that one has, and it may be necessary to say sometimes, "This happens to be something I really do know something about" or even, "That is not true." As such it is a proper introduction of difference. It only becomes dangerous where the claim is to a knowledge about the other person, or about life as a whole, and where this becomes a subtle way of imposing one's will on another. The difficulty with a claim to knowledge, or rightness, or responsibility for another is that it is normally much too absolute.

Persuasion, preaching, parenting, and the use of personal authority are the methods of help that the world has relied on over the centuries. They are still the most usual methods resorted to. Undoubtedly they can be useful at times but they have not in general proved too successful. Indeed reliance on them is in general the chief reason that help is so often of no avail. They are all efforts in one way or other to impose, however much for the helped person's good, the will of an elite, whether this be of the moral, the wise, or the scientific.

Many people obviously believe that what has gone wrong in the past is that they have been applied inappropriately, without sufficient knowledge, or by people who were not sufficiently aware of their own motives to be able to distinguish a desire to help from a desire to control. They assert that we have now acquired such knowledge and such self-discipline in the person of the professional helper that these traditional methods can now be made to work. There remains the other possibility, that there is a helping process, glimpsed at times, still imperfectly understood, based in principles which are more or less universal but which have been rarely applied to helping, which is to some extent available to anyone who really wants to help and which will lead to a type of helping that is both practical and treats people as fully responsible individuals not basically different from one's self. It is in this faith that this book has been written.

X. HELPING IN VARIOUS SETTINGS

One of the things that has been suggested about the helping process is that it has about it something of the universal. It therefore should be usable in many different settings, perhaps not directly associated with help in the ordinary sense of the word. For the most part the examples which have been used in this book have been taken from a one-to-one relationship in which the attempt to help is clearly the purpose of the encounter. These have been varied, it is true—the social worker with his client, the minister with a church member, the teacher with a student whom he is advising. It has also been made clear that the process does not require that the helped person seek out help on his own initiative. It is as applicable to the work of the probation officer, the judge, and the protective worker as it is to the family counselor. Reality, in these situations, is perhaps of a different nature and includes the authority of the law or of the helper's special function, but the principles are the same.

We might ask then at this point in what other settings the process might operate. Does it apply, and if it does, what modifications are apparent, in situations of a more personal nature, where other and perhaps different relationships exist, such as marriage or child-rearing? Does it apply in the business world, in politics, in public administration, in endeavors to bring about change in a community, and to groups as well as to work with individuals?

In order to try to answer these questions, we may need to recognize that man is likely to enter into a relationship with another for one, or possibly more than one of three reasons.

(1) *To share with another.* Here the expectancy is that both will contribute and that the decisions to be made will be, as far as possible, to their mutual benefit. This is the kind of relationship characteristic of marriage, friendship, and business or other partnerships, although both control and helping factors may exist at the same time or indeed replace mutuality, sometimes helpfully but sometimes in a somewhat disastrous way.

(2) *To control the other.* This has a very wide variety of forms. It

includes not only overt forms of domination, but persuasion (except in the form, perhaps, of logic divorced from partisanship), influence, seduction, exhortation, pleading, and demanding. It exists wherever a person brings into the relationship a will that something shall be done, and that the other shall give way to it. It makes no difference, for this discussion, whether the thing to be done is for the other person's good or wholly for one's own, or indeed for a third party's. The other's will must be overcome, whether it be by a salesman trying to sell a product, by a beggar attempting to beguile a patron, by a mother trying to influence her son, or by a debater arguing his point of view.

(3) *To help him*. Here the distinguishing characteristic is that the ultimate decision is left with the person being helped. Although the helper may very much wish for certain things to happen, he is for some reason or other prepared to risk that it will not, and that the other will make the final decision.

It is perhaps important to see that there is not, at least as far as motivation is concerned, an easy hierarchy of moral values to be attached to these relationships in themselves. Controlling is not necessarily bad, and helping necessarily good. A baby or a small child may need control. Some criminals must be controlled. The person who wishes to control may do so from the highest motives and may choose this kind of relationship only because he does not believe that another will bring about a bearable result. Control is only to be deprecated when it infringes the right of another to solve his own problems, when it is exercised without a clear mandate to make use of it, when it belittles another, or when the goals to be reached are denied because it has been substituted for help. It is an inferior relationship, it is true, in terms of democratic or even theological ideals, but in a real world may sometimes be necessary. And mutuality, of course, is a very real human need.

It might also be observed that certain actions, like compromising, can be a part of the process of more than one of these relationships. Compromise may be, for instance, a way of reaching a mutuality or it may represent the limit to which an attempt to control can go. In the first case it may be wholly accepted; in the second it may be a somewhat uneasy and temporary resting place.

The three processes are, however, distinct and quite different in their methods. Although there may be in any one relationship times when one or another may be employed, it is in general necessary to be clear which one is doing at any one time. Indeed it is quite possible that it is a failure to make this distinction which is at the root of the belief, often heard expressed today, that social casework has failed. Social casework, as it was conceived of in the 1930s and 1940s, was almost entirely a helping process, and like all true helping processes, could not ensure results that could be measured in any concrete form.[1] The results of helping are predominately internal and often intangible. Social workers, however, found themselves increasingly expected to exercise social control, to prevent problems occurring, and to bring about statistical improvements in such matters as the assistance or the crime rate. These preventive social functions are not, however, at present obtainable solely through a helping process with individuals. One cannot rebuild society brick by brick when the basic structure is awry. Despite its many faults, perhaps, the most effective preventive programs in America to date have been those of public assistance coupled with some of the training programs of the war against poverty. In England it has been the Health Service.

But, instead of recognizing this fact, social workers, in America, who have been primarily oriented toward a helping process on a one-one-one basis, have tended to try to make this process do what it cannot possibly do—become a control as well as a helping method. This may in fact account for the amount of control philosophy which even caseworkers now so often express.

We said, in chapter 1, that a helping process cannot subsume *any* goals except the self-fulfillment of those it attempts to help.

This is the reason why some doubt must be expressed about any assumption that the helping process is just as applicable to a community as it is to an individual. Although most social reformers or planners recognize that there may be some sort of helping process involved in introducing planning to those whose cooperation is necessary for the planning to be carried out, and that people may need help in making use of the product, a planner or social reformer usually has his own concept of what is necessary and quite often a very strong will of his own. It may not be, and usually is not, a selfish will. It represents the needs of a group in the community. But out of his knowledge or out of his commitment to this need, the social planner has

1. Halmos has an interesting discussion on this which he calls the "Mirage of Results" and in which he attempts to show that for many helpers the relationship itself and not its outcome is the goal. See *The Faith of the Counsellors: A Study in the Theory and Practice of Social Casework and Psychotherapy* (London, 1965), pp. 146-55. It is hard to agree with him completely since there are results in helping, but these are often not measurable and sometimes possibly not even communicable.

a goal he cannot very well give up. Kenneth Pray recognized this when in spite of his belief that community organization could be what he called "social work practice" (by which he meant a helping process) he observed that the "process of organization often follows, rather than precedes, goals."[2] However, he limited community organization to a process whose "objective is not to make over either the environment or the people involved in it, but rather to introduce and sustain a process of dealing with the problems of social relationships and social adjustment which will enable and assist those involved in the problems to find solutions satisfying to themselves and acceptable to the society of which they are a part."[3]

Ronald Lippitt, in his *Dynamics of Planned Change,* goes in fact further. He describes a process of diagnosis, clarification of issues, and coming to a decision that very closely resembles a helping process that might be offered to a man. While this is not exactly the helping process described in this book—it depends too much on a process of diagnosis or treatment—it does see the community as more or less of an organism which may decide to change "after experiencing pain (malfunction) or discovering the possibility of improvement."[4] He comments that "where reports of attempts to change attitudes describe efforts of persuasion or indoctrination, these are not collaborative and do not involve a helping relationship."[5] He even questions whether "the process of change itself, if it is properly conducted, will determine the goal," which suggests a process of self-discovery closely related to the experience of being helped, or whether "the change process must be organized from the beginning in terms of a distinct, outlined objective."[6]

But with this a modern social planner is rarely content. He recognizes in the community not a desire to come to a decision "satisfying to itself" but a vast number of conflicting desires, based in general on a need to maintain or to gain control and likely to shut out the interests of the group to whose need he is responding. He therefore sees himself needing to gain control and persuade, influence, or manipulate decisions his way. He deals frankly with power, and particularly in ensuring power for the group which at this time is

2. Kenneth Pray, "When Is Community Organization Social Work Practice," in *Social Work in a Revolutionary Age* (Philadelphia, 1949), p. 282.

3. Ibid., p. 277.

4. Ronald Lippitt, Jeanne Watson, and Bruce Westley, *The Dynamics of Planned Change* (New York, 1958), p. 10.

5. Ibid., p. 57.

6. Ibid., pp. 99-100.

disadvantaged or is not receiving its fair share of community benefits. To leave decision to whatever process a community or a committee uses to come to it would be to maintain the present power structure.

There is much to be said for this view. A community or a committee is not in fact a person and its processes are different. It would, for instance, be a false analogy to ascribe its inability to make up its mind to take some particular action to ambivalence. It is much more likely to be a difference between individual points of view. A community proceeds by compromise rather than commitment. If one really wants it to do certain things, it is probably necessary to control it by reinforcing one point of view. But, if one takes this position, one must be clear what one is doing. One is not helping these people in themselves. One may even be destroying the people with whom one is working for the good of someone else. This is quite a big responsibility for one man to undertake and certainly demands a great deal of sureness that one is right.

Some of this can be overcome by limiting the process to the needs of a neighborhood. That is, there is a process of helping a group of people with somewhat similar interests discover what they want to do and put it into practice, to create, perhaps, a "neighborhood house" or a social resource, such as a recreation facility or an educational project. Here much of what we have said about helping may hold true. Principles that might have particular significance might include listening to feeling rather than content, helping the group express what it wants and then work towards how much of this is possible, partializing the problem, leaving room for modifications when giving advice, and being interested in the feelings of an angry or rejecting person, but in fact all the principles we have suggested may be important.

If the group has some common feeling and arrives at conclusions through responding to certain more or less shared goals, it may in fact be helped through this process. The board or staff of an agency may be a good example. As a consultant to many such groups, I find them, for instance, particularly able to use what we have called "alternative advice" or consultation which involves them in going back to consider their own specialized knowledge of the particular before committing themselves to a course of action. They are quite responsive to the reality of such things as falling enrollment and to the understanding of their goals. They can take considerable difference if there is empathy too and if they are quite clear that the consultant does not wish to control them.

It is a prerequisite of all good consultation that the consultant create a likeness by accepting the essential framework that gives an agency or a group identity. A Protestant can act as consultant to a Catholic agency only if he is willing to accept certain Catholic doctrines not as true for himself but as important to a Catholic and if he has some feeling for where this importance lies. The difference has, in fact, to be bridged by empathy.

The same is true for a consultant working with an agency whose values even in helping are somewhat different from one's own or which one might consider old-fashioned or lacking in skill. It is only by working with an agency on what it wants to do, within a very broad framework of shared values, that a consultant can be of use. I once knew a community council, for instance, which spent several years trying to sell a common, interdenominational social work service to a group of agencies whose only reason for existence was their denominational pride. While this pride might have been helped eventually to evolve into something else, for the moment it effectively blocked the council's attempts to help them and actually hindered the development that might have been possible if each had been encouraged to develop its own service.

Groups, in fact, may or may not be amenable to help through the helping process. This will depend on their structure, their possession of a common goal, their voluntary or enforced nature. A group which has chosen to be a group is more likely to act as an individual in this respect than one which exists perhaps because of mere propinquity. Sometimes the helping process can be brought into play in helping a group become more unified, but often compromise may play a big part.

Yet there is much to be learned from the helping process even in dealing with power. A powerful person is often one who wishes, as does anyone, to maintain the status quo. He is afraid of change. Sometimes he can be classified as "angry or rejecting." Opposition, or defense of those he is angry against, may lead to a hardening of his attitudes. Power is often countered with power, and sometimes it may be wiser to try to help rather than to overcome. The problem is all too often that we are too fearful to take this risk.

Here we might consider particularly the question of dealing with power, in the form of pressure brought on oneself or on one's organization to do what the powerful person wants. To this there have usually been two recourses: (1) the acquisition, somehow, of counter-power (2) attempts to present one's point of view through reason or persuasive logic, often designated as "interpretation" of the true state of affairs. To do (1) is not always possible, and, even if such counterpower is obtainable, is apt to result in a state of opposition that will mean that should the focus of power change again, the power exercised on one may be even more oppressive. Yet there have been situations where the power to disrupt has won concessions which are unlikely ever to be withdrawn. The labor movement is an example. So apparently are the black and the student power movements. Although there may be some backlash, it is highly unlikely that blacks, or students, will ever lose all that has been conceded to them, any more than labor has done.

But in many situations counterpower is not obtainable. Most of us then turn to (2), or the power of explanation and interpretation. This sometimes works and sometimes does not. All too often it puts the other person on the defensive. The director of a state-financed adoption agency found himself under constant political pressure to make specific placements. Normally, in such situations, he had found himself telling senators that adoption was a complex and difficult process, that one could not start from the needs of those wishing to adopt, that one must start from the need of the baby for a particular kind of home—true material, possibly very helpful if distributed through mass media of some sort, but in the individual situation tending to throw doubt on the senator's knowledge and judgment and even his concern for children.

On one particular day the director, trained to listen to feeling, caught something in a senator's tone that troubled him. Instead of becoming defensive he said, "Senator, I would not have your job for a million dollars. The pressures on you must be enormous." The senator began to tell him what he had to put up with and ended, "You know, I don't believe these people would make good adoptive parents. I just want to get them off my back." The director offered to take the blame if a placement was not made and the senator left, full of gratitude for the understanding he had been shown. The administrator, in fact, knew that when one is dealing with an angry or rejecting person one must keep one's interest on his feeling and not come to the defense of what he is feeling about.

Similarly a social work student in an administrative sequence found herself suddenly confronted by a grand jury investigation into the Aid to Families with Dependent Children program, which it believed to be contributing to illegitimacy. Instead of producing statistics to prove that this was not so or asking whether the grand jury intended that little children should starve, which I have heard asked in similar situations, the student acknowledged the grand jury's concern and her own at the amount of illegitimacy in the county. She told them what she had tried to do and invited suggestions. As a result the grand jury became interested in the whole problem and ended by indicting not the Welfare Department but the whole community for its failure to meet this problem. It suggested that one thing that might be done would be to increase the number of welfare workers.

The third situation, somewhat similar, has to do with decisions that are made by someone who has a right to make them but who is acting irresponsibly. A child welfare office was much concerned by the decisions of a juvenile judge which seemed to them capricious and often ignored social considerations. Child welfare workers would strongly recommend certain actions and the judge would do the opposite, sometimes, it seemed, almost in order to spite them.

A new consultant suggested that if the judge were ever to learn to be a judge he must make his own decisions. She suggested that the office, instead of making recommendations, try to clarify for the judge what were the issues in a case and what might be, from their experience, the likely results of a decision one way or another. In doing this they could express empathy for the difficulty that some of these decisions would entail, the conflicting interests that might have to be balanced and their willingness to try out whatever the judge might decide would have to be done. The judge made one or two bad decisions for which he had to take sole responsibility, but very soon learned to trust the child welfare office's experience of what might result from his actions. From being a notorious critic of social work he became in the course of a year or two one of its firmest supporters.

These three instances could be looked at in a number of different ways. It could be said, for instance, that the senator, the judge and the grand jury were basically well intentioned. They did not attack social work programs with malice or with a settled desire to control them—although the judge was at least determined not to allow them to take over his work. This might suggest to some that a helping method should or could only be used where one is not up against implacable opposition. Yet this is hard to distinguish. Initially in each case the opposition was there. It was the administrator's empathy in each case which made it possible for the opposition to be withdrawn.

It might also be suggested that the administrator was, in each case, simply using a subtle form of control. Despite the risk he took that the other's decision would be inimicable, he was simply relying on the likelihood of things going his way. He was using a "soft sell." But this, I believe, discounts the fact that empathy, if it is to carry conviction, must be genuinely felt. The director who faced the senator did not think out a strategy. He was genuinely for a moment feeling for the senator. The consultant who advised a change in relationship to the judge was convinced in her own mind that judges have a right to decide. It is much more that by giving up their own immediate interests these people found that help was possible to those who looked at first unhelpable. That this help also resulted in the other person's cooperation with one's own ends was in a sense an accident. It arose because a person who has been helped is in general more rational and more able to share than a person who is not, but in the instant of helping it was the other person who mattered.

Perhaps all we are saying here is that the helping process reflects so accurately the actual nature of man that in all human relationships it is generally what will bring people together in cooperation. Man is basically more attuned to being helped than to being controlled. On the other hand man's first reaction on being attacked, or opposed, is to try to control. This is obvious, for instance, in international affairs, where interests are enforced by attempts to control the other and where the acquisition of power inevitably calls up a counterresponse of power. Without wishing here to enunciate a total philosophy of life, I would suggst that there is evidence that this is not the way in which human differences actually get resolved. We turn to power or to control because we do not know how to help.

There are many, however, who would suggest that the reverse is true—that these three administrators turned to helping methods out of weakness. They risked the senator's, the grand jury's or the judge's negative decision because they were powerless to control them. Realism might suggest that in fact the number of such situations in which help can or should be used are small. They might be limited to situations in which some good will is possible, or in which we do not have the power to control in any other way. But this assumes not only that control is a really effective method of getting our own way, but that the purpose of life is to get our own way in it. To believe this makes it very important that we are sure that our own way is right.

What is of course very difficult is to see something that we care about very much attacked, and not fight for it. There are situations in which this may have to be done. But it is also true that much more often than we recognize that the best way to protect something we care about is not to try to protect it, to risk it, and to try to help its enemies with their need to attack it.

Another problem is that we find it very difficult to think in terms of helping those who are our superiors, or even our equals. Helping still implies to most of us our superiority. A superior or an equal also usually has the power to hurt us in the way an inferior does not. We struggle to assert our will for fear the other's will will overcome us. It takes a great deal of courage and confidence in oneself to see in the insistent senator, the investigating body or the overruling judge someone in need of help, someone who is trying to solve problems in his own way and is perhaps not entirely happy about it. Even the most committed helping person is apt to fail in such a situation, and yet the more one becomes convinced that this is the way in which people actually change and grow and the more one sees it work in practice the more one comes to believe that if men are to live and work together helping must grow at the expense of control.

Another administrative setting in which the helping process plays a large part is that of supervision. Although the supervisor may be thought primarily to be one who controls, in actual fact the supervisor who sets up controls as an objective reality for the worker to encounter, and then helps him with these is using a helping process. There is a great difference between controls and control.

This is particularly observable in one supervisory function which to many people would seem to have a very strong control factor. Evaluation is often seen as a necessarily judgmental process, involving a superior who judges and an inferior who is judged. But if the organization has developed an adequate set of standards of performance which are related to the job and not to the person doing it, then the supervisor can really be a helping person. Instead of "supervising"—that is, exercising judgment and control—he can help the worker face what objectively needs to be done and offer his support. But in such a situation the wrong question often gets asked. The first and the most important question is not, "How can I help you meet this standard?"—logical as this may seem. That comes only as a result of a certain answer to a much more fundamental question, "Do you, in fact, want to do it? Is the price that you would have to pay to come up to standard in your work one that you would be willing to pay? If so, I am here to help you, if you want me and can use me. If not, you had better start looking for other work. And only you can decide."

It is surprising what strength failing workers of all kinds can muster when they are really helped to face reality in this way. Some, naturally, resign. The price that they would have to pay—the acquisition of self-discipline, the willingness to arrange matters of concern to them outside their work, is too much for them to pay. But most will respond with a genuine effort and a clear understanding that they are being helped, although it may be the supervisor who has to make the final decision about their work. And those who leave usually do so with their heads held high. The decision has been basically theirs.

The examples we have considered to this point have been drawn from the social work field. Yet some of them are clearly applicable to other organizations where public relations, supervision, and evaluation are important.

In the world of business there are a number of situations in which the helping process applies. There is, for instance, no more crucial place for the exercise of good helping than in the loan department of a bank. The applicant is asking for help. He has selected one way of solving his problem, that of applying for a loan. This may or may not be realistic in terms of his active will to make productive use of the money. Both his interests and those of the lending institution are concerned. Although the lender must rely to a certain extent on diagnosis, based on past performance, it is also in considering the terms of the loan, its size and period of repayment as well as what it will cost, that lender and borrower come to understand each other and make a sound and useful loan. It is also through this process that the borrower can discover what he really wants to do, and the likelihood that he can keep up his payments will depend to a great extent on his having discovered this. If he borrows unrealistically, or for something that will not give him satisfaction, he is much more likely to find difficulty in repayment.

The helping process may also have much to do with customer satisfaction. An architect is or should be trained in helping his customers express and in fact come to decisions about what they really want in a house. This means the kind of life they lead or hope to lead. If the architect imposes on his customers his idea of what a house ought to be like—a complaint frequently voiced about some members of this profession—he may find that he is making impossible what his customers really want to do with their lives. Traffic control may be wrong, so that parts of the family obtrude on each other's interests or, conversely, do not come together enough. There may or there may not be ways to include provision for an ill parent, or grandchildren. The result will be full satisfaction or discontent. Architects, too, may be wise to follow the helping principle of discovering what someone really wants and then helping him come to terms with how much of it he can have, rather than feeling discontent that his hopes have not been taken into account.

Businessmen who provide a service would also be well-advised to consider what the helping process might tell them about false reassurance. All too often businessmen will promise something that they cannot fulfill, but rather than face this reality with the customer right away, they resort to reassurance. The customer in the end is much more dissatisfied. One airline, for instance, apparently makes the practice of trying to cushion the disappointment that a delay may cause by postponing the plane's estimated time of arrival twenty minutes at a time. This may be justified for short-time purposes in that one's tendency is to hang on, hoping against one's better judgment that the airline means what it says, but in long-term reputation it does the line a lot of harm.

These are not, perhaps, strictly helping processes. The businessman, despite his protestation that he exists to serve his clients, is usually more concerned with his profit than with change or growth or even "satisfaction of need" in those he serves. The very fact that he works so strenuously to stimulate this need is an indication of this. But to take the position that because the businessman's ultimate motive is selfish, he does not help, or need to know about helping, is far too absolute. It ignores the fact that the helper also has needs. The question is rather whether the man in business is so intent on profits in the here and now that he permits this to override the interests of the client, and this the wise man of business does not do, for in general he depends in the long run on the goodwill of his clients and their willingness to trust him. There are many people in business who do, moreover, have a real feel for helping, and many helping people—doctors, for instance—who are at the same time engaged in making a profit. While perhaps most businesses rely more largely on a control relationship—advertising and salesmanship—helping principles are often applicable to much that they do. Even the "soft sell" is based on the recognition that negatives may have to be faced and dealt with. It is probably true, however, that only a superior product can be promoted by helping principles. An inferior product is not close enough to reality.

Helping also takes place in less structured situations. In considering first relationships within a family, mutuality, rather than help, is, perhaps, of the first importance. This immediately suggests principles that may contradict those of helping. The very fact of a common interest may suggest that there are times when sympathy rather than empathy may be the more appropriate. People may need to share their sorrows and their joys. But marriage is in some aspects a mutual helping relationship, in which one partner perhaps offers help at one time and the other at another, or both offer help but in relation to different things. There are clearly situations in which helping does take place and in such situations the process is an important guide— where, for instance, one partner is troubled and turns to the other, or should, but does not.

It is perhaps easier to see the times when helping goes obviously wrong—the husband who cannot face reality with his wife about the financial situation, the wife whose support is clearly conditional, the partner who feeds into the other's hypochondria or depression by sympathizing with it. But so much else is involved—their need to live together, the compromises and adjustments they may need to make, even the possible unreality that may have to be manufactured to render this possible at all. Therefore one might say that where relationships are so close and often so total, the basic principles of helping are good to keep in mind and occasionally to use, but one needs to be very sure, first, that helping is what one needs to do.

Helping theory does, however, help us to see some of the limitations of total mutuality. As one sociologist has put it, what is needed in marriage is "co-operative individuality" rather than complete unity.[7] Kahlil Gibran, although his archaisms are somewhat hard to bear, expresses this neatly when he says of marriages, "Let there be spaces in your togetherness."[8]

With children it is another thing. One may quite often need to help. In fact the whole process of rearing is in a sense a form of help. A mother may need to help a child go to the dentist. As we have said, it would be foolish to tell him that it will not hurt. Instead she needs to be real about it, to permit him not to like it and above all to assure him that she will be with him in the experience.

Even to punish a child can be an attempt to help and in most cases the how is much more important than the what. While punishment can, of course, be used to enforce demands or compel submission, and as such is far from helpful, the helping factor—"This is it. I know it must hurt. I am here to help you if you want me and can use me"—might have been written in the first place by someone about to

7. Robert O. Blood, *Marriage* (New York, 1962), p. 347.
8. Kahlil Gibran, *The Prophet* (New York, 1923), p. 15.

administer a mild spanking. It can, in fact, make of a spanking or any other quick punishment what is its only justification—that it is a sharp and immediate reminder that a limit has been transgressed, must be paid for, and will result in a restoration of grace. As such, it differs enormously from the punishment of any kind in which the parent continues his displeasure for a length of time, or uses some form of the statement, "This hurts me more than it hurts you." Here the attempt is not so much to remind and restore as it is to maintain control and to diminish the child's will. It is the difference between the setting of controls, which can be helpful things if they are not too confining, and may lead to added strength, and the control of another, which in a long-time situation almost always leads either to conquest or to rebellion. That is why children often like and admire the teacher who is strict but fair, and who makes his limits clear, but despises the one who nags, who pleads, or who is "hurt" by their behavior, even though he may be the more permissive.

It is a sad but perhaps inevitable fact that child rearing is becoming, in the United States at least, less a matter of controls, within which the child made many decisions for himself within a framework of clear limits, enforced perhaps too rigorously, and much more a matter of control. Children's play is much more supervised than it used to be. Much more adult "guidance" and "leadership" is given. The times have largely vanished when a child disappeared and engaged in his own pursuits for most of the day, appearing perhaps only for meals, as did Tom Sawyer, Penrod, or Elizabeth Nesbitt's children.

Part of the reason for this may be the objectively far greater hazards of life today, part the living habits of an urban society, but part certainly is due to the kind of beliefs which have stressed "togetherness," manipulation, and persuasion rather than command, and have confused freedom with permissiveness. The least free school I ever taught in was one in which there were no punishments but a constant pressure on the children to be productive, to create, and to absorb adult values. While reality for the Victorian child, in terms of adult sanctions, may have been too harsh, and empathy often lacking, reality has too often been ignored of late and subtle control put in its place. Parents have in fact lost their role to represent reality for a child, and this has often been a growth-inhibiting factor.

As the child grows older, parents will find it much more possible, and indeed necessary, to use a helping process. While most of us would, I think, see the failure in communication between many teen-age children and their parents as due to too much difference in desires or values, I doubt that this is really the problem. What has happened is that the process of control has broken down as the child becomes more able to think and act for himself. A true helping process has never been set up. There are no recognized limits and little empathy and support in meeting them. Negatives towards these limits have not been recognized or allowed since negatives threaten control. The parent has not in fact been different enough, and so is unable to help with the child's new-found difference. A control function cannot, in fact, tolerate difference. Therefore, as many parents can testify, a child may find it more possible to go for help to someone outside the family, to a minister, teacher, or friend, not because of any lack of closeness with his family but for the very opposite reason. With the parent too much is shared. Difference—difference in ideals, in ways of looking at things, in challenges to established patterns—may be too difficult to express or too unlikely to be found.

There are, therefore, many situations and many settings in which the helping process can and will be of use. One of the nicest bits of helping I have myself received came from the mouth of a tough first sergeant in the American Army in World War II. I and many others had been drafted, pulled from our families much against our wills but had been, except at home, unable to express our hurt. The culture demanded that we be proud to make this sacrifice, that we pretend that we were going willingly, when the very reverse was true. I do not mean that in any way we would try to dodge what we saw as a necessary and unpleasant task, but it was very hard to like. It was only when the sergeant asked how many of us were happy to be here and no one answered that he said simply, "I don't blame you. It's a dirty and difficult business. But it's here and so we had better tackle it. It's my job to show you how." From that moment most of us were able to make at least a partial commitment to the unpleasant task ahead.

Help often is not planned, as it was not planned with the senator discussed earlier in this chapter but arose from a sudden feeling for him, as it may sometimes not be planned in a quarrel when one ceases to think of all the retorts one might make, the justifications, and the deliberately wounding remarks, and is for a moment struck with what the quarrel may mean to the other. It may in fact occur almost casually, as it were. I have no doubt that the child whom I probably helped most in twenty years' work with Children's Homes was one to whom I never spoke but whose face I found interesting—that is, strong, watchful, and inquiring—when I saw her in a crowd. I mentioned my feeling about this child's quality to somebody and found that she was considered a most unsatisfactory and rebellious child in danger of dismissal. The person to whom I spoke asked if she could tell Barbara what I had said. I never saw Barbara again, but three years later, when she graduated with an excellent record, Barbara was asked by someone how she had managed to change so much. She said that the change had begun when she had been told of my interest. "I figured," she said, "that if someone who sees as many children as he does singled me out I had something to live up to." Barbara must have been, of course, almost ready for change, and the real helping was done by the person who recognized her need and relayed my comment, but the thought of how accidental the straw may have been that tipped the balance is a disturbing thought. How many times have we not done the helpful thing that, in this case, meant so much?

The helping process, then, is something which operates both in and without the formal helping situation wherever one's primary concern is for the person one encounters and one is willing to give up, even for a moment, one's own will, even one's will for him, to help him find something for himself. It is an entirely different process from that we use to control another, however, good for him or for others that control may be. It is a difficult process and one that involves quite a bit of risk but is probably much underused and certainly much misunderstood. Confusion with such general concepts as that of doing good or being kind to people, failure to distinguish it from subtle processes with control, equating it with permissiveness and the conviction that in order to help one must know a lot about the other person have concealed much of its precision and its universality. To what extent it really expresses something that is basic in man and indeed in the universe as a whole is probably a matter of faith, but it is a faith that is based on some experience. The helping process, in fact, works.

XI. A SHORT HISTORY OF HELPING

The history of helping throughout the ages is not easy to disentangle and cannot be found in any one place. Part of the difficulty is that until this century it has been confused with another problem, that of dealing with the poor—a problem that has broad political, theological, and social aspects and has influenced man's thinking about how he should help. The history of charity, has, for instance, been very well annotated by such writers as Lallemand,[1] Uhlhorn,[2] and Troeltsch,[3] that of social measures to overcome and relieve poverty by many writers, notably for the early period Eden[4] and Devine,[5] and in the later de Schweinitz[6] and many others. There have been several accounts moreover of the development of the first specifically "helping profession"—social work—by Witmer[7] and Fink,[8] for instance, in the United States and Young and Ashton[9] in Britain.

What is attempted here, however, is to give some account of the ideas that have guided man's relationships to those who are in trouble. That these ideas are largely theological, and until the Enlightenment, at least, expressed in theological terms, will not be surprising to those who are aware that until the end of the Middle Ages the church was the primary "helping agency." Even where provision for the poor or the sick, for instance, became a governmental function the culture demanded that it act on, for the most part, Christian principles. That the Jews developed their own methods and attitudes is also true, and

1. Leon Lallemand, *Histoire de la Charité*, 3 vols. (Paris, 1902-6).
2. G. Uhlhorn, *Christian Charity in the Ancient Church* (Edinburgh, 1883).
3. Ernest Troeltsch, *The Social Teaching of the Christian Churches*, trans. Olive Wyon (New York, 1931).
4. Sir Frederick Eden, *The State of the Poor: Or, An History of the Labouring Classes in England, from the Conquest to the Present Period*, 2 vols. (London, 1797).
5. Edward T. Devine, *Principles of Relief* (New York, 1904).
6. Karl de Schweinitz, *England's Road to Social Security* (Philadelphia, 1943).
7. Arthur Fink, Merrill Conover, and Everett Wilson, *The Field of Social Work* (New York, any edition since 1943).
8. Helen Witmer, *Social Work: A Social Institution* (New York, 1940).
9. A. F. Young and E. T. Ashton, *British Social Work in the Nineteenth Century* (New York, 1956).

unfortunately we do not have time here to consider the enormous contribution this group has made to helping—a contribution quite disproportionate to their numbers—except to note their insistence on justice, their sense of community, and their refusal to punish those in need of help by supplying them with less than their basic needs.[10] Nor is any attempt made in this book to explore the helping principles that have emerged from Islam or from Eastern religions and cultures. Such a study, made by someone who had real competence in these fields, would be enormously interesting and might in fact add a lot to any attempt to formulate a more universal theory.

Nor, although man's view of himself and his relationship to the universe lies at the heart of any helping theory, can we forget that social conditions and economics often influence attitudes and theory. It is easier, for instance, to understand the comment, made in 1889, that "kindness to an individual means cruelty to a class"[11] if one has some conception of how hopeless the life of the poor was at this time, and how ineffectual and deluding an offer of material help might be. The social and economic history of helping is of the greatest importance and a case might be made for considering it as the primary subject for research. I shall treat it here only as it has influenced basic theory since the problem of the poor and the problem of helping, though interconnected, are not the same.

Rather little is known about what helping meant to people in the pre-Christian era although, except in Hebrew culture, there is some evidence that the poor and the unfortunate were all too often left to starve. But by the time that Christianity became the West's official religion it could be said that here were four basic motives for helping others that had to some extent been amalgamated. These four principles can be very broadly correlated with the ideas of four different cultures. The Greek attitude to helping was largely what might be called, for lack of a simple English word, eudaemonistic. The man who helped others furthered the development of his own soul. Thus helping could be extended to one's equals, but man could continue to be insensitive to the plight of whole segments of society. The Romans, judging from the form in which material help was given

10. For a good account of the development of Jewish thought, see Herbert H. Aptekar, *The Dynamics of Casework and Counseling* (Boston, 1955). Also of interest is Alfred J. Kutzik's *Social Work and Jewish Values* (Washington, D.C., 1959).

11. W. Bury, "Poor Law Progress and Reform," *Poor Law Conference Reports* (London, 1889), p. 319, excerpted by Gertrude Lubbock, *Some Poor Law Questions* (London, 1895).

and as might be expected from the nature of their law, felt deeply about the responsibility of a man for his dependents and particularly for those who gave him service in return. In terms of purely material aid estimates vary in assigning from one third to three quarters of the Roman population to a dependent status.[12] The great Jewish contribution was the concept of justice. Kindness and mercy, giving to the poor, are associated throughout the Old Testament with the just disposition of disputes and honest principles of commerce as aspects of man's relationship towards those less fortunate than himself. For every mention, for instance, in the Old Testament to "kindness" or "mercy" there are two to justice and even in Micah's summing up of God's requirements justice is given the first place.[13] To this the Christian had added, or developed, the ethic of love to one's fellows as a response to the love of God for man.

It is curious how in fact these four basic impulses still exist. In particular the Greek and Roman concepts still operate within, and to some extent vitiate, the legacy of Judaism and Christianity. Much helping today is blatantly eudaemonistic, although perhaps not so crudely as it was in the Middle Ages where it chiefly took the form of earning one's own salvation through one's almsgiving. Nowadays it takes the form of helping others to satisfy one's own conscience, or to minister to one's desire to be liked, to control others, or to establish one's own superiority. The sense of responsibility for one's own, a more or less happy state of affairs if everybody does in fact have a place in society, still troubles us in its negative aspect when people make distinctions between those they are willing to help and those they are not and is at the root of much disclaiming of responsibility as well as much assumption of it.

The feeling for justice is fortunately still with us. It is the wellspring of much of the present concern for the poor and for oppressed racial minorities. How much the concept of Christian love in its original form—that is, the impulse to share what one has received—is still a real motive for helping is debatable. In one sense it is the only really helpful motive for helping and lies behind the humanist's as well as the Christian's or Jew's concern for others. In another, except in

12. Uhlhorn in his *Christian Charity in the Ancient Church* calculates that in the later days of the Roman Empire there were 580,000 persons receiving some kind of public subsidy to 90,000 self-sufficient (p. 38) and Lallemand says that under Julius Caesar there were 320,000 recipients of relief (annonae) in the city of Rome alone (*Histoire de la Charité*, vol. 1, p. 139).

13. Micah 6:8.

certain explicitly religious forms of helping, it has become divorced from its original rationale. And although it was what gave the ancient Western world its primary impulse to help, it was soon perverted and moreover came into conflict with two other human desires—the desire to further morality through judging and controlling those whose conduct offended one, and the desire to maintain order in the state.

The problem of judgment arose early. This may at first have been purely prudential. When love needed to be expanded from the little, closed group of Christians to the world at large, it became obvious that there are people who ask for help that they do not need and those who use help to gain unworthy ends. And while we would recognize that to help such people in the sense of giving them simply what they say they want is bad helping, man's easiest response to the problem is to make a moral judgment that these people are undeserving of aid.

Most early writers on charity, or concern for others, struggle with this problem. Their handling of it ranges all the way from St. Basil, who says that great experience is needed to distinguish between those who are really poor and those who dissemble[14] to St. Clement of Alexandria, who warns against fastidiousness and "setting oneself up to try" who is fit for one's benevolence.[15] There is even an apocryphal saying of Jesus specifically damning those who "hypocritically take" and "while they could help themselves, rather take alms from others,"[16] which shows how deeply an early writer must have felt about the problem.

It is in St. Chrysostom towards the end of the fourth century that we find the finest flower of the purely Christian attitude to these problems. "Be we as large-hearted as we may," he writes, "we shall never be able to contribute such love towards man as we stand in need of at the hand of a God that loveth man,"[17] and reminds his congregation that God has never said to them what they have said to those who asked alms of them, such as: "Stand off, since thou art an impostor, always coming to Church, and hearing my laws, but when abroad setting gold, and pleasure, and friendship and in fact anything above my commandment."[18]

St. Chrysostom, indeed, is extraordinarily modern. He was able to see what few can see even today, that to ask for something one does

14. Quoted by Uhlhorn, *Christian Charity*, p. 269.
15. St. Clement of Alexandria, *Quis Divos Salvus*, p. xiii.
16. *Constitutions of the Apostles*, 4:3.
17. *Fourteenth Homily on the Book of Romans*.
18. Ibid.

not need may be the result of being in need in other ways, which he says, may force a man "to put on such a character"[19] and he was unwilling to restrict aid to the citizens of Alexandria when in charge of their giving there.[20] He wished alms to be given to anyone in need, irrespective of their residence or their acceptability to the local church.

It was not however judgmentalism that proved to be the major perversion of love in the medieval church. The medieval church was in fact less judgmental than its later offspring. The major perversion of the helping impulse in the Middle Ages was the growth of the idea that the purpose of giving was to ensure salvation for the soul of the giver. Even St. Chrysostom believed that the poor were useful to the rich so that the rich might get rid of their abundance and win treasure in heaven[21]—a sentiment that we find almost exactly echoed by John Wesley thirteen hundred years later, when he became concerned about the riches which religion would necessarily produce and urged the religious to "gain all they can and save all they can" but to "give all they can" and "the more they will grow in grace, and the more treasures they will lay up in heaven."[22] Others went much further. St. Cyprian characterized charity as "needful for the weak, glorious for the strong, assisted by which the Christian accomplished spiritual grace, deserves well of Christ the Judge, accounts God his debtor."[23] Uhlhorn in fact suggests that almsgiving was one of two officially recognized substitutes for martyrdom (fasting being the other) as a clear-cut way to salvation. Christianity became the religion of the state and martyrdom was no longer easily sought.[24] The clearest example of this thinking comes, however, not from this early period but from an Anglican divine in 1716. "Whatever is laid out in charity, God accounts an Offering and a Loan to Himself; and accordingly He engages to repay it."[25]

While these comments have perhaps more to do with giving than with offering help, the effect on all kinds of helping must have been

19. *Fourth Homily on Lazarus.*
20. *Fourteenth Homily on Romans.*
21. *Seventeenth Homily on Second Corinthians.*
22. Quoted by Richard Niebuhr, *The Social Sources of Denominationalism* (New York, 1929; Living Age ed., 1957), pp. 70-71.
23. Quoted in this instance from Lillian Brandt, *How Much Shall I Give?* (New York, 1921), p. 85.
24. Uhlhorn, *Christian Charity*, pp. 212-13.
25. Edmund Gibson, Bishop of Lincoln, *The Peculiar Excellency and Reward of Supporting Schools of Charity* (1716), quoted by Betsy Rogers, *The Cloak of Charity* (London, 1949), p. 11.

tremendous. Even where the more selfish motive was not glorified, where giving was done ostensibly to fulfill God's demands, giving and help were divorced from the needs of the helped person. Sir Thomas Browne, for instance, could write in 1672, "I give no alms to satisfy the hunger of my brother, but to fulfill and accomplish the will and command of my God. . . . I relieve no man upon the rhetoric of his miseries, nor to content my own commiserating disposition, for this is still but moral charity, and an act that oweth more to passion than to reason."[26] This is, in fact, a divorce between the two halves of the Great Commandment which Jesus had put together. It is difficult to know to what extent this divorce affected treatment of the poor—there were other elements present—or how much the treatment of the poor affected other kinds of helping, but it is true that from St. Chrysostom to perhaps the end of the Middle Ages there is very little indeed to indicate a concern with what those in trouble needed. The emphasis is on what helping can do to the helper.

There are, of course, exceptions. St. Francis of Assisi is one. Another is the poet Langland, who, although he accepted wholly the medieval concept of order, which is one of the factors that undoubtedly discouraged attempts to help the poor, combined a deep sense of personal unworthiness with a deep feeling for those in trouble and a strong desire for justice. He is perhaps unique in that he asked for people "some manner of joy/ Either here or elsewhere. else it were ruth,/ for amiss he were made. who was not made for joy."[27] Later, too, there was the remarkable work of Juan Luis Vives in his plans for caring for the poor of the cities of Bruges and Ypres. Vives charged his "prefects" with the duty of ascertaining not only the condition and health of the poor but also "their homely and secret griefs and—as near as can be—their merits."[28] He also believed strongly in "visiting, comforting, helping and in executing the deeds of pity."[29]

We cannot deal here at length with the efforts of scholasticism to

26. Sir Thomas Browne, *Religio Medici,* 7th ed. (London, 1672) , p. 48, quoted by de Schweinitz, *England's Road to Social Security,* p. 14.

27. William Langland, *The Vision of Piers Plowman,* C, cvi, lines 299-301. A fuller version of pertinent passages can be found in *Visions from Piers Plowman,* trans. Nevill Coghill (London, 1949) , but these lines are quoted here from Christopher Dawson's *Mediaeval Religion and Other Essays* (London, 1934) , and are a less free translation.

28. Juan Vives, *Forma Subventionis Pauperum* (1535) , trans. William Marshall and excerpted by de Schweinitz, *England's Road,* p. 34. *The Forma Subventionis* refers to the City of Ypres. His *De Subventione Pauperum,* which refers to Bruges and is very similar, has been translated by Margaret M. Sherwood and is also excerpted by de Schweinitz.

29. *Forma Subventionis,* p. 35.

consider almsgiving an act of justice rather than one of charity since this question relates more to the constitution of society than to concepts of helping. St. Ambrose discusses benevolence under the general helping of justice[30] and St. Thomas Aquinas recognizes a "certain moral debt"[31] to the poor and unfortunate, but considered commutative justice, which would ensure to man his basic rights, less important than distributive justice which rewarded man in relation to his contribution to society and both of them subordinate to general justice, which assured the good order of the state.[32] Suffice it to say that justice, and particularly the legal right to assistance in need, became dormant as a basic incentive to helping and St. Thomas's main contribution to helping theory is, according to one writer at least, his concept of prudence or rational action and involves a relationship of superior to inferior, since "it is only insofar as we are superior to others that we can be of help to them, supplying their needs."[33] This does not deny, however, certain ways in which Thomism supports helping theory, particularly its insistence on the uniqueness of each individual, and the necessity for man to try to understand himself.

What happened at the Reformation is one of the saddest stories known to man of the perversion of what should have been a liberating force in freeing man's impulse to help his fellows. The rediscovery of a God who grants unmerited grace and before whom there is "no distinction, since all have sinned and fallen short of the glory of God" might have been thought to lead naturally to a vast compassion, or at least fellow-feeling, for those in trouble. The temptation to salvific eudaemonism was destroyed. But in actual fact the reformed theology led to almost the exact opposite—to the identification of God's grace with worldly success and to the "intolerable rule of the saints."

Quite how this happened may be in doubt and there are a number of theories, some social and some theological. Some have attributed it to the rise of a bourgeois class and the consequent reevaluation of work as a major moral value.[34] The troubled person is often unable or apparently unwilling to work. Some give the same intolerance of those

---

30. *De Officio Magistrorum*, I, xxxii.

31. *Summa Theologica*, II-II, Q. 63.

32. Ibid., II-II, Q. 117.

33. Mary J. McCormick, *Diagnostic Casework in the Thomistic Pattern* (New York, 1954), esp. p. 196. A separate "school" of Thomistic social workers exists in the United States. See Herbert H. Stroup, "The Minister and the Thomistic Social Worker," *Illiff Review* 17, no. 2 (Spring 1960): 27-31.

34. This is the view of H. N. Robertson in his *The Rise of Economic Individualism* (Cambridge, England, 1933), which he put forward in opposition to Max Weber's more theological views in *The Protestant Ethic and the Rise of Capitalism*, trans. Talcott Parsons (London, 1930).

who did not work a more theological explanation, basing it on Luther's "evaluation of the fulfillment of duty in worldly affairs as the highest form which the moral activity of the individual could assume."[35] Others attribute the growth of judgmentalism to the new concern Protestantism appeared to have for moral issues in the whole population.[36] The gnawing fear that one might not oneself be among the elect and the consequent searching for external signs of grace undoubtedly played a part,[37] and one writer makes the interesting suggestion that moral judgment became the principal way of dealing with social ills because morals were in the Puritan's "sphere of competence" whereas psychological and economic causes of distress were not.[38]

The net result, whatever its causes, was to create a separate class of the "poor" who needed from their better-placed fellows exhortation, strict control, and deliberately harsh living conditions to spur them to greater effort. Kindness toward this group was a mistake. The group, also, despite efforts to classify them as deserving or undeserving were in general lumped together and treated as all undeserving. And while this feeling was directed chiefly towards those who were in need of financial help, there is no doubt that it permeated all relationships between helper and helped. This was seen almost inevitably as a relationship between someone who was whole, and moral, and someone who was neither.

That this concept persists in many quarters today is only too apparent. It is the source of what we have called the puritan-capitalist ethic, now in many of its manifestations divorced from its original theological roots, although often using religion to buttress its principles.

How deeply it affected man's relationship to those of his fellows who were in trouble is evidenced in the Poor Law with its vicious principle of less-eligibility—that is, the theory that the way to make people better themselves is to make their present situation as uncomfortable as one can. Young and Ashton ascribe to this principle the workhouse which "was made as uncomfortable as possible by irksome regulations, few social amenities, poor food and a general and deliberate encouragement of gloom and despondency."[39]

---

35. Weber, *The Protestant Ethic*, p. 80.

36. Troeltsch, *The Social Teaching*, p. 512. See also C. S. Loch, *Charity and Social Life* (London, 1910), and Weber, *The Protestant Ethic*, pp. 36-37.

37. Weber, *The Protestant Ethic, passim,* but esp. pp. 111, 122, 159.

38. R. B. Perry, *Puritanism and Democracy* (New York, 1944), p. 95.

39. Young and Ashton, *British Social Work*, p. 47.

Two attitudes were predominant. One was that to make the life of someone in trouble more bearable was to encourage him in his weakness. It took, in fact, Dr. Samuel Johnson to state, entirely contrary to the tenor of the times, that "we do not always encourage vice when we relieve the vicious."[40] The other was the belief in God's providence. As a nineteenth-century writer held, "to lay down any general rule that the old are to be maintained, the fatherless to be provided for, the sick to be taken care of, is to render null God's ordinances in favor of prudence and foresight in the shape of the ordinary changes and vicissitudes of life."[41]

Evangelicalism might have offered something different. But although evangelicalism was a religious movement that emphasized love and, according to one source, "began to mean . . . that all men had equal dignity in the eyes of God, and should therefore be so regarded by other men,"[42] its actual results were not so much an understanding of the plight of the individual, but large-scale reforms such as Factory Acts and child-labor laws, as well as the founding of many philanthropic and educational institutions. It added little to helping theory. Richard Niebuhr attributes this to its essential middle-class nature and to the sins it sought most strenuously to eliminate—vice and laxity, the traditional sins of the troubled person, rather than pride or greed, the typical sins of the successful. As Niebuhr states, "Wesley was more offended by the blasphemous use of the name of God than by a blasphemous use of His creatures."[43]

It was indeed from Calvinist sources that the next advance might be said to have come. Thomas Chalmers, an eighteenth-century Presbyterian, is held up by many writers on Puritanism as a thoroughgoing example of smug judgmentalism, particularly because he opposed state measures for the relief of the poor and wished to make them dependent on the compassion of the rich. But his principal reason for doing so was his belief that the governmental system promised more than it could deliver. "It is playing fast and loose with people—first to make a declaration of their right and then to plant obstacles in the way of their making it good."[44] He could also say, most surprisingly for a man of his time—no age was more conscious of social distinctions

40. Samuel Johnson, *Works* (Oxford, 1825), IX, 303, quoted by Lubbock, *Some Poor Law Questions*, p. 241.

41. Thomas Walker, *The Original*, quoted ibid., p. 166.

42. Young and Ashton, *British Social Work*, p. 41.

43. Richard Niebuhr, *The Social Sources*, p. 67.

44. *Chalmers on Charity: A Selection of Passages and Scenes to Illustrate the Social Teaching and Practical Work of Thomas Chalmers, D.D.*, ed. N. Masterman (Westminster, 1900), p. 106.

—that in putting oneself under the roof of a poor neighbor "we in a manner render him for the time our superior."[45] Although he maintained many of the attitudes of the morally superior, he insisted on a rigorous social investigation accompanied with friendly interest and personal service. His spirit is not unlike that of Vives.

Chalmer's insistence on a social investigation is in fact a tentative beginning towards social diagnosis, that science which has dominated helping from that day on. It replaces the moral diagnosis of the Puritan with something more inclusive but it includes within it the same dangers of becoming an incentive to exercise control in the name of the culture.

When the distribution of government aid or charity is concerned, some sort of judgment is of course necessary, and one can in general choose between four sources of judgment:

—the judgment of the "saint," or what it is thought that man deserves;

—the judgment of the social scientist, or what it is thought man needs;

—the judgment of law, or what man is entitled to;

—the judgment of the helped, or what man wants and is willing to do.

It is the third of these that has become the basis of most public assistance plans, and of the three it is probably the least personal and the least affected by transient changes of theory or values, but it is always attacked by those who believe that their morality or their knowledge gives them the right to a more personal decision. And this sort of judgment which has to be made for prudential reasons where material aid is concerned very easily spills over into all human relationships in which help is concerned. The fourth sort of judgment —what a man wants and is willing to do himself—is rather easily obscured.

Chalmer's dual insistence on investigation and friendliness and personal service led to the Charity Organization Society and to the Friendly Visitors, and these have been described in many accounts of the development of modern social work. In part they were a reaction against indiscriminate and eudaemonistic giving; in part a protest against mass measures. They certainly began to place a great value on human relationships in the helping process.

There was, perhaps, for the first time, a belief in the importance of

45. Ibid., p. 228.

the troubled person participating in his own recovery and a good deal of belief in his ability to do so. In fact, the pendulum swung too far, and all material support came to be depreciated and helping became almost entirely a matter of counseling and encouragement. There was a tendency, also, to place the whole responsibility for how a man dealt with his problems onto himself, with little regard to the realities of his struggle against almost overwhelming social conditions, so that devoted as were such leaders as C. S. Loch, Edward Dennison, and Octavia Hill there is a curious lack of true empathy in them. There is something disquieting about a man of whom it could be said that "the poor soon came to understand the man who was as liberal with his sympathy as he was chary of meat and coal tickets."[46] They were still so convinced that man could solve his problems through their counsel and encouragement that they found his failure to do so very hard to bear. They always carried within them the hope that the individual might be reformed.

At the same time there was growing, chiefly outside the church, a new consciousness of the evils of society which took the emphasis off the individual once again. The "sin" which had previously been ascribed to the individual now became ascribed to the society he had created. Beatrice Webb describes this as a "new ferment" and believed it to be the result of "a new consciousness of sin among men of intellect and men of property"[47] and in England it led to a more humane treatment of the poor and the beginnings of social security, curiously enough to the virtual exclusion of advances in theories of personal helping. In America, on the other hand, there was a longer tradition of puritanism, which, however harshly, did concentrate on the individual. There were very different economic conditions and political organization. There was perhaps a more genuinely classless society and there was far greater optimism about the possibility of an individual rising above his environment. At the same time John Dewey had laid great emphasis on environmental factors in overcoming ignorance, and science of any kind enjoyed a very high status. The coming together of all these influences led to the rapid development of a new helping method which came to be known as social casework.

The virtual founder of this new discipline was Mary Richmond. Miss Richmond borrowed from medicine the concept of diagnosis and

46. R. H. Bretton, *A Modern History of the English People* (London, 1930), p. 689.
47. Beatrice Webb, *My Apprenticeship* (London, 1926), p. 173, quoted by de Schweinitz, *England's Road*, p. 166.

treatment. She proposed a system of minute inquiry into all the circumstances of a client's life and a somewhat rigorous testing of this evidence. A typical schedule for inquiry about an unmarried mother, for instance, in her book *Social Diagnosis,* includes as one of forty-six items:

When did the girl's sexual experience begin? Under what circumstances—was it with a relative, an employer, an older man, a school boy? Has she accepted money from any man or men for unchastity, or has she received only a good time—theaters, dinner, etc.—or board? Has she lived for any period as the wife of any man or men? Has she supplemented her income through men or made her whole livelihood in this way? If so, for how long and when? Has she been a common prostitute, has she had a succession of "friends," or has she been intimate with only the one man? Has she a court record? From what she, her relatives, friends and employers say, does she seem to seek wrongdoing, or does she merely yield when evil approaches her?[48]

As can be seen, Miss Richmond's diagnosis was carefully constructed from many different sources of knowledge. She was very careful that it should be evidential and spent considerable time in distinguishing between social and legal evidence. Her remedies, however, for the conditions she discovered were less explicit than her perception of what had gone wrong. They consisted largely in manipulation of the environment. She stood quite clearly outside her client, looking at him as a doctor would look at a patient. At the same time she was aware of the importance of the client participating in plans for his recovery. In a curious sentence she sums up what she considers most necessary for treatment: "encouragement and stimulation, the fullest possible participation of the client in all plans and the skillful use of repetition."[49]

It was against this background that the theories of the analytical psychologists burst upon American social work, and, more slowly, upon the American public, in the late 1920s. It was not so much the content of the new knowledge that made it important, although it did help to explain many of the discrepancies that had become apparent between the predominately environmental theory of man's growth and what had been observed in practice. It was rather its dual emphasis on man's common frailty and on treating him as "subject" rather than "object" that made the difference. As a writer of that time put it:

By virtue of its new scientific character the perspective of all social work shifted from an "external" view previously held by social reformers, theorists and philanthropists alike, in which the poor, the sick, the criminal or the neglected child appeared mainly in contrast to the normal and quantitatively

48. Mary Richmond, *Social Diagnosis* (New York, 1917), p. 416.
49. Mary Richmond, *What Is Social Casework?* (New York, 1922), p. 256.

solid mass of the population, to an analytic view as from the angle of the client himself. The social worker in this new conception was no longer an agent serving the social mechanism as much as an instrument of adjustment manipulated in the interest of the client upon the physical and social environment of the client.[50]

It was this change in point of view and the rediscovery, as it were, of a doctrine of "original sin"—Freud's insistence that all men were to some extent neurotic—that made a theory of helping possible and put great emphasis on the quality of the relationship between helper and helped person. It occasioned what can only be thought of as a great outpouring of love in the helping relationship and it stood in marked contrast to the moralistic attitude of most of the churches at that time.

This philosophy is the one that we have called humanist-positivist-utopian. As was made clear in an earlier chapter, such a philosophy has its dangers. What was not so clear, however, was that the real helpfulness of this new humanism lay not in its scientific character, but in what it had to say in quite a different and possibly a quite unscientific realm—that of human relationships.

The clue to this lies in the very quotation given above, and principally in the opening phrase. Was it really "by virtue of its new scientific character" that this shift had taken place? It can be equally scientific to contrast "the poor, the sick, the criminal or the neglected child" with "the normal and quantitative mass of the population." In fact this—comparison of a group with some norm—is one of social science's most approved methods.

Analytical psychology is one of the less exact sciences and has been held by many not to be a science at all. The shift was not from a nonscience to a science, but from an external or objective science to one that is largely internal or subjective and the difference between these is largely one of values. America did not so much adopt analytical psychology as the mainspring of its emerging helping philosophy because it was more scientific than anything it had had before, much as it may have believed itself to have done so, but because this particular science expressed certain values in its culture. It can even be shown, for instance, that America adopted some of Freud's work but not other, generally later, formulations. It accepted, for instance, the Freud of the optimistic oral-anal-genital progression and not the Freud of the death-wish; the Freud who believed that

50. Philip Klein, "Social Work," *Encyclopedia of the Social Sciences,* ed. Howard W. Odum (New York, 1930-34) , vol. 14, p. 168.

repression caused anxiety and not the Freud who, recanting, recognized in man a primal anxiety which caused repression.[51]

The implications of a science of man, in which he inevitably becomes object rather than subject, was obscured, and its manifestations held in check by a number of factors, including the great sense of oneness and common vulnerability occasioned by the depression of 1929 to 1937, the belief in psychic determinism and even, as Lionel Trilling has pointed out, biologic determinism, which "is actually a liberating idea. . . . It suggests that there is a residue of human quality beyond the reach of cultural control, and that this residue of human quality, elemental as it may be, serves to bring culture itself under criticism and keeps it from being absolute."[52] There was also at that time a deep sense of awe in the face of this new knowledge.

As early as 1930, Virginia Robinson foresaw that the new knowledge could be used in two ways, either to offer to the client "a new environment," relationship with a helping person, which gives him "opportunity to work out his own problems"—the basic tenet of this book—or a point-to-point relationship in which the worker "manipulates the client's inner life as before she manipulated his environment."[53] Thus she saw the basic difference between the helping and the control process.

Of the history of social work in America, and in particular of what Grace Marcus once called "our Chinese war of ancestor worship"[54]— Freud or Rank—which is not really that at all, but an argument on the essential safeguards which one must put round man's tendencies and growing ability to control these he seeks to help, there is no need to speak here in detail. Social work is not necessarily a helping profession, despite its general classification as such. It always exists in tension between its responsibility to those it helps and to the society which

51. This point is made very forcibly in regard to psychiatrists by Norman O. Brown, *Life Against Death* (New York, 1959), p. 112, and in regard to social work by Gisela Konopka, *Eduard C. Lindeman and Social Work Philosophy* (Minneapolis, 1958), p. 185. Freud's "recantation" can be found in his *New Introductory Lectures on Psychoanalysis* (London, 1933), p. 192.

52. Lionel Trilling, *Freud and the Crisis of Our Culture* (Boston, 1935), p. 48.

53. Virginia Robinson, *A Changing Psychology in Social Casework* (Chapel Hill, N.C., 1930), pp. 183-84.

54. In her verbal introduction to her paper, "Some Changes in the Theory of Relief Giving" at the National Conference of Social Work in Atlantic City, 1941, on the day following Gordon Hamilton's attack on the "functional school" of social work in her "The Underlying Philosophy of Social Casework Today," *Proceedings of the National Conference of Social Work, 1941*, pp. 237-54. Quoted from memory.

sanctions it. Its theory and that of helping are not necessarily synonymous.

Its tendency to control has been outlined in several places in this book. There is no doubt of the increasing tendency of this profession during the 1950s and most of the 1960s to use control methods, to identify with the culture, to abandon its internal and subjective relationship to its clients, to see those whom it helps as "sick" and to turn to sociology and even to behavioristic psychology rather than to analytic psychology as the social science in which it puts its trust.[55]

Recently there has been evidence of a change in this trend. This has come partly from those who have shifted their interest from the individual to the reform of society, through community social work, which has taken from social casework its, I believe, mistaken mandate to solve society's ills, and tended to return it to a true helping method, so that it may once again become at least in some programs what it was in the 1940s, when it was described by one writer as "completely oriented to the individual and his very personal needs . . . trying to serve his purposes only, flexibly and in a non-directing way."[56]

But partly this countermovement has come from clients of social agencies, who, in the new "participatory democracy" that many social workers now envisage, are increasingly saying that they are not sick, and they do not wish to be controlled. They are not as yet saying that they do wish to be helped, except on their own terms. In fact, at the moment, they discount skill in helping, perhaps because skill has meant to them more skill in control than skill in helping.

Both these trends are however more or less problems for a particular profession torn between two somewhat conflicting loyalties and do not affect the existence or nature of a helping process. This will continue to be necessary in a hundred different ways, however our major social problems may be solved. It will always be there for those who care and dare to use it.

55. I have traced this development in greater detail in a paper, "Self-Determination and the Changing Role of the Social Worker," in *Values in Social Work: A Re-examination,* Monograph IX, in the series sponsored by the Regional Institute Program, National Association of Social Workers (1967). See also such articles as Alvin Schorr's "The Tendency to Rx," *Social Work* 7, no. 1 (January 1962) : 59-66, and, as expressions of this trend, Elliot Studt's "Worker-Client Authority Relationships in Social Work," *Social Work* 4, no. 1 (January 1959) : 18-28; Robert K. Taylor, "The Social Control Function in Casework," *Social Casework* 39 (January 1958) : 17-21; and many others.

56. Hertha M. Kraus, "The Role of Social Casework in American Social Work," in Cora Kasius, ed., *Principles and Techniques in Social Case Work* (New York, 1950) , p. 139.

XII. HELPING AND RELIGIOUS BELIEF

In one sense all helping has a religious base. The desire to help another is not, as far as we know, instinctual. All worldwide religions have stressed to some extent responsibility for one's fellow man, kindness or justice to the needy, or self-fulfillment through service.

But this is very far from saying that helping, in the way we have described it, is compatible with a particular theology or belief. Indeed at first sight it may appear not to be so. Certainly many of the insights into helping that we have learned have not come from religious sources, and equally certainly many humanists and agnostics have shown far more ability to understand and practice the process than have those who profess religious faith.

Yet the relationship between religion and the helping process is important for a number of reasons. First, a great deal of helping takes place under some sort of religious auspices. The range of this helping has increased greatly in the last few years as more and more churches are interpreting their mission as one of service to the world instead of preoccupation with the state of grace or the afterlife of its individual members. Secondly, much modern helping theory has been developed in opposition—one might almost say reaction—to theological ideas and to so-called religious attitudes, and this naturally disturbs those who care about religion. And thirdly, religious people, and religious organizations, are wondering if they have anything in particular, beyond good will, to contribute to helping. Some churches believe, for instance, that the right thing to do today is to cease any distinct "religious" effort and to support governmental and community helping programs.

Let us suggest, then, three questions, which we will attempt to answer in part:

—why do many helping people look still with great suspicion, despite some recent attempts at reconciliation, at religious motives for helping?

—is the helping process compatible with religious belief?

—does religion have anything particular, or indeed different, to add to helping theory?

In the following discussion most of my comments will be directed to the Christian understanding of things rather than to the Jewish, not because I think the latter unimportant but because these questions have been raised in much more acute form about Christianity than they have about Judaism. Jewish points of view have never been as extreme, or as dogmatic, as have Christian, and the Jewish concern for justice, which has been its outstanding contribution to helping practice, has been something of a constant over the centuries. Jews, too, have been less identified with prevailing class and power structures. Their contribution to helping theory has been quite out of proportion both to their numbers and to the positions held by them in government and community leadership. Perhaps, too, they have been less quick to identify helping efforts with their religion in a superficial way.[1]

The first question can be answered to a great extent in terms of the three sets of assumptions that we discussed in chapter 8. To the extent that Christian doctrine has been identified with capitalism, to the extent that it assures, even implicitly that worldly success and grace have anything to do with each other, to the extent that there is any room in it for judgmentalism, or distinction between people on the basis of their supposed goodness or badness, to the extent that it rejects the sinner rather than his sin, the church is operating on CP assumptions and deserves all that the humanists have said about it. Indeed the wave of humanism that swept over the country in the 1930s can be considered a most beneficial chastening of its theory and practice.

It is the kind of religious identification with CP assumptions that is so strenuously attacked, and rightly, by a humanist such as Bisno in his *Philosophy of Social Work*.[2] He takes exception to such religious beliefs as the value of suffering in creating character, or seeing it as the just desert for sin, to a philosophical division between the body and the soul and to the identification of certain instinctual drives as "bad" or "immoral." But these are not actually beliefs in the Judeo-Christian

1. For good discussions of Jewish religious thought as it affects helping and social welfare, see Herbert H. Aptekar, *The Dynamics of Casework and Counselling* (Boston, 1955), and Alfred J. Kutzik, *Social Work and Jewish Values* (Washington, D.C., 1959).
2. (Washington, D.C., 1953).

or biblical tradition. They are perversions of these beliefs in the capitalist-puritan set of assumptions.

It could also be said that in the 1930s when much of our present helping theory began to develop, the church, as it was represented in social work, in the activities of church groups, and in its general attitudes, was either CP, paternalistic, or insensitive to need. Indeed HPU thought appeared to offer an alternative. At that time the sense of a new relationship, loving, helpful, respecting the other, transcending caste or culture which liberal humanists and Freudian psychiatry created appeared to give new expression to much of what many of us thought religion should be about. In addition, it dispensed with many of the biblical faith's more uncomfortable features, such as problems of sin, judgment, and personal responsibility.

But, as we have seen, HPU thought contained in itself the seeds of its own deterioration. And because, for a moment in time, the church was put to shame, it does not follow that religion must become humanist or deny its essential doctrines if it is to help people. Although in the nineteenth century it was those churches who had no concept of "original sin," the Unitarians and the Quakers, who had most to give to the social scene,[3] the fault lay not with the doctrine itself—it is the greatest deterrent to pride that can possibly exist—but with the identification between sin and lack of social or material success. It was the divorce between original sin and grace, the puritan habit of ascribing the one to others and claiming the other for oneself, that made of "original sin" such a dangerous helping concept.

There were other problems, too. The tendency to divorce religion from life in this world, to insist on "spiritual" or other worldly values rather than on what is happening in the social scene, is another result of the development of the CP set of assumptions. Theology can be perverted to support capitalist assumptions, but, if it is to do so, concepts such as concern for people, relationship with a loving Father, repentance, and justice have to be limited to some area of operation— the "spiritual"—which does not affect everyday life and relationships.

Yet there exists an extraordinary and indeed very close analogy between the process of help as we know it empirically and the processes described in traditional theology.

Consider first the description, in chapter 2, of the demands that are made on the person to be helped. These were listed as: to recognize

3. A. F. Young and E. T. Ashton, *British Social Work in the Nineteenth Century* (New York, 1956), p. 36.

that something is wrong with, or lacking, in his situation which he can do nothing about by himself; the willingness to tell someone else about this problem; according to this other person a limited right to tell him what to do or to do things for him; and the giving up of his present and familiar adjustments in favor of a possibly dangerous but probably more satisfactory life.

These demands have long been familiar in religious thought. Indeed, because they have been familiar in this setting for so much longer than they have in the context of human helping, the church has developed single terms for what helping theory has at the moment to express in somewhat clumsy phrases. The recognition that something is wrong and that one can do nothing about it oneself the church calls repentance, which does not mean, let it be said, simply being sorry for what one has done and resolving to do better, but just this very recognition of one's own helplessness and a turning to God for help. The willingness to tell another the church calls confession. The granting to another of control of one's affairs it speaks of as submission; the undertaking to change it calls commitment and the willingness to give up the known for what, as Paul points out bluntly, is unseen and unknown, it designates by the word faith.

The agnostic, considering this phenomenon, will see this simply as an indication that the process has been known for a long time. When man, he would say, invented God and sought help from his invention this was the process he described because this is the way that people actually are helped.

But to the Christian such an analogy begins to raise the question whether what he believes and what the helping process requires are not related in a very particular and intimate way—whether in fact the helping process as we struggle to know it is not a faint reflection, but a true one all the same, of a divine relationship. And if he does begin to suspect this, he should not be too surprised. He might even expect that in a consistent universe this might be so.

It is not exactly the same process. That would be too much to expect. The process of repentance, confession, submission, and faith is in relation to a divine Person. Submission needs to be much more absolute than it does in the human context. In fact, in the human context it needs to be carefully limited because the person to whom one submits is a person like oneself, and could and might use the relationship to exploit one.

We may feel the same about God. We do, sometimes. Yet it is exactly that quality of God that makes submission possible: that He does not exploit us—that His service is perfect freedom.

Nevertheless we do resist Him and in doing so we may see more clearly how those we help may and will resist us. How often, for instance, do we not protect ourselves from Him by going through all the motions, attending all the services, praising Him exaggeratedly or fulsomely, singing all the hymns, involving ourselves busily in what we imagine to be "His work" and kidding ourselves that this is all He demands?

An understanding of these evasions may help us appreciate more accurately what is meant by "disarming" those who try to help one, or why people demand help on their own terms. Just as it is a fearful thing to fall into the hands of the Living God, so in a lesser way it is fearful to fall into the hands of a helper.

Having seen this correspondence between a human and a divine process, we are then faced with the question of what this implies. Is it just a coincidence, or merely a useful analogy, or does the pattern follow through? Are we here on the edge of a synthesis between our beliefs and our helping activity which might have real significance? Obviously faith might wish it so, and this is the great temptation, to go looking for analogies as some people search the Bible for texts to support their theories or prejudices.

Yet it is hard not to be impressed with what happens when we begin to examine the other side of the helping relationship, what the helper puts in to it.

In chapter 5 we developed an analysis of the helping factor into three elements—reality, empathy, and support. We said of them then that they were triune, necessary to each other, needing each to be present in any helping situation, and incomplete without each other.

This statement was developed on a purely pragmatic basis. This is what helps. Yet one might suggest with some diffidence that there are characteristics of another triune phenomenon, Father, Son, and Holy Ghost, that correspond very closely to reality, empathy, and support.

God the Father, the Creator, is in Christian thought certainly the author of reality—both the reality of things and that of the moral and natural law, as well as of the laws of causality and consequence. He is also the Wholly Other, the One who is different, who is "God, not man."

Biblical history, as Christians read it, certainly suggests that this reality was not enough. Man could not, of his own will, face reality and change in relation to it alone. There was needed an act of empathy, and there is no more characteristic or total act of empathy than that described in the Incarnation—a God who became man and yet remained God, "who in every respect has been tempted as we are, yet without sinning." Indeed, the whole theology of "very God and very man," the refusal to consider Jesus as either less than God and not wholly man, or part God and part man, the insistence that he is a single person "without conversion, composition or confusion,"[4] as the Westminster Confession of Faith asserts, is a struggle with the same kind of problem as that which troubled us a few pages back—how a person can feel another's pain and yet remain separate from it. Both require the concept that in doing two apparently different things at the same time, one does not do either less completely.

Again, the name given to the Spirit, both in the Bible and the Prayer Book, is the Comforter. Although the word to "comfort" has suffered a weakening of meaning since the seventeenth century, its derivation is from *cum* = with and *fortis* = strong. A comforter is therefore one who is "strong with you," and there is no better one-sentence definition of support.

Reality, empathy, and support—Father, Son, and Holy Ghost—the analogy may seem blasphemous at first, despite a similar handling of the mystery of the Trinity in Dorothy Sayers's *The Mind of the Maker*,[5] where she applies the doctrine to the creative process.

It is, however, logical, that if the person asking for help is analogous to the recipient of grace, then the helping person must, as far as it is possible for a finite, fallible being to do so, model his helping on the actions of God himself. One almost wishes at this point that one believed, as did Freud, that man created God in his own image instead of the other way round, for then one would be dealing only with an additional resource—theology—to help one with insights about one's helping, and not with an imperative that demands of us the near impossible—that imperative, incidentally, that is summed up in the Last Commandment where the American R.S.V. has clarified the meanings of "as" by the addition of "even"—"Love one another even as—in the same way as —I have loved you."

Supposing then this double analogy to be significant—and there is plenty of room for an honest skepticism still—what are some of its implications? It follows, I think, that help becomes in a new sense the expression of one's religion, not just as the term is often used, one's

---

4. *Westminster Confession of Faith*, chap. 7, art. 2. The Belgic Confession describes the nature as "not divided or intermixed" (art. 7).

5. Dorothy L. Sayers, *The Mind of the Maker* (London, 1942).

general but unspecific goodwill towards men, but what one actually believes. It follows too that the helping process is real, that it is not merely a collection of pragmatic principles, that it deserves much closer study than it has received to date, and that where we have got it right it is much more than a set of useful techniques. It has about it some of the nature of a universal, although we can never, as it were, argue from this point backwards. The first requirement of any process is that it can be shown to work. And it suggests that there are other ways in which the biblical schema is relevant to our work.

These are in fact of two kinds. One exists when something which is already known in the helping process is both confirmed and illuminated by a theological doctrine. One example of this is not so much the fact that man is a deciding, choosing creature, which we probably know anyhow, but the nature of that choice—not a selection of alternatives, as we have seen, but a far more total orientation of one's energies to a goal. Here religion provides us with a much more understandable term in the form of "commitment." We might add, too, that the risk which God took in allowing man free will, rather than creating him as a subservient being, throws some light on the helper's need to treat human beings as capable of choice. The distance between the wisdom of God and the wisdom of even the wisest human being is surely greater than that between us and even the sorriest and most confused person we might want to help.

Again, in struggling to express the quality of the helped person's concern (a word in itself borrowed from religious writers) that has nothing to do with liking or approval and can even be exercised towards those whom one thoroughly dislikes, the concept of agape and in particular Paul's short but quite exact analysis of it in I Corinthians 13, can be of very great use.

Other instances in which an understanding of religious processes may throw light on helping practice have been mentioned at various times in this book. They include:

(1) the understanding that the environment does not wholly, although it may partially, explain human behavior—it was in Paradise itself that man first got into serious troubles.

(2) that progress, in a man or a program, is not simply a matter of linear progress, or even a Hegelian dialectic of thesis, antithesis, and synthesis. Man's tendency is in fact, to start towards a goal and gradually to deviate from it, so that in time he finds himself going in a reverse direction. From this he can be rescued, or set aright, only by going back once again to the source of his inspiration, a function

which was fulfilled in biblical times by the prophets. Indeed this movement is perhaps the major lesson of the Old Testament.

(3) that problem arises not so much by a reversal or denial of the good but by a gradual perversion of it, a one-sidedness or an emphasis on part of the whole. This follows from (2) above.

There are also probably many instances where the key to phenomena we may have observed but do not know how to explain lies in the biblical schema. One that has begun to intrigue me lately, but which I cannot document, so tentative are the clues at present, has to do with the kind of involvement that is required in intercessory prayer. Another has to do with the meaning of suffering and there has, for some time, been a dialogue between the church and psychoanalysis attempting to understand and perhaps categorize the two-edged sword of guilt.

But the illumination that arises from seeing one's beliefs and one's helping practice as part one of each other is not a one-way street. Just as in my own experience I came much nearer to an understanding of what was meant by support when I considered the implications of God's unconditional love for man, so the practice of helping illuminated religious concepts which up to that time had been vague or had gathered to themselves debased or what I call Sunday School meanings. Thus repentance is seen more clearly as a turning to God in one's helplessness rather than a simple resolve to do better because one knows from helping people that this is what works. Forgiveness becomes more clearly a continued concern for the sinner despite his sin rather than "cheap grace" that minimizes the fact of sin, because this is the kind of forgivenesss people need when they are helped. Even some glimmering may be possible of what it means to love one's enemies when one has felt concern for people one cannot possibly like.

I might suggest also, although this may seem presumptuous, that a study of helping might raise some questions about some current trends in theological thought. The tendency in this age is not only to demythologize God. It is to depersonalize him, too, and to replace him with something like a Tillichian "ground of our being" which does not act except through people and is purely immanent. This is expressed in modern theology by the belief that the transcendent, acting, God is dead. I have every sympathy with attempts to get rid of outworn concepts and express the essential truth in ways more comprehensible to the twentieth-century mind. We have ascribed to God many little personal actions in which in all probability He was not, at least, directly concerned, and some of our images of Him ought to die. But it is the very personal, or suprapersonal acts of God and the ancient formulations of His transcendence as well as His immanence which are relevant if we wish to study how we can help others. Is it possible that there is a relevance of the gospel to the world which does not depend in its recasting in less anthropomorphic terms as much as it does a new understanding of what the ancient formulas mean?

A word of warning would seem to be pertinent here. We have commented elsewhere that much of the most important work on relationship during the past twenty years has been done by theologians of an existentialist bent, notably Berdyaev, Buber, Tillich, and Maritain.

Yet it is very important that we, who are devoted to helping others, do not surrender our own practical judgment to what theologians believe, as so many helping people have surrendered theirs to the external findings of sociology or psychology. We are the doers, the pragmatics. We can care only for what works. Insights, ways of conceptualizing, we can draw from them in plenty but we cannot allow them to tell us how, in fact, one really helps.

The same is true of our own religious beliefs. We cannot in our discovery of the likeness of the human and the divine processes deduce one entirely from the other. We have, in helping people, to hold rigorously to what experience and research in helping people tells us is useful, even if it should at first appear to conflict with a religious belief. But if this belief is a true one the conflict should not arise. We can, and should, however, use our beliefs to help us discriminate between goals, or to examine the presuppositions on which a piece of research is based.

This brings us to our third and final question. Does religion have anything in particular, or indeed different, to add to helping theory? This can be asked both of the Christian who practices some form of helping and of the church-sponsored agency or helping endeavor.

Let us be clear that our question relates to the person or organization who professes definitely Christian beliefs, of a theological nature, and not to the mere fact of being culturally related to or influenced by the Judeo-Christian tradition. We are not talking here of a belief in the Golden Rule, which antedates Christianity, or of a general beneficence. We are talking of the helper, whether he helps in a church-setting or a secular one, who is at the same time a sincere and professing Christian who can subscribe, say, to the Apostles' Creed, or of the agency or service that is probably denominationally owned or supported. Does either help in any distinctive way, and does the latter need to exist?

Let us put aside for the moment any specifically evangelistic argument, either ecumenical or denominational. There are reasons both for proclaiming and for not proclaiming that a service is church-sponsored. And let us again for the moment not consider the importance to the church and its members in being engaged in some sort of social service. All that can concern us here is the effect of the service's or the helper's Christian belief on those who are helped or on the general practice of helping.

The first thing perhaps that we can say about a Christian agency, or a Christian helper, is that the Christian has certain guidelines, or touchstones, that enable him to make certain kinds of judgment about trends in helping theory or practice. When new knowledge becomes available, and it is doing so every day, it tends to take over the field and become the fashionable or even the only socially sanctioned way of helping. It is easy to fall into the humanist belief that the new knowledge is always the best, or that it supersedes the old. And in the humanist world there is no way to call a stop to the process, to go back to fundamentals and ask whether a new piece of knowledge or a new fashion is indeed an advance, or whether it may not be leading to that very reversal of values and outcomes which the Christian knows to be the fate of so much human endeavor.

The Christian has a number of such touchstones. One is that very knowledge that this "drift" is the major problem with all man-made plans, which change subtly and almost imperceptibly from good to bad unless there are ways from time to time to return to the source of one's inspiration.

Another is his knowledge that pride is the mother of all the deadly sins. A third is that all men are sinners—that is, fallible creatures—and that this includes the helper as well as the helped. A fourth is that one we spoke of when we said that it was in Paradise itself that man first got into serious trouble.

A fifth is that relationships matter, that a man lives through his relationships with others. A sixth is that each individual matters, and that his good cannot be subjected entirely to the good of the whole. A seventh is that suffering and loss, though never good in themselves, may be necessary steps to growth. And an eighth is that force or violence, while it may bring temporary advantages, is in the end less powerful than love.

These touchstones are more or less absolutes. They are, in their various ways, necessary parts of the Gospel, deducible not from texts, although texts could be found to support them all, but inherent in the whole biblical schema or stance, from Genesis to Revelation, as it has been understood in the mainstream of theological thought from Paul to Barth. They cannot be altered by any temporary shift in the culture or the intellectual climate. It is true that at some periods Christians have forgotten one or more of them. There was nothing any more prideful than the Puritan attitude towards the poor, and church institutions are just as liable to drift as are secular ones. Nor is the history of the church in any way a nonviolent one.

Yet these principles are there and in time Christians always come back to them, sometimes in opposition to the prevailing culture. This the humanist cannot do. He may at any one time believe in any one or more of them, but if the culture changes he must change with it. This can be seen today in a gradually shifting attitude among humanists towards violence as a way of ensuring social change, towards control methods instead of helping ones, and towards willingness to subject the interests of the individual to the good of the whole.

The Christian agency or helper then has a role as a critic of society's efforts to help or to control, as a check on drift and as a guardian of and witness to certain important values. He, or it, will be suspicious of certain trends, such as the increase of "parenting" situations, and of the negative diagnosis that declares a person unable to take help, the tendency to solve situations the easiest and least painful, but also the least responsible way, the reduction of human problems to a prescription or a conditioning that ignores or excludes feelings and relationships, a total concentration on community to the exclusion of the individual's needs and rights, and the encouragement of violence.

At the same time to be a guardian of external values must never mean holding to the past, doing things the same old way, not welcoming new knowledge, or not seeing in these very trends of which he is suspicious a large element of salutary correction of drift in the opposite direction. It is exactly in the attempt to hold to the past that drift is most apparent. The Children's Home, for instance, that once fulfilled a most valuable function as an orphanage and that does not change with the times, use new knowledge, find a new helping role now that there are very few true orphans to care for, suffers a drift all the way from a truly helpful service to one which sacrifices children and their families to institutional pride.

All these trends, too, are in a sense reactions against unwise or even unfeeling practices in the past. Helpers have allowed, or rather encouraged decisions that people could not or should not make. They have been too optimistic. They have sometimes ignored knowledge by concentrating solely on feeling. They have ignored the injustices of society and have come near at times to demanding adaptation to an unjust and unnecessary social scene, and they have been afraid of conflict or confrontation.

It is not therefore these trends themselves that are bad, but the extent of them and where they could themselves lead if they are not kept in balance.

In his own practice the Christian helper will have certain characteristics that follow from these beliefs. He will be a person who is concerned with individuals as well as with society. He will accept "parenting" roles reluctantly and always with some sense that they are at best pragmatic answers to his and mankind's lack of knowledge and skill. He will be chary of prescribing for others. He will care about relationships and he will constantly seek ways that avoid violence.

He will have other characteristics, too. He will be both compassionate and forgiving. He will stand by people to the last, even when they seem hopelessly lost. He will have faith and the kind of respect for people that survives all disappointments—in fact one of the outstanding characteristics of the Christian will be that he cannot be disappointed. The Christian has a reason to believe in people that the humanist does not have. The humanist believes in man, but the closer he looks at him, the more disillusioned he is bound to get. Obviously man is a mess. The Christian knows this. He doesn't have to be disillusioned. He never had the illusion or the delusion in any case. But he does know that man has an ultimate worth, and that nothing that the man can do can destroy this. To put this another way—the humanist's belief in man is a belief in his behavior, which can easily be destroyed; the Christian's a belief in his destiny, which is forever sure. Berdyaev makes this clear when he says of humanism both that it is a dialectic movement in the revelation of human personality, which we have stressed, and that:

> The error of humanism certainly did not lie in the fact that it laid too great an emphasis upon man . . . but in the fact that it did not give sufficient emphasis to man, that it did not carry its affirmation of man through to the end, that it could not guarantee the independence of man from the world and included within itself a danger of enslaving man to society and nature. The image of human personality is not only a human image, it is also the image of God.[6]

6. Nicolai Berdyaev, *Slavery and Freedom,* trans. R. M. French (New York, 1944), p. 44.

The Christian helper will be a little tough. This may sound surprising. Christians are not supposed to be tough. They exalt a Man who told them always to turn the other cheek. But in fact the Christian will rely more on helping people face reality than on taking people's problems away from them. He will be less likely to say, "Poor fellow, you never had a chance," and more likely to know that even the chanceless have a choice. Reinhold Niebuhr, in a book published in 1932,[7] said that only the "shrewder insights of religion" could save from sentimentality the liberal Christianity of his time, which was shared by many humanists.

But there are some characteristics which the Christian helper will not have, despite certain stereotypes that others may expect of him. He will not be pietistic, dragging the name of the Lord into all his dealings with those he helps, who may at that time not even be able to trust the people around them, much less the Lord that they cannot see. Christ may have solved the helper's problem, but the most dangerous helper of all is the man who has solved his problem and has forgotten what this cost.

And, need I say it again, he will not be in any way moralistic. That is not what is meant by saying that a Christian is unsentimental—that he is "tougher" on sin, or refuses to sanction what a humanist would condone. Rather the opposite. To a humanist, sin is neutral, a maladjustment in someone else, something to be put right. But, to a Christian, sin is something in which he lives himself. He has it too. The humanist sees particular sins (maladjustments) from which he himself is free. The Christian knows that there is no distinction; all, all have fallen short of the glory of God. This is particularly true of the particular sins against which one's own branch of the church witnesses most—perhaps drunkenness and lust—for these are the things that one can see. They are the mote in one's neighbor's eye, but one's own sins are hidden from one and this should keep the Christian particularly aware of how presumptuous it would be to condemn the sins he sees. Richard Neibuhr has pointed out that what prevented the Evangelical movement from establishing a true source of understanding of the needs of the oppressed and limited it to a kindly paternalism was the fact that poor and rich were guilty of quite different sins.[8] This still might be said of the poor and the middle class today, and even if one

7. Reinhold Niebuhr, *The Contribution of Religion to Social Work* (New York, 1932), pp. 67-68.
8. Richard Niebuhr, *The Social Sources of Denominationalism* (New York, Living Age ed., 1929), p. 67.

were able to convict the recipients of public assistance of both sloth and lust (which I doubt one can do), most of us would hate to be compared with them in respect to envy, gluttony, and pride.

It is interesting to note in this respect that Jesus' pronouncements on giving and helping others never tell us what to demand of others, only what to demand of ourselves. He shows a curious lack of interest in that subject that so engrossed the concern of the church from Clement of Alexandria to the Christian Socialists—even to Glasser's reality therapy, despite its essentially Christian base—the effect of our help on the character of the person helped. It is the effect on the character of the giver which concerns Him. To formulate a theory of self-determination, for instance, that forbids certain behavior because it is morally bad is not a religious act. It is the act of a moralist or a busybody or someone who thinks that he is good.

Nor will the Christian helper be one who is spiritually inclined, who puts counseling or psychotherapy above such things as decent relief, or clothing, or getting a job. Quite the reverse. Despite the tendency in all of us to twist the Scriptures and make blasphemous use of our Lord's dictum that man does not live by bread alone, even to the point of substituting "service" for what He said we needed, Christianity is the only religion whose founder exhorted His people to pray for bread. It is the most down-to-earth of all possible religions, the least world-denying. Christ did not say, "When saw ye me in need of psychotherapy?" He said, "When saw ye me hungry?" What he has called the Christian helper to is not the announcement of his Kingdom but the plain, down-to-earth, service of man.

One final point needs to be made. The insights we have claimed for the Christian helper in no way constitute any superior wisdom or deeper insights. Our Lord the Spirit is not the property of the church or its adherents. Christianity's insights, in this context, are simply and only the logical results of accepting man as a creature responsible to a loving Creator. There is no claim that the Christian will behave in any more democratic, kindly, or generous way, or be a better helper.

His only claim is that he has certain insights about the way things really are that will temper and regulate his helping and perhaps at times throw light on its processes. This in itself is a big enough claim.

INDEX

A

Action: as confirming decision, 127–28; as symbol, 130
Adaptation, 9, 211
Adaptive efficiency, 29; as goal of helping, 12
Adoption, 73–74, 120, 158n
Advice, 128; taking literally, 24–25; "alternative," 129–30, 173
Agreements, written, 119
Aid to Families with Dependent Children, 175. *See also* Public assistance
Alcoholics Anonymous, viii, 59, 134
Ambivalence, 34–35, 42, 163, 173
American culture: ignores negatives, 62; avoids reality, 79; adopts Freudian concepts, 197
Angry person: method of helping, 113–14, 175
Aptekar, Herbert, 16, 168n, 201n
Aquinas, Saint Thomas, 191
Aristotle, 48
Ashton, E. T., and A. F. Young: quoted, 192
Augustine, Saint, 42
Authority, 78, 118–19, 128; help possible in situations of, 10–11; of helper, 55, 164, 167
Awe, 143

B

Bad Seed (film) , 74
Baker, Inez: quoted, 154
Basil, Saint: quoted, 188
Berdyaev, Nikolai, 12n, 146, 208; quoted, 211
Bible, 140, 204, 207
Bisno, Herbert, 139, 143, 145, 201
Blood, Robert O.: quoted, 181
Brainwashing, 33
Brown, Norman O., 146, 192n
Browne, Sir Thomas: quoted, 190
Buber, Martin, 146, 208

C

Capitalist-puritan ethic, 138–50, 192, 201–2
Carkhuff, Robert R., 17–18
Chalmers, Thomas: quoted, 192, 193
Character disorders, 104, 156–57, 163
Children, 58, 153, 182; deep feeling of, 72; desire to be loved by, 90–91; alignment with, 92; ability to face reality, 154–55
Children's Homes, viii, 42, 72, 86–87, 99, 183, 210
Choice, 31, 35–45, 60, 149; alternative, 36, 38; active and willing, 37–39, 43, 47; positive and negative, 39–43; intensely personal nature of, 43–46; repetitive nature of, 45
Christianity, 186–87, 201, 208
Chrysostom, Saint: quoted, 188–89
Church, 200, 202, 209, 210; as helping agency, 185
Clement, Saint: quoted, 188
Client: as term for recipient of help, 50
Colonialism, 162
Commandment: Great, 190; Last, 205
Commands, 33
Commitment, 37, 206
Community, ix
Community organization, 171–73
Compromise, 170, 173, 181
Comte, Auguste, 140
Concern, 105–8, 145, 206
Condescension, 139
Confession, 203
Confidentiality, 119
Confrontation, 211
Consequences of choices, 42
Consultation, 25, 75, 90, 129, 173–74
Control: differentiated from helping, 8–12, 17, 151; political implications of, 11; diminishing need for, 11; justification for, 32; feasibility of, 33; social workers as agents of, 53–55; occasions

where needed, 86; of conditions of help, 116–18; argument that people desire, 136; mechanist view of man leads to, 145; turned to in 1950s and 1960s, 147, 199; and "parenting," 164; helpers who desire, 165; social workers increasingly making use of, 166, 171; one of motives for relationship, 169–70; empathy questioned as means of, 176; helping must grow at expense of, 178; differentiated from controls, 178; parents use subtle means of, 182–83

Controls: differentiated from control, 178, 182

Counterpower, 174–75, 177

Courage, 97–100, 121

Court: juvenile, 22, 49, 54, 78, 113

Crisis, 27, 30, 31

Cultural deprivation, 159, 163

Cyprian, Saint: quoted, 189

D

Davis, Annie Lee, 159n; quoted, 54n

Decision: effect of manipulation on, 11; thrust on helper, 24–25; end interview when made, 125–26

Decisions, 14, 28, 29; hard to make, 64; confirmed in action, 127–28

Defensiveness, 84, 98

Dennison, Edward, 66, 195

Dependency, 9

de Schweinitz, Karl, 17; and Elizabeth, 167n

Deviancy, 8, 138, 197

Devil's advocate, 77

Dewey, John, 140, 195

Diagnosis, 6–7, 44, 69, 81, 128, 164, 194, 195

Dialectic, 206

Difference, 59, 65, 74, 76, 124; criteria for introducing, 74–77, 131

Disciplined spontaneity, 93–94, 95

Drift, 99, 209–10

Drug Therapy, 69

Dying, 156

Dysfunction, 8, 102–3

E

Economic factors, 186, 192, 195

Empathy, 71, 75–76, 79–85, 105, 176; distinguished from sympathy and pity, 80–81; act of loving imagination, 81; feeling in, 82, 177; paradox of, 82; lacking in public assistance, 160; in Incarnation, 205

Environment, 195, 206; manipulation of, 196, 198

Epidemiology, 68–69

Erickson, Erik, 16

Eudaemonism, 186–87, 191

Existentialism, 142

Expert, 26–29, 32; as generalist, 128–29

F

Faatz, Anita, 16, 38, 67n; quoted, 37, 45, 117

Failure, 42–43, 79, 123

Faith, 203

Faith of the Counsellors. See Halmos, Paul

Families: "hard-core," 159, 161

Federal Extension Service, viii

Feelings: need to respond to, 110–12; early recognition of, 112–13

Foster home care, 48, 72, 73, 99, 144, 190

Fromm, Erich, 106–7, 136n; quoted, 90

Freud, Sigmund, vii, 36, 140, 143, 197–98, 205

G

Gandhi, Mohandas K., 144

Gennaria, Marion, 144n, 153n

Gibran, Kahlil: quoted, 181

Gibson, Edmund: quoted, 189

Gilpin, Ruth, 95n

Glasser, Melvin, 16, 48, 69, 152

Goal: of community organization, 172

Goals: of individuals, 173

God, 138, 191, 203–8, 213

Grace, 191–92, 200

Greeks: influence on helping theory, 186–87

Groups: do not act as individuals, 174

H

Halmos, Paul, 7, 146, 171n

Help: going to waste, 3; nature of, 3–4, 11, 12–15; inappropriate, 4; nature of, 11; resistance to, 20–32, 61, 86; conditions of accepting, 20–21, 103, 116–18; action to force, 22; on own terms, 24; those who do not ask for, 30–31; readiness for, 32; accepted by unlikely people, 44; particularization of, 58; material, 66–67; resistance to, 86; conditions of, 103; given to superiors, 178; given to enemies, 178; unplanned, 183; to deserving only, 192

Helper: century of, 3; qualities of, 3, 97–108; not necessarily trained in psychosocial diagnosis, 7; values of, 29; authority of, 55, 164, 167; not selfless, 90–91, 108; not afraid of self, 91; not necessarily adjusted, 93; as agent of process, 104–5; function as, 116–18; as ego-ideal, 161; Christian, 209–10

Helping: literature of, 15–18; as art or science, 17–19; unrealistic, 87, 160; not everyone's métier, 89–90; historians of, 185; religious base of, 200

Helping factor: attempt to define, 67; as reality, empathy, and support, 71; all three elements necessary, 88

Helping process: not permissive, 10; those who can use, 11; teachability, 19; trust in, 131; existence of, 168; universality of, 169, 184, 206; reflects nature of man, 177; in business, 179–80; relation to theology, 202–8; works, 206

Helping professions, vii

Helping relationship: mutual, 47; not necessarily pleasant, 48–50; knowledge and feeling in, 50–51; single purpose of, 51–53; in here and now, 56–57; offers something new, 59; must offer choice, 60; nonjudgmental, 63–65; as means of learning to help, 95; must be risked, 99; human relationships in, 194

Hill, Octavia, 66, 195

Houwink, Eda: quoted, 167

Humanism, 141, 148, 210–12

Humanist-positivist-utopian value system, 139–50, 197, 202

Humility, 17, 100–105, 121, 168

Hutchinson, Dorothy, 15n

Hypnotism, 33

I

Image, 56–57, 75, 111. *See also* Persona

Imagination, 81, 108

Individualism, ix

Individuality: contrasted with personality, 13

Indulgence, 87

Influence, 167, 170, 172; as force, 39–40

Institutionalization, 86, 157

Interpretation, 69

Intervention, 31–32

Interview: end when decision made, 125; leave something for next, 126–27

Investigation, 194

J

Jesus, 190, 205; quoted apocryphally, 188; sayings of, 213

Jews, 148, 185; contribution to helping theory, 187, 201

Johnson, Samuel: quoted, 193

Judeo-Christian tradition, 140–50, 201–2, 208

Judgment, 188, 194

Judgmentalism, 63–65, 101–3, 163, 188–89, 192, 212

Justice, 186; almsgiving on act of, 191

Justification, 78

K

Kierkegaard, Soren, 43, 44

Klein, Philip: quoted, 196–97

Knowledge: as aid to empathy, 82–83; of services, 96; based on actions, 128

Kraus, Hertha: quoted, 199

Kutzik, Alfred, 186n, 201n

L

Lallemand, Leon, 186, 187n

Lane, Lionel, 158n

Langland, William: quoted, 190

Law, 55, 165, 194

"Leap in the dark," 43, 44

Lenin, V. I., 147

Lewis, C. S.: quoted, 13–14

Likeness, 59–60, 65, 74

Liking and disliking, 48, 82, 105–8

Lippitt, Ronald: quoted, 172

Listening, 67, 71, 104, 115

Littner, Ner, 153n

Loch, C. S., 195

Love: Christian, 95, 106, 187–88; God's for man, 187, 207

Love and hate: close to each other, 42

Love and joy: as goals of helping, 13, 16, 29, 116

Luther, Martin, 192

M

McCormick, Mary J., 142

Mahoney, Stanley C., 16–17, 71

Man, nature of, 137–50, 160, 198, 211

Manipulation, 9, 10; effect on decisions, 11; of the environment, 67

Marcus, Grace: quoted, 36n, 198

Marx, Karl, 140

Material support, 195

Maturity, 44, 139

Mental illness, 133, 152

Micah, 187

Morality, 188, 192, 194
Mouse, era of, 68
Mutuality, 169, 180–81

N
Negative feelings, 60–63
Neighborhood, 173
Neurosis, 21
Niebuhr, Reinhold: quoted, 212
Niebuhr, Richard, 212; quoted, 193
Nonchoice, 31, 34, 35, 72
"Nondirective" counseling, 16, 59, 116

O
Objectivity, 50–51
Old Testament, 187
Opposition, 176–77
Optimist Clubs, 62
Original Sin, 156, 197, 202
Overton, Alice, 31n

P
Paradox, 146; of empathy, 82; of In-
    carnation, 205
Paranoia, 133
"Parenting," 154–68, 210–11
Parents and children, 22, 24, 48, 59, 158,
    181–83
Partialization, 124–25
Participation, 195–96, 199
Paternalism, 160, 162
Patience, 105
Paul, Saint, 42, 106, 115, 203, 206
Perlman, Helen Harris, 16, 36
Permissiveness, 10, 35, 42, 182
Perry, R. B., 139
Persona, 26, 76
Personal helping, vii–viii
Personality: contrasted with individual-
    ity, 13
Persuasion, 33, 39–40, 156, 168, 170, 172,
    182
Pity, 80
Poor Law, 192
Power, 172–77
Praise, 132
Pray, Kenneth: quoted, 43–44, 172
Pride, 150, 163, 164, 209
Probation, 40, 53, 70, 79, 122–23
Problem: need to take seriously, 72; for-
    mulate at intervals, 123–24
Professionalism, 50–51, 93–95
Prophets, role of, 207
Protectiveness, 73, 79

Protective services, 53, 83, 100, 126, 156
Prudence, 191, 193
Psychic determinism, 102, 198
Psychoanalysis, 68, 92–93, 102, 143, 146,
    152, 165, 196–97, 202
Psychology: behavioristic, 199
Public assistance, 52, 58, 73, 84–85, 86,
    142, 160, 171, 194, 213
Punishment, 33, 48, 64, 138, 181–82

Q
Quakers, 202

R
Ramsey, Ruth, 106n
Rank, Otto, 198
Rapport, 48
Reality, ix, 71–79, 104; not necessarily
    good, ix; client's desires as a form of,
    121; need not to defend, 122; helping
    to change, 123
Reality Therapy. See Glasser, Melvin
Reassurance, 72–73
Rebellion, 40, 162
Recipient of help: moral judgment on,
    4; intelligence of, 153
Reeducation, 151
Reformation, 191
Regensburg, Jeannette, 162n
Regression, 131
Relationship, 5, 143, 209. *See also* Help-
    ing relationship
Religious belief, 200, 201; relevance to
    helping theory, 203–8
Religious experience, 45
Repentance, 203
Request: starting with, 109
Research, viii, 136
Resistance to help: positive aspects of,
    25; universality of, 25–26; less in crisis
    situations, 27; and expertise, 27–29;
    cultural, 30
Responsibility: as motive for helping,
    187, 198
Retardation, 153–54
Rewards, 138
Reynolds, Bertha: quoted, 36
Richmond, Mary, 195; quoted, 196
Risk in helping, 43, 98–100, 161, 178
Robinson, Virginia: quoted, 198
Rogers, Carl, 16, 59, 68
Romans: influence on helping theory,
    186–87
Rousseau, Jean-Jacques, 140, 147

S

Sayers, Dorothy, 205
Scherer, Lorena, 159n
Scholasticism, 190
"Scientific Method," 140, 146
Self-determination, 36–37, 149–50, 163, 164, 213
Self-discipline, 19, 84, 93, 95, 163, 164, 165
Self-fulfillment: as goal of helping, 12
Self-knowledge, 91–93, 163, 164
Senility, 155
Separation, 145
Service: payment for, 119–20
Sin, 195, 202. *See also* Original Sin
Social casework, 54, 171, 195, 199
Social conditions, 186
Social science, 28, 50, 137, 164, 165, 194, 197
Social Security Act, 52
Social work, vii, ix, 36, 95, 166, 194, 196, 198; "functional" school of, viii, 16, 38; and control, 8, 10; schools of, 19; students in schools of, 26; training, 95–96
Social workers, 49, 53–55, 171
Sociology, 146, 199
"Soft sell," 177, 180
Soyer, David, 78, 123
Stretch, John J., 142n
Studt, Elliot: quoted, 167
Submission, 203
Suffering, 143–45, 201
Supervision, 96, 178–79
Support, 71–79, 85–88, 105
Symbolism, 130
Sympathy, 80–81, 167, 181

T

Tact, 77
Taft, Jessie, 13n
Tawney, R. H., 139
Theologians, 146, 208
Theology, 139, 191–92, 202; relationship to helping, 202–8
Theories of help: as models, vii; possibility of unitary, 5–6
Thomism, 142, 191

Tillich, Paul, 207–8
Time: need in helping, 57, 120–21
Training: in-service, 96–97
Trauma, 144–45
Trilling, Lionel: quoted, 198
Trinity, 205
"Trolley diagram," 61, 83
Trust, 48, 50
Truth, 73–74
Turning point, 14

U

Uhlhorn, G., 187n; quoted, 189
Unconscious, the, 68
Unconscious feelings, 22, 23, 28
Unitarians, 202
Unmarried mothers, 144, 158, 196

V

Values: systems not susceptible to proof, 10; as affecting decisions, 28–29, of helper, 41; religious, 138–39; of organizations, 174; "spiritual," 202
Violence, 210–11
Vives, Juan Luis, 190, 194
Voegelin, Erich, 140
Vulnerability, 198

W

Walker, Thomas: quoted, 193
"War on poverty," 67
Webb, Beatrice: quoted, 195
Weber, Max, 139
Welfare. *See* Public assistance
Wesley, John, 193; quoted, 189
Why: futility of asking, 68–69, 132
Will, 22, 23, 33–34
Wills: battle of, 84, 112
Wiltse, Kermit, 159n, 161; quoted, 53
Witte, Ernest, 160n
Wooton, Barbara, 5, 50n
Work, 138, 191

Y

"Yes man," 39
"Yielding," 160–61
Young, A. F., and E. T. Ashton: quoted, 192

DATE DUE

MAR 7 '79	MAR 8 '79		
JUL 9 '79	JUN 29 '79		
OCT 5 '79	SEP 24 '79		
	DEC 18 '79		
NOV 19 '79			
MAY 8 '80	APR 29 '80		
APR 10 '81	APR 10 '81		
APR 30 '81	APR 22 '81		
MY 02 '86	MAY 1 '86		
GAYLORD			PRINTED IN U.S.A